A Christian Guide to Psychology and Counseling

A Christian Guide to Psychology and Counseling

Geoffrey Buckley, Ph.D.

Pepperdine University

Bassim Hamadeh, CEO and Publisher
Amy Smith, Senior Project Editor
Alia Bales, Production Editor
Jess Estrella, Senior Graphic Designer
Kylie Bartolome, Licensing Associate
Natalie Piccotti, Director of Marketing
Kassie Graves, Senior Vice President, Editorial
Jamie Giganti, Director of Academic Publishing

Printed in the United States of America.

cognella® ACADEMIC PUBLISHING
3970 Sorrento Valley Blvd., Ste. 500, San Diego, CA 92121

Brief Contents

Preface . . . xi

Chapter 1 Of What Value is Psychology? . . . 1

Chapter 2 The Movement Forward: A Brief History of Psychology . . . 11

Chapter 3 How Therapy Works . . . 21

Chapter 4 The Therapist and the Therapy . . . 35

Chapter 5 Denial and the Mechanics of Escape . . . 45

Chapter 6 Problems and Promise . . . 55

Chapter 7 On Being Human . . . 63

Chapter 8 Depression, Anxiety, and Other Troubling Emotions . . . 71

Chapter 9 The Helping Professions: Pastoral, Social, Psychological, and Medical . . . 79

Chapter 10 Mental Illness, Evil, and a Fallen World . . . 85

Chapter 11 The Psychology of Couple Relationships . . . 99

Chapter 12 The Psychology of Community and Connection . . . 109

Chapter 13 Temperament, Gifts, and Calling . . . 119

Chapter 14 On the Psychology of Worship . . . 129

Chapter 15 Counseling and the Laity . . . 141

Chapter 16 Church Hurts . . . 149

Chapter 17 The Psychology of Survival . . . 155

Chapter 18 On the Sacredness of Therapy . . . 163

Appendix . . . 171
References . . . 181
Index . . . 185

Detailed Contents

Preface . . . xi

Chapter 1 **Of What Value is Psychology?** . . . 1
Chapter Preview and Learning Objectives 1
What Happened on the Road to Damascus? 2
A Jew Born in Tarsus 2
What Is Psychology? 4
Speaking of Psychology 5
Stories About People 7
The Best Story 9
Questions for Review, Reflection, and Discussion 9

Chapter 2 **The Movement Forward: A Brief History of Psychology** . . . 11
Chapter Preview and Learning Objectives 11
Forward Movement in Psychology 12
Stages of Human Development 15
Thinking Differently 17
Recent Developments 18
Today 19
Questions for Review, Reflection, and Discussion 19

Chapter 3 **How Therapy Works** . . . 21
Chapter Preview and Learning Objectives 21
Why Talk About Problems? 22
Why Talk About Feelings? 24
Emotion and Memory 25
How Does Talk Therapy Work? 28
Healing, Holding, and Helping 32
Questions for Review, Reflection, and Discussion 34

Chapter 4 **The Therapist and the Therapy** . . . 35
Chapter Preview and Learning Objectives 35
Different Problems, Different Approaches 36
What Makes Counseling Christian Counseling? 39
The Therapeutic Person 39
Gifts and Calling 40

The Journey 41
Questions for Review, Reflection, and Discussion 43

Chapter 5 **Denial and the Mechanics of Escape** 45
Chapter Preview and Learning Objectives 45
Denial—The Good Kind 46
Denial—The Bad Kind 47
Existential Denial 47
Three Paths 48
Defense Mechanisms 49
Questions for Review, Reflection, and Discussion 53

Chapter 6 **Problems and Promise** 55
Chapter Preview and Learning Objectives 55
Problems with Psychology 56
Integrating Psychological Languages 57
Promise 58
The Rise of Christian Counseling 61
Questions for Review, Reflection, and Discussion 61

Chapter 7 **On Being Human** 63
Chapter Preview and Learning Objectives 63
A Living Spirit 66
Fully Human 66
Psyche 68
Relatedness 69
Questions for Review, Reflection, and Discussion 70

Chapter 8 **Depression, Anxiety, and Other Troubling Emotions** 71
Chapter Preview and Learning Objectives 71
Depression 72
Cognitive Therapy for Depression 72
Existential Therapy for Depression 73
Anxiety 74
Existential Anxiety 76
Shame 77
Healing 77
Questions for Review, Reflection, and Discussion 78

Chapter 9 **The Helping Professions: Pastoral, Social, Psychological, and Medical** 79
Chapter Preview and Learning Objectives 79
Different Professions for Different Needs 80
Licensed Clinical Social Workers 81
Marriage and Family Therapists 81
Licensed Clinical Psychologists 81
Psychiatric Nurses 82

Psychiatrists 82
Physicians 84
Questions for Review, Reflection, and Discussion 84

Chapter 10 **Mental Illness, Evil, and a Fallen World** 85
Chapter Preview and Learning Objectives 85
Evil 86
Fear 86
Pride 87
Psychosis Versus Neurosis 89
A Fallen World 90
Existential Option 1: "I Hid Myself ... Because I Was Afraid." 92
Existential Option 2: "I Will Be Like the Most-High!" 93
Existential Option 3: "Blessed Are the Poor in Spirit." 94
Little Gods 95
The Ruler of This World 96
Questions for Review, Reflection, and Discussion 97

Chapter 11 **The Psychology of Couple Relationships** 99
Chapter Preview and Learning Objectives 99
These Two Shall Become One Flesh 100
Limbic Resonance 100
Stage 1: Romance 100
Limbic Regulation 101
Stage 2: Connection 101
Limbic Revision 102
Stage 3: Becoming One 102
Stretching 102
Two Kinds of Pain 103
Two Ways to Die 104
Reenactment 104
Questions for Review, Reflection, and Discussion 107

Chapter 12 **The Psychology of Community and Connection** 109
Chapter Preview and Learning Objectives 109
The Value of Community 110
The Costs of Isolation 111
Life Groups 112
The Corrective Emotional Experience 113
The Parent, Adult, Child Model 114
Mean People 116
Turning the Other Cheek 116
Questions for Review, Reflection, and Discussion 117

Chapter 13 **Temperament, Gifts, and Calling** . . . 119
Chapter Preview and Learning Objectives 119
How Do Gifts Differ from Talents and Temperaments? 120
Temperament 120
MBTI Explained 123
Developing Temperament Strengths 124
Spiritual Gifts 125
Temperament and Gifts 126
Gifts and Calling 127
Questions for Review, Reflection, and Discussion 128

Chapter 14 **On the Psychology of Worship** . . . 129
Chapter Preview and Learning Objectives 129
On the Nature of Worship 130
Misplaced Worship 132
A Life Devoted to Worship 133
Worship—Opening to the Heart of God 134
The Sweet Spot 135
Personality and Worship 136
Undressing the Clergy 137
Sign and Symbol 138
Freedom to Worship 139
Questions for Review, Reflection, and Discussion 140

Chapter 15 **Counseling and the Laity** . . . 141
Chapter Preview and Learning Objectives 141
Counseling by Laypersons 142
Limitations to Lay Counseling 142
Pastoral Counseling 142
Spiritual Gifts 143
Equipping the Laity 144
Counseling Skills—The Basics 144
Preparation 144
Listening 144
Attunement 145
Joining 145
Practice 146
Questions for Review, Reflection, and Discussion 147

Chapter 16 **Church Hurts** . . . 149
Chapter Preview and Learning Objectives 149
Maturity 150
Perspective 150
Fathers 151
At Church 152
The Healing Work of the Church 153

Questions for Review, Reflection, and Discussion 154

Chapter 17 **The Psychology of Survival** 155

Chapter Preview and Learning Objectives 155
Standing Firm 156
Choices 156
Spiritual Strength Training 159
Surviving Your Calling 160
The Work of the Cross 161
Survival Skills 161
Questions for Review, Reflection, and Discussion 162

Chapter 18 **On the Sacredness of Therapy** 163

Chapter Preview and Learning Objectives 163
A Frame of Orientation 164
On The Sacredness of Therapy 164
The Thin Place 166
Learning to Die 167
The Heart of Christian Psychology 168
Questions for Review, Reflection, and Discussion 169

Appendix 171

Speaking of Psychology: You Know More Than You Think 171
Family Rules Exercise 172
Family Roles Exercise 173
Understanding and Helping Families 174
Therapeutic Approaches 174
Guidelines for Good Communication 175
Taking Turns 175
The Heart of the Work: The Goals and Breadth of Psychotherapy 177
The Goals of Therapy 177
The Breadth of Therapy 177
The Heart of Therapy 178
BBPI: The Buckley Burnout Prevention Inventory 179

References 181
Index 185

Preface

Do Christians need a book that explains psychology? There is so much good psychology in Scripture that this book may seem redundant. But there is so much about psychology that reinforces and amplifies the wisdom of Scripture that it is well worth reading. I have read many books describing the relevance of the Christian faith to the task of helping people. There are books with titles like *Jesus, the Greatest Therapist Who Ever Lived*; *Biblical Psychology*; *Living from the Heart God Gave You*; and so forth. But you will not find very many books describing the relevance of psychology to the Christian faith. Is knowledge of psychology relevant to the Christian faith? I hope this book will answer that question.

I was raised in a Christian home. We went to church most Sundays, said grace before meals, and were taught traditional Christian values. In college, when I did not have to go to church, I did not. My faith was revitalized in the Navy. As a junior officer I was tasked with primary and collateral duties. My primary duties were as a diving officer and preventative maintenance officer. My collateral duty was "special services," relating to the welfare of the ship's company. In the early 1970s, I was on a large ship where sailors would inevitably find ways to get into trouble. Drugs and alcohol were some of the ways. I suggested to our ship's chaplain that it would be good to have a place where sailors could meet for education and support regarding substance abuse. I did not realize it at the time, but that was the beginning of my counseling career.

From that rewarding experience, I thought about becoming a Navy chaplain. I attended seminary for the Master of Divinity degree required to return to active duty as a chaplain. While in seminary, I was required to have 2 years of internship as a seminarian. For my second internship I was invited to be a youth pastor at a Presbyterian church. I loved it. I worked with junior and senior high and college-age youth and did a lot of counseling with kids and families. I spent 8 years at the church and decided not to go back on active duty. I enjoyed the counseling I did at the church so much that in 1981 I went back to school, and in 1984 I graduated with a master's degree in marriage and family counseling. I was licensed in 1985 and recently retired after a 36-year career as a therapist.

In 1994 I went back to school again and received a PhD in clinical psychology. I have always enjoyed teaching and knew that the degree would be important for me to teach in graduate school. My first teaching assignment was in 2001 at Pepperdine

University's Graduate School of Education and Psychology. It is now 20 years later, and I am still teaching at Pepperdine. For many years I also taught in the graduate psychology school at California State University, Northridge, and also at California Lutheran University. I have taught almost all of the various graduate counseling classes offered. Apparently, I like school.

The point of my story is that in the many years I have studied and taught the tenets of psychology, my faith in Jesus Christ has not diminished. It is stronger. The more I understand psychology, the more I appreciate the Gospel and the wonders of God's creation. The Christian faith is nothing less than brilliant. It reveals the saving work of Jesus Christ and offers the perfect solution to life's many challenges. It provides guidance for mental and emotional well-being and is the best answer to life's most perplexing questions.

Psychology is not a belief system that challenges the Christian faith. It is simply a collection of ideas and stories about people and how best to help them with their problems. Most of these ideas and stories are useful in understanding human nature and the emotional problems that people face. There are many therapists who believe in God and count on their faith in Him for wisdom and direction. And there are therapists who do not. My experience in the past 40 years is that more and more practicing psychotherapists have a good understanding of the importance of faith as a foundation for mental health. In fact, in 1999 the American Psychological Association published a collection of articles in a book titled *Integrating Spirituality into Treatment: Resources for Practitioners.* The first paragraph in the introduction to this text states:

> For as long as people have been able to record their thoughts, they have conceived of reality in a way that is not limited to sensory experience and intellectual knowledge. Most generations and cultures have taken for granted that "this is not all there is," that there is a spiritual dimension of reality and of human nature beyond this material world we know through our senses. To be sure, the degree of emphasis on spirituality varies in pendulum fashion over the years. At the moment, in American culture at least, we seem to be coming out of a period of extreme materialism experiencing anew the hunger for that which is transcendent in and beyond us. (Miller, 1999, p. xvii)

It would be hard to find a practicing psychotherapist today who did not believe in the power of faith or the importance of a foundation of vital beliefs. The essential task for the Christian Church is to explain the importance of having a faith that is grounded in the atoning work of Jesus Christ and a foundation of vital beliefs that is grounded in the Gospel.

On the other hand, could it be beneficial for Christians to understand how psychology and counseling work? The workings of the human brain, the dynamics of human development, the processes of attraction and attachment, the diverse challenges of living, and how counseling is able to help people heal and grow are just a few of the aspects of psychology that can enhance one's appreciation for the Gospel and ultimately strengthen one's faith in Jesus Christ. The deeper one's faith, the more appreciation for the psychology in Scripture.

CHAPTER 1

Of What Value is Psychology?

> "For to me, to Live is Christ."
>
> Phillippians 1:21

Chapter Preview and Learning Objectives

Beginning with the psychological transformation of the apostle Paul, Chapter 1 introduces the conviction that understanding the workings and applications of psychology can be beneficial for pastors, laypersons, and students studying psychology from a Christian perspective. The chapter describes the triune nature of human beings as spirit, soul, and body, focusing on the soul (psyche) as relational—a connection within ourselves, with others, and with nature. The chapter concludes with a description of the major languages of psychology as useful and engaging stories about people, problems, and how to help them.

Learning Objectives

Students will do the following in this chapter:

- Learn how understanding psychology is valuable for Christians.
- Explore the nature of human beings.
- Understand the nature and function of soul (psyche).
- Learn the five major genres (languages) spoken in psychology.
- Appreciate the value of stories as ways to understand human nature.

What Happened on the Road to Damascus?

There is no good reason to doubt that the apostle Paul met the risen Jesus Christ on the road to Damascus. Why is that? There are two answers to that question. One answer is that it is reported in Scripture. And that is a perfectly good answer. Another answer follows from an understanding of Paul's psychology. Of what value is understanding psychology to the Christian? The answer is that psychology, along with other disciplines, has the potential of deepening our faith and our understanding of God's brilliant design in his creation. The prophet Jeremiah said, "You shall seek and find me when you seek me with all your heart" (Jeremiah 29:13). The Astronomer and Professor Owen Gingerich wrote beautifully about *God's Universe* (2006). The head of the human genome project, Francis Collins, wrote *The Language of God: A Scientist Presents Evidence for Belief* (2007). Whether one looks into the starry heavens or into a human cell, Jeremiah promises that you will find Him if you seek Him with your whole heart. Human beings are extraordinarily complex and complicated. Psychology helps us to understand ourselves. And in looking deeply into His creation, we find His hand at work.

The story of psychology is a story about searching: searching the heights and depths of the human soul. Psychology is interested in people, their motivation, their behavior, their problems, and how to help them. Psychology's search spans a continuum between art and science and speaks the languages of both measurement and metaphor. The search is to help people find answers to life's problems and ways to help people to heal and grow. We are all psychologists. We have a keen interest in ourselves and others. We observe people all our lives. The best of us make efforts to love and care about others.

What does it mean in Psalm 139 to be "fearfully and wonderfully made"? It means that God's creation is beyond amazing. As we reflect on the intricacies of the human brain, our capacity for creativity, for wonder, and for appreciating the world around us, it is hard to deny that a human being is a miracle of creation. Think about the workings of the human brain. Try to grasp the billions of brain cells that combine to create the associations we call "memory." How does the brain store intimate details of daily life and organize experience to give us a sense of continuity and a sense of identity and history? How does the brain manage to achieve the unimaginably rapid progression of a baseball player at bat, standing at home plate, seeing the trajectory of a fastball, and hitting it out of the park? The more we understand psychology, the more we are in awe of being fearfully and wonderfully made.

A Jew Born in Tarsus

Before his journey to Damascus, the apostle Paul, from his own account, was living a life he believed that God Himself was applauding. Paul was worshiping God in what he was convinced was the best and only true religion. He had no need for another. He was "blameless, according to the law," saying, "I am a Jew, born in Tarsus of Cilicia, but brought up in this city. I studied under Gamaliel and was thoroughly trained in the law of our ancestors. I was and zealous for God, as any of you are today" (Acts 22:3). Paul was also a citizen of Rome by birth, and "circumcised on the eighth day, of the people of Israel, of the tribe of Benjamin, a Hebrew of Hebrews; in regard to the law, a Pharisee" (Philippians 3:5). Paul had risen to the top of his social and religious community. Why give all of that up?

What happened to the apostle Paul was a profound spiritual and psychological transformation. One could imagine, as many people might, that what happened to Paul was only psychological and not spiritual. They think something must have happened to him. Maybe he felt guilty for his part in rounding up and murdering Christians. Maybe he came to doubt his Jewish faith. Perhaps he had been betrayed by another of the Pharisees. Certainly, something must have happened to explain his mental condition.

Yet the problem with doubting Paul's own account of what happened to him is that no one with a mental condition or a guilty conscience could work so courageously, tirelessly, and intelligently for 30 years of his life to consistently bear witness to a lie. Or was Paul mentally ill? Was he in the category of people that C.S. Lewis described as someone who thinks he is a poached egg?

In Acts 21, Paul was warned by Agabus not to go to Jerusalem, where he could be recognized as one who "teaches everyone everywhere against our people and our law." Paul insisted on going, however, anticipating that he may even be killed there. People did recognize him in Jerusalem, accused him of preaching against the Jewish faith, attacked him, and tried to kill him before the Romans intervened and took him away from the mob. They were planning to scourge Paul when he asked, "Is it right to scourge a citizen of Rome?" On many other occasions, Paul was tortured, beaten, jailed, and shipwrecked, all for the sake of what he was convinced was true: He had seen the risen Christ. He had many opportunities to recant and escape his fate. Instead, he willingly agreed to go to Rome to stand trial. While under house arrest for 2 years, he established a church in Rome before Nero had him put to death.

In the context of his letter to the church at Philippi, Paul is saying that if anyone could boast in doing good works, he could. But he continues, saying that it is not about good works; it is about faith in Jesus Christ. Paul is contrasting his old beliefs with his new awareness. By reciting his former life in detail, he is saying, in effect, "I didn't need a new religion. It was working for me just fine. Now I know better."

What is instructive about the passage in Acts above, as well as his letter to the Philippians, is that Paul was referring to his former psychology. Something happened to me, he is saying, that radically transformed the way I think and the way I live. Because of what happened, I no longer believe what I had believed. Paul defended his new awareness by acknowledging the intense psychological grip of his old religion contrasted with his profoundly new psychological perspective. He is referring to his former psychology in defense of his newfound faith. He is saying, in effect, "I didn't need a new religion." And in his letter to the church at Philippi, Paul is saying that the religion he had previously thought was the all-in-all has now been eclipsed by Christ.

Of what value is psychology? In addition to a deeper appreciation of God's miracle of creation, psychology helps us to understand people. Psychology helps us to understand ourselves, our motives, our emotions, our development from children to adults, the effects of our early parental conditioning, how we have been taught to think, feel, and act, what challenges we have faced, and how life has wounded us. Psychology helps us to understand our relationships, our friendships, our families, and our romantic attractions and attachments.

Again, trained or not, we are all psychologists. We are all interested in people and in ourselves. We study human nature and ask questions like, "What was he thinking!?" "Why do people act that way?" "Why do I keep dating the wrong guys?" We are all curious about life: what is important, how to be happy, how to be a better person. Psychology can help us to answer some of those questions.

What Is Psychology?

Psyche is Greek for "breath" or "soul," and *logia* means "the study of." The concept of "soul" is first introduced in the Hebrew Bible in Genesis 2:7: "Then the Lord God formed a man from the dust of the ground and breathed into his nostrils the breath of life, and the man became a living being." "Dust," "breath," and "living being" are three different words in Hebrew: *Ruach Elohim* (the breath of God/Spirit), animates *Adamah* (earth) and man becomes a living *Nephesh* (soul). Genesis describes human being as a complex mixture of transcendent Spirit and dusty biology. Soul (neshama or nephesh), in this case, is the place of connection between the two. In other words, Soul is relational. It is the connection between the breath of God and the dust of the earth. Soul is a relationship—a connection, a conversation, a wrestling match between Sprit and biology. Psychology, the study of the psyche (soul), is the study of the relationship one has with one's own life, with one's Self or Spirit, and the relationship one has with other people. It is the study of our wrestling and relating both internally and externally. Soul connects our spirit to our biology and connects our life to the lives of those around us. Jesus warned us that if we lose that vital connection, if we pay too much attention to the things of the world, we risk losing our soul, our connection to others and to God.

I checked out my thinking about Genesis 2:7 with a local rabbi. We had an enjoyable conversation, and he agreed with the concept of "soul" as that part of human existence that seems to link biology to Spirit. He also directed me to additional Jewish commentaries confirming the nature of soul. The Hebrew understanding of nephesh/soul is somewhat different than how English speakers customarily refer to it. English speakers might say "we *have* a soul." The Hebrew understanding is that "we *are* a soul." Soul, in this sense, refers to the entirety of the person. Soul so profoundly connects and relates Spirit to biology that it encompasses, infuses, and contains both. To love God with your whole nephesh is to love Him with your entire being, your whole existence.

Soul is connective tissue. We breathe in God's Spirit, which nurtures and sustains our life. "In Him we live and move and have our being" (Acts 17:28). Soul connects our life to God and to the lives of others. At a deep level, soul connects everyone who feels called to do a certain work in the world. Soul communicates calling. Soul connects people to the work that God is doing in us and through us.

The concept of "soul" is of interest to other disciplines besides psychology. Soul speaks the languages of philosophy, theology, literature, music, and other of the arts. An enlightened psychotherapist along with the minister, the priest, and the rabbi are all concerned for the care of the soul. The poet and the musician are instruments of soul. Professional and amateur bakers often say, "Love is an ingredient in everything I bake." The soul speaks in many ways that reflect the heart of the creator. The art of therapy is the capacity to skillfully draw from depths of soul to invite connection with the soul of the other.

> When a person is singing and cannot lift the voice and another comes and sings, another who can lift the voice, then the first will be able to lift the voice too. That is the secret of the bond between spirit and spirit."
>
> Martin Buber, *Tales of the Hasidim*

Soul connects Sprit to biology and also integrates the personality and the spiritual calling of the therapist. Soul integrates the art and science of psychology and the faith and wisdom of the practitioner. When Jesus was quoted in Deuteronomy 6:4–5 as saying, "Love God with all your heart, all your soul, and all of your strength," he was sharing the key to living life. Loving God with every aspect of your being integrates spirit, soul, and body; connects you with your true Self, with God, with others; and confirms the design of God to live a transformed life—a life useful to God.

Speaking of Psychology

Since psychology is both an art and a science, a student in training will learn many different psychological languages. Some of these languages will be evidenced-based, empirical languages. These may include the languages of diagnosis and assessment, treatment modalities, statistics, psychopathology, psychophysiology, and psychopharmacology. They will also learn the art of helping people. They will learn the tools of communication, empathy, nonjudgmental listening, attunement, acceptance, and genuineness. They will learn the many different theories and methods that can be used with a diversity of people, for a diversity of problems, and in a diversity of contexts. Over time, students will become practiced at knowing which approach to use with which person and problem, and in what contexts.

Students in training learn a vast vocabulary of psychological terms. In fact, I recall telling my students in the introduction to courses in personality theories that they could think of the course as a language class, that, in addition to the theories on how people have understood human nature, they would also be learning the specific vocabularies in which those theories have been described. They will be learning languages.

In brief, there are five main psychological languages. These are psychodynamic, humanistic/existential, cognitive/behavioral, systemic, and medical/biological. These represent different stories and languages about people and the diverse approaches to understanding and helping them. These stories might also be thought of as a variety of genre in the literary world of psychology. Recall that genres are compositions in art, music, and literature with similar styles, forms, and subject matter. Psychology also has its literary genre.

Psychodynamic languages tell a story about *what happened*. What happened in our life that has contributed to our development, our childhood conditioning, the quality of our early attachments, the significant people who guided us, and the culture we were raised in all play an important role in who we become. Psychodynamic languages also speak of emotional wounds and traumas: life experiences that may have affected us, perhaps made us stronger (or weaker). A psychodynamic perspective provides not only insight into these issues but also many tested and successful strategies for helping people heal from developmental deficits, abuses, and psychological wounds from the past.

Humanistic and existential languages are about *what is important*. The work of Carl Rogers and Abraham Maslow were foundational in what has been called the "humanistic or human potential movement." Rogers was confident that when a therapist offered unconditional positive regard, empathy, and acceptance, as a truly genuine person, people benefit. Roger's ideas were originally termed "client-centered therapy." It soon became obvious that his ideas worked in all relationships, not just in therapy. Consequently, Rogers's work is now called "person-centered therapy."

Christians already understand that people need to experience acceptance and love, especially when they are hurting. Carl Rogers's research reinforced and restated the significance and power of Jesus's commandment to love one another. Truth is truth, whether from Scripture or scientific research. The three psychiatrists who worked together to write *A General Theory of Love* understood the value of love when they wrote, "People do come to therapy unable to love and leave with that skill restored. But love is not only an end for therapy; it is also the means whereby every end is reached" (Lewis et al., 2000, p. 169).

Many Christians have a problem with the word "humanism." They fear that humanists advocate people working to improve themselves by themselves. And most Christians know that that is a misguided idea. Yes, there is much a person can do to improve their life. But the deep work of finding healing and wholeness is only found in the work of the cross. The problem with the human-potential movement is that it can point people in the wrong direction and promise what it cannot deliver.

A cousin of a humanistic approach to therapy is the language of existential therapy. Existential therapy falls into two camps, Christian and non-Christian. Humanistic and existential therapy are related in that they share a common approach to therapy. That approach is the conviction that people are extraordinarily valuable and, if given a nurturing environment, healing and growth can happen. The two approaches are often linked together by the term "humanistic-existential therapy." Again, their shared languages are about what is important. What is important is finding meaning, making some sense of the trauma and the turmoil of living. Existential therapy is often used when someone has lost a loved one or is going through a terrible loss of hope and faith in life. This kind of therapy requires that the therapist comes alongside and stays on the journey until hope has been restored.

Cognitive and behavioral languages are about *what is needed*. What people often need is to better understand their thoughts and behaviors. The "cognitive" approach in therapy is learning to manage your thoughts more effectively. The "behavioral" approach in therapy is about how to manage or extinguish self-defeating behaviors. Since thoughts, feelings,

---

and behaviors are all interrelated, people can make a change in one area and see changes in the other two. Scripture provides encouragement in all cognitive behavioral therapy (CBT) contexts of thinking, feeling, and doing what God has made possible for us and is the approach of choice when people suffer from depression, anxiety, addictions, and other problem behaviors.

Systemic languages have to do with *what is involved*—the systems we live in and how they have influenced us. We are influenced by the rules, roles, and rituals with which we were raised. We are also affected by social and cultural contexts. Family systems therapy, for example, is about becoming more aware of the impact of our familial and social influences and learning to make more adaptive choices. Marriage counseling is another example of a systems approach. Partners create the dynamic of circular causality, as each partner reacts to the others' reaction. Marriage therapists help couples illuminate hurtful patterns of interaction and develop healthier ways to communicate and resolve conflicts. The languages of statistics, social psychology, and cultural contexts also fall under the heading of "systemic languages."

The fifth major psychological language is *medical and biological—what helps.* Some problems have an organic origin. Mental and personality disorders, genetic impairments, issues related to chronic pain, debilitating depression, and panic disorders are just some of the many serious problems that require medical attention. Competent therapists always consider the origin of presenting symptoms and, when necessary, make referrals to physicians and psychiatrists. Patients routinely continue with their therapy with the added benefit of medication.

Psychological languages have been around a long time. Our day-to-day conversations are filled with psychological terms. We use language to communicate ideas, desires, and problems. It is good to be familiar with the psychology of relationships, of mental and emotional health, and of life challenges. Test yourself. I bet you know more psychological terms than you realize. There is a brief exercise in the Appendix to find out how fluent you are in speaking psychologically. Added to these psychological languages are the stories (i.e., case studies) that describe people and their problems as well as a variety of approaches to treatment. I also think of these different stories as literary genre, stories about people and how to help them on their journey.

Stories About People

Psychology consists of stories about people. For the ancients, those stories existed in the form of myths, fairy tales, legends, and sagas. The modern story of psychology begins in 1879 when Wilhelm Wundt established the Institute for Experimental Psychology at the University of Leipzig solely for the study of psychology. Wundt was the first person to call himself a psychologist. Prior to this, psychology had been a branch of philosophy, an inquiry into human nature going back to ancient Greece and Egypt. I would argue that psychology, as the care of the soul, actually had its origin even further back in time to the first time a mother comforted her infant.

Therapists listen to stories—many stories—day after day and week after week. We listen to stories about pain and heartache, about betrayal and trauma, about confusion, frustration, and exhaustion. Our training provides us with many different ways to listen to our client's story and many ways to respond to it. It is important for us to know whether the story we are listening to is our client's story or our own. I once ordered pancakes at a restaurant. When they arrived, I stared in disbelief: They were overlapping the plate. "The cook's hungry," the server said with a smile. We both laughed. I seldom give advice, but when I do, I make sure to reflect on whether the advice is for my client or for me.

People live inside of the stories that their brains tell in order to make sense of themselves, their experiences, and the world around them. The psychologist Dan Siegel (2007) says that our brains "narrativize" experience and self-awareness to create autobiographical memory. The resulting *schema* (belief system) informs our perceptions, beliefs, automatic thoughts, and emotional imprinting from which we construct our reality. As a client tells their story in therapy, we notice how the story reaches into the past for illustrations, circles around present problems, and anticipates the challenges of the future. We may have to construct this format, however, since stories told in therapy rarely follow a linear progression. Our client's brain searches for antecedents and consequences with which to create a narrative—an accumulation and representation of events and meaning selected to invite us into their inner life and the challenges they face. Which of many possible stories are we listening to? What is the story our brain is telling us about the story our client is telling?

The theoretical orientations we study in our training to become psychotherapists provide a library of storied possibilities. In the same way that we study psychological languages, we also study the stories that contain those languages. We study psychodynamic stories about people as they grow and develop, their early attachments and the significant people in their lives, their family and cultural conditioning, their developmental milestones, and the impact of childhood wounds. These are stories about how the effects of the past continue to inform and challenge the story we are living today. We study cognitive and behavioral stories about how thoughts, feelings, and behaviors are all interrelated and that each domain is impacted by the choices we make and rehearse. Our training enables us to become more conscious of the central task of counseling and psychotherapy: to enable people to become more aware of the choices they have in their own stories. We help them to realize that perception itself is a choice, that they have options in choosing how they think, feel, and behave. The goal of our work is to help our clients become more skillful in making healthier and more adaptive choices.

"Freedom," "choice," and "responsibility" (meaning, literally, our "ability to respond"), are terms we become familiar with as we listen to the existential story of human experience. Many of our clients will be trying to make sense of their lives, to find meaning in the problems they face. Others of our clients are trying to make better choices in their relationships, set better boundaries, and deal more successfully with their families. They are telling us about problems in their relationships—a systems story. They want to work on becoming aware of the impact of their families of origin and to be more conscious of healthy ways to think, feel, and behave more independently as separate and unique individuals with the ability to respond from the choice to love rather than to react from feelings of guilt or shame.

The families we grow up in, the cultural norms and expectations surrounding us, and our life experiences create our stories. We cannot abstract ourselves from the influence of the story we live in or the language in which we experience that story. Language lifts experience into consciousness. Language enlivens and deepens experience into story. The diverse studies in the multifaceted languages of our profession equip us to listen more deeply to the stories we are being told in therapy and to hear those stories against the background of the many psychological languages and stories we have been taught. Listening to clients tell us about their challenges and the stories they choose to use to illustrate these challenges, revealing not only their problems but also the way in which they perceive their problems. The host of theoretical orientations we study in psychology classes become the narrative genre that informs our choice of the best way to hear the story and the best way to respond. Of what value is psychology? The study of psychology is the study of the search to understand people: the search to understand the best way to listen to the human story and the best way to help people to live a better story.

The Best Story

All the languages and stories that therapists learn in school are important sources of insight into people, their problems, and the best way to help them. Christian therapists know another story, the best story. The Gospel of Jesus Christ tells us about God's grace, forgiveness, and power to heal hurts, restore relationships, and help people grow. The Christian faith provides answers to existential questions; healthy ways to think, feel, and behave; the best ways to be with others; and insight and wisdom for growth as a human being. I cannot imagine what it must be like to spend hours and hours with hurting people without having faith that God can help them (and me) to deal with their challenges. I know that there are competent therapists who do not have a relationship with Jesus Christ. However, having that relationship provides an extra measure of wisdom, confidence, and endurance. The apostle Paul knew the best story. He lived it. He was gripped by it. The Holy Spirit inspired him to give his life to writing and living the story. People's lives are transformed by Jesus Christ. Their psychology is transformed. Understanding some of what psychology teaches helps us to know more about the transforming power of Christ.

Questions for Review, Reflection, and Discussion

1. How might an understanding of psychology benefit your life?
2. Describe the triune nature of human beings.
3. How would you describe "soul"?
4. What are the five major psychological languages?
5. How would you know if the story you hear is your client's or your own?

CHAPTER 2

The Movement Forward

A Brief History of Psychology

> "God of Your promise, if all reveals Your nature so will I. I can see Your heart in everything You say. Every painted sky a canvas of Your grace. If creation still obeys You, so will I."
>
> —Hillsong United "So Will I"

Chapter Preview and Learning Objectives

The Christian church has evolved since the days of inquisitions and burning witches, and so has psychology. Modern psychology, beginning with Freud, has evolved by developing meaningful stories of people and the ways to help them with their problems. People have evolved as well. A brief look at the stages of human development helps to track the progress of human beings, the corresponding social changes affecting parenting and communities of connection, and the increased acceptance by psychology of a spiritual foundation for healthy living.

Learning Objectives

Students will do the following in this chapter:

- Understand how modern psychology has evolved since the time of Freud.
- Understand how the science and application of treatment has developed.
- Review Erikson's stages of the lifestyle and its impact on culture.
- Appreciate the value of an integrative perspective in clinical treatment.
- Be introduced to *Integrating Spirituality into Treatment*, an APA text.

According, to Hillsong above, everything "evolving in pursuit of what you said?" In 1975, Ray Anderson, a professor at Fuller Theological Seminary, wrote a book entitled *Historical Transcendence and the Reality of God*. Anderson traces the history of God's people from Genesis to Jesus and the evolution of God's working out his plan of salvation. This transition and transformation of God's people may be summarized in Ezekiel 36:26:

> And I will give you a new heart, and a new spirit I will put within you.
>
> And I will remove the heart of stone from your flesh and give you a heart of flesh.

Israel's heart of stone required severe parenting. The Old Testament often describes God as a rigid and exacting father. God's people had not yet matured sufficiently to be entrusted with the grace and freedom purchased for us by Jesus Christ. Anderson recounts God's progressive identification with his people, first with Abraham and the Abrahamic covenant, then with the giving of the law to Moses, establishing the temple and the temple requirements, working through His prophets and judges, and His final identification and promise to humankind in the person and work of Jesus.

One can also see the evolution of the church. The apostle Paul envisioned a "charismatic" community governed not hierarchically but by gifted people of God (1 Corinthians 12:4–7). Later, the church adapted elders and deacons to accommodate the growing needs of the community. Then, gradually, a hierarchy of priests and bishops came into being as the church faced divisiveness within and enemies without.

During times of reformation, the church continues to evolve as polity and liturgy are modified and adopted to remain current with changing cultures. Gratefully, the days of literal witch hunts, torture, burning people at the stake, and, in most cases, requiring rigid adherence to particular forms of worship have passed. The Gospel continues to be robust and attractive to newer generations of believers. The church and God's people, moved by His Spirit, continue to "evolve in pursuit of what You said" (Hillsong United, 2017).

As the Church has evolved, so has psychology. Recall that the downside of the era of "enlightenment" was to question "truths" that could not be proved empirically. The unfortunate consequence of enlightened thinking was to create a deep rift between faith and science. It seems that that rift may be narrowing.

Forward Movement in Psychology

Sigmund Freud published *The Interpretation of Dreams* 121 years ago. Freud was 44 years old and a practicing psychiatrist in Vienna. Having graduated in neurology from the University of Vienna, he was especially interested in the workings of the mind. In his training, Freud inherited the scientific structure of his day, placing the enlightenment tenet of the sovereignty of reason as the supreme test of truth. As such, Freud had no room for faith or traditional religions. What he did accomplish, however, was to demonstrate the effectiveness of helping people recover from biological symptoms that had no organic etiology. He rightly understood that emotion is energy, and when blocked, physic energy can show up as physical symptoms. Psychoanalysis was the technique Freud developed using talk therapy, including dream interpretation, to explore repressed emotion and the resulting biological and psychological symptoms.

It was not until recent advances in fMRI (functional magnetic resonance imaging) technology that science htas actually understood how talk therapy is able to help people. Without the aid of modern instrumentation, Freud had to resort to a subjective interpretation of his clinical observations. Many of those observations were surprisingly astute, and some were pretty far-fetched. Alongside many ground-breaking theories of human behavior, Freud also developed some pretty strange reductionist ideas to explain human behavior. These ideas were typically rejected by his contemporaries, and many are still scoffed at today. Freud's major failing was his arrogance. Without any spiritual foundation or safeguards for his own ego, he lacked the humility to learn and adapt. His ideas were challenged by many of his early followers, some of whom left his inner circle because of his inflexibility. Freud did evolve some of the theories over time but rigidly clung to his most notorious ideas, specifically those regarding repressed sexuality as the single origin of neurotic behavior.

In 1911, Alfred Adler was among the first to leave Freud's circle of followers. Adler noticed how often children developed ways of compensating for being small and feeling inadequate and less powerful than their parents and older siblings. Children, he thought, often create imaginative ideas about ways to feel more powerful and important. Adler called this tendency a child's "guiding fiction." "Someday," kids imagine, "I'll be somebody important," (Ansbacher, 1956, p. 98). We see this tendency today when kids are drawn to comic books and movies about superheroes and heroines. Marvel comics have always been popular. It is interesting to speculate why, in the last few years, people (not just little kids) seem to have become even more eager to escape into a world (via movies and television shows) where powerful figures fight to right wrongs.

For Adler, this idea of "compensation" was a key to understanding human behavior. Normal, healthy people, he thought, seem to strive for success in ways that are socially acceptable and commendable. Immature people (Adler used the term "neurotic") on the other hand, strive for superiority or avoidance (Ansbacher, 1956 p. 104). Personality disorders, according to Adler, might be understood as people who manage anxiety by needing to be better or have more than everybody else. Other methods people use to manage anxiety are hiding out and keeping their world small and safe. Mature, well-adapted people have a healthy amount of social interest. They have learned in their families to be concerned for others.

Adler was very interested in how families conditioned children to think about themselves and others. When parents rewarded their kids for being kind and compassionate, they grew up to create a life that was socially productive. Adler's term for this, "social interest," was exhibited in a lifestyle characterized by productive contributions to society. When kindness and individual effort were not practiced at home or rewarded, when there was no validation or modeling for being a socially mature person, kids could become bullies as children and continue this behavior as adults. With little social interest, people may tend to become exploitive. Because of his interest in how families raise children, Adler is given credit for being one of the first psychologists to think in terms of "family systems." Today, you are able to find Adlerian family therapy and therapists who practice Adlerian therapy online.

The apostle Paul characterized love as being patient and kind. He instructed husbands and wives to work lovingly together to raise children to be obedient to parents, to be kind to one another, and to love God. Paul not only gave instruction to families but modeled loving-kindness and acceptance to his large family of churches. Perhaps the apostle Paul, inspired by the Holy Spirit, is the one who should be considered the first family systems therapist.

Carl Jung was another who left Freud's inner circle because of differences. Jung was one of the first psychiatrists to adopt a "teleological" understanding of human development and behavior. The word "teleology" comes from the Greek *telos*, having to do with how things end up—the end point of a process. *Ology* is Greek for "the study of." A teleological perspective of human development is a consideration of the trajectory and goal of life.

Broadly speaking, psychology includes two major branches, causal and teleological. *Causation* is the idea that nature and nurture interact with each other to create the traits and tendencies of character and personality. The effects of DNA, family and cultural conditioning, and life experiences, including psychological wounds and trauma, are thought to be the causes of both adaptive and maladaptive behavior.

A teleological perspective has to do with what has been called the "actualizing tendency." The actualization tendency comes from the study of biology and affirms that living things have an internal drive to grow—to reach their potential. A teleological perspective of human development is that there is a type of internal "blueprint," or "actualizing tendency," that accounts for our particular interests and life trajectory. Alfred Adler, Carl Jung, Erik Erikson, Carl Rogers, and Abraham Maslow were theorists who believed that even as children we begin to feel the pull of a particular story. If we are fortunate, the story unfolds throughout our life as it twists and turns through wrong directions and dead ends until we emerge, more or less, in a good place in our lives.

Jung called this process "individuation." Individuation, in Jung's mind, was an inner journey. Through the course of our lives, we become more aware of our Self and better able to handle the internal conflicts and confusion that compete with the unfolding of our journey toward wholeness. The term "Self" is Jung's teleological expression of this inner blueprint that guides our preferences and direction in life. Jung would not have argued that behavior can be caused. However, he also believed that the pull of individuation would move us in the direction of wholeness despite our background and life challenges.

Jung's understanding of human nature and the process of individuation is popular with many Christians, largely because Jung developed additional language and insights that help to support the existence of the soul and the processes of spiritual growth. I have not found any evidence that Jung was a practicing Christian. Jung's father was a pastor in the Swiss Reformed Church. Jung was raised with an understanding (and probably an appreciation) of the Christian faith, but it does not seem as if Jung had a personal relationship with Jesus Christ.

When asked whether Jung believed in God, Jung replied that he did not need to believe; he knew (that God exists). I think that Jung found it hard to be a practicing Christian because he saw his father's struggle with his own faith and because, at that time in history, Jung believed that his psychology would have been dismissed by the scientific community if he were to openly profess faith in Jesus Christ. Jung was quoted as saying that he could prove that the *idea* of God existed but that he would leave the study of God to theologians.

What I appreciate from reading Freud, Adler, Jung, Erikson, and others are the insights and thoughtful confirmation that God has created human life with an instinctive drive toward health and wholeness. From these early pioneers in the science of human behavior to the present, one finds intelligent people exploring the human condition, learning about the brain, and searching for the best ways to help people meet life's challenges.

Stages of Human Development

Drawing on a teleological perspective and the actualizing principle, Erik Erikson developed a fascinating theory of human development. Erikson's model suggested eight major stages of human development. Each stage has a positive and negative outcome depending on individual, parental, and social conditions. These stages are:

- trust vs. mistrust: ages 0–2
- autonomy vs. shame and doubt: ages 2–4
- initiative vs. guilt: ages 4–5
- industry vs. inferiority: ages 5–12
- identity vs. role confusion: ages 12–18
- intimacy vs. isolation: ages 18–40
- generativity vs. stagnation: ages 40–65
- integrity vs. despair: 65+

In brief, Erikson is saying that human beings have developmental mile posts that mark their growth as individuals, their maturity, and their progress in life.

When caregiving is adequate, an infant attains the ability to develop confidence that the world is a safe place and that their basic needs will be met. But if care is sketchy or inadequate, the child may miss out on the very first developmental task of life: basic *trust*. With potty training, walking, and praise for self-regulation, *autonomy* is developed. When exploring their world is rewarded, a toddler develops *initiative*. With progress in school and other forms of skill building, a child learns to be *industrious*. An older child begins to develop self-confidence and sense of *identity* as a prerequisite for the ability to make friends and date. With the onset of legal adulthood, a young person is able to make life choices to follow occupational paths and form lasting relationships, *intimacy*. Being a contributing member of society, raising children, and developing creative passions and enjoyable pastimes are possibilities for most adults. Erikson called this stage *generativity*. Each of these eight stages of the life cycle can be accomplished successfully or unsuccessfully. A mature individual has successfully worked through the stages sufficiently to have lived a socially productive life.

The final stage of life in Erikson's model is similar to the teleological goal Jung called "individuation." Erikson found a similar word. He called it "integrity." Erikson was thinking of the less familiar and older idea of integrity, not just about honesty but about things "holding together." In the Navy we used the term "water-tight integrity" to affirm that the ship did not leak. Life "holds together" when we are able to reflect back on our lives with confidence that it was lived well, without too many leaks. Abraham Maslow's "self-actualization" is perhaps the best-known idea describing life's goal of realizing one's full potential. I used the term "fortunate" above because, according to Maslow, one has to be fortunate enough to live in a time and place where one is not preoccupied with survival and can enjoy the luxury of thinking about one's life as opposed to struggling just to stay alive.

This fact was very clear to Maslow, who is best known for developing his theory of the hierarchy of needs. Maslow understood that the most fundamental and primitive human need was survival. One needs to eat, drink, have shelter, and deal with daily subsistence. People also need to be safe and not have to worry about being attacked or threatened. Unfortunately, for too many human beings, staying alive is the horizon of their vision. But along with the needs for subsistence and safety, human beings need each other.

The next level in Maslow's hierarchy of needs is love and belonging. All humans need love and a sense of connection. Vivek Murthy, a former U.S. Surgeon General, wrote *Together: The Healing Power of Human Connection in a Sometimes Lonely World*. We are wired for connection, Dr. Murthy reminds us. Our physical and mental health are severely impacted by isolation and loneliness. Our overall health is improved when we feel connected to others.

> We know we are attending to those connections when we feel 'at home' with a closely knit group or family. We're wired to associate belonging with the sharing of stories, feelings, memories, and concerns. That's why our bodies relax and our spirits lift when we connect in genuine friendship and love. (Murthy, 2020, p. 32)

Hebrews 10:25 admonishes us not to forsake meeting together. It is in community and caring for the well-being of others that we most truly experience our value and the joy of knowing that we are gifted by God. We are gifted by God for the work He has for us. Maslow calls this our need for esteem. Christians understand that it is not as fruitful to seek the esteem of others as much as the esteem and value we experience when we are about the work God has prepared for us.

Maslow's term "self-actualization" is the culmination of his hierarchy of needs. It is the confluence of our doing with our being where what one *does* is an extension of who one *is*. For a fortunate few, reaching a state of self-actualization is achieving a sense of right fit. Again, this is a teleological perspective, underscoring the possibility that one can experience a particular type of "being" that fits and is congruent with one's sense of self. When we know who we are in Christ and we are doing the work He has given us to do, we know the joy of combining our doing with our being. Scripture calls this process *sanctification*, a word that means "to be set apart." "Integrity," "individuation," and "self-actualization" are all terms that describe becoming a unique individual, a person set apart for God's work. God is able to equip and inspire all of his children to do important work. It is inspiring to know the joy of experiencing God's presence and pleasure promised in His Word through Jesus Christ.

Clearly, the teleological perspective is at the heart of most religious thinking, as Rick Warren's *The Purpose Driven Life* (2012) attests. A fundamental tenant in theology is the notion that the soul is a unique spiritual endowment with the capacity to energize and direct one's journey. Interestingly, this teleological perspective also seems to show up in business literature from time to time. Steven Covey's *The 8th Habit* (2005) is a good example. The subtitle of the book, *From Effectiveness to Greatness*, heralds Covey's encouragement to find one's "authentic voice" and to help others to find theirs. In his view, enlightened business practice creates opportunity for individuals to experience their unique contribution and individual voice. It is useful and empowering to imagine that one's story exists as both the push of one's DNA and life experiences as well as the pull of that something more that belongs to each individual and can potentially influence the direction of their life. Christians know that that "something more" is the Spirt of God at work in a human life. A human being is, at the core, that particularization of the Spirit of God that is assigned to each of us.

Thinking Differently

As psychology evolved, researchers began developing theories about human behavior and clinical treatment that could be more rigorously applied to the empirical method of testing and prediction. Many people are familiar with the work of Ivan Pavlov, the Russian physiologist who popularized the concept of "classical conditioning." *Classical behavioral conditioning* is paring two stimuli together to create a new learned response. B.F. Skinner amplified the notion of behavioral conditioning by introducing *operant conditioning*, an understanding of human behavior based on rewards and punishment. Parents praising a child's performance in school or removing privileges for poor performance is the most basic (and likely the most common) form of operant conditioning. This type of conditioning is clearly the most often used by parents, teachers, and law enforcement officers. The blessings and curses God promised to Abraham in the book of Deuteronomy was not the first occasion when human behavior was reinforced or punished by classical and operant conditioning.

Cognitive behavioral therapy (CBT) is directly related to the work of Skinner and others. For example, Albert Ellis (1961) popularized the ABC model of cognitive therapy. Ellis pointed out that an emotional consequence (C) is not directly related to an activating event (A). The emotional consequence is actually related to the belief (B) about the event. This formula is certainly the underlying premise of most self-help books. Of course, the most powerful approach to CBT is in the pages of Scripture. Phrases such as "new creation," "child of God," "chosen," and "beloved" help to align our self-perception with the truth of how God sees us. I often recommend to clients to take time to memorize Scriptures that affirm God's love and grace and the value He places on each human life. I especially recommend that they memorize the 23rd psalm. Once the psalm has been internalized, it is available in times of stress and doubt. I know of no better CBT intervention for Christians.

The mistake that some people make is in imagining that it is easy to change habits of thinking and feeling. When God spoke to Joshua (1:8), saying, "*Keep this Book of the Law always on your lips; meditate on it day and night, so that you may be careful to do everything written in it. Then you will be prosperous and successful*," God was stressing the importance of daily rehearsing and confirming what is truly valuable: who God is, what He has done, who God says we are, and what He has promised. Memorizing and meditating on Scripture daily is an effective use of CBT to internalize God's word.

Recent Developments

In 1969, English psychiatrist John Bowlby published the last of three volumes under the title *Attachment and Loss* (*Attachment*; *Separation: Anxiety and Anger*; and *Loss: Sadness and Depression*). The ideas described in these books have become, to great degree, the current thinking in psychology about the origin of human behavior and human problems. Bowlby's work added to the work of the theorists that came before him and offers valuable additional insight into the importance of early attachments. Psychology has always accepted that understanding early childhood conditioning and life experience was key to anticipating behavioral challenges later in life. But the work of John Bowlby and his colleague Mary Ainsworth has made their research on attachment theory one of the most important recent developments in understanding human behavior.

A simplistic explanation of attachment theory is that in the first few months of a child's life, the quality of the infant's attachment to their mother or primary caregiver may create a lifelong trajectory of behavior. When the quality of care is adequate, a child experiences the benefits of secure attachment that will promote healthier and more mature relationships in the future. If the primary care giver, usually mom, is needy herself and tends to be overprotective and invasive, the child may develop an anxious or ambivalent attachment. The child may then become preoccupied with needing contact and vigilant about maintaining the connection. If, on the other hand, the infant care is inadequate, the child may develop a dismissive and avoidant defense against feeling the chronic disappointment of an abandoning mother.

This understanding of the importance of primary care has become accepted in mainstream psychology. In 1999, Dan Siegel wrote *The Developing Mind: How Relationships and the Brain Interact to Shape Who We Are*. Siegel's work underscored the value of understanding the process of *epigenetics*, how neurons responsible for brain development are "switched" on or off depending on the environment. Siegel (1999) states, "Caregivers are the architects of the way in which experience influences the unfolding of genetically preprogrammed but experience-dependent brain development. Genetic potential is expressed within the setting of social experiences" (p. 85).

When you add "what happened" (the results of childhood experiences and conditioning) to "what's important" (finding valuable and life-sustaining beliefs) and to "what's needed" (practicing healthy ways to think and perceive), you then need to have a good understanding of "what's involved."

"What's involved" is having a clear grasp of the blessings and challenges of living in a family and in a particular culture. Family therapy, including marriage counseling, dates back to the early 1950s. Pioneers in marriage and family therapy understood that people are embedded in families and in cultures and that it would be incomplete to treat individual clients without that understanding. In many cases, the family itself needs help. Families and couples become the "patient." Many successful treatment approaches have been developed in recent years to treat families and couples. These approaches are covered in detail in Chapter 11. All of these developments in treatment approaches alongside a thorough understanding of the many psychological languages used to understand human behavior will give you a pretty complete picture of how to help people. Add the overarching truth of humankind's need for the grace of God, the saving work of Jesus Christ, and the comfort and counsel of the Holy Spirit, and you have a powerful source of healing.

Today

Today, therapists in training typically become familiar with all of the major genres in the languages of psychology. Before students graduate with a master's degree in counseling, they can speak the major languages of their profession. Each language group is an extension of philosophical presuppositions and attendant therapeutic skills. State licensing requirements include many hours of supervised training and exams to ensure that the state can represent to the consumer that an individual is qualified for a state license in counseling. Thankfully, these exams require knowledge of traditional psychodynamic, CBT, humanistic-existential, and family systems. In addition, students must pass ethics exams and be well-versed in cultural awareness, the ability to recognize potential self-harm and suicidality, and contexts that require mandated reporting.

The practice of psychotherapy has evolved and continues to evolve as it searches to find the best approaches to help hurting people. As the discipline of psychotherapy has evolved, so too have clinicians. There was a time when religious and spiritual awareness was deemphasized. Today, the American Psychological Association has endorsed what we have intuitively known: that faith, prayer, and community are important. Below is an additional quote from the preface of the APA text *Integrating Spirituality into Treatment*:

> It is an underlying theme in this book that an understanding of people, individually and collectively, is incomplete without knowing about their spirituality. (Miller, 1999, p. xvii)

This openness to the value of spiritual disciplines is certainly a step forward. As Christians, we understand that true and health-giving spirituality must be grounded on the work of the cross. Following Christ is the surest path to spiritual and psychological wholeness. In 1856, Soren Kierkegaard said that "so soon as psychology has finished it must turn the patient over to dogmatics." Kierkegaard understood that psychology is illuminating and useful, but a complete work of healing is in the saving grace of Jesus Christ.

Questions for Review, Reflection, and Discussion

1. How might you characterize the forward movement in psychotherapy?
2. What is the value of an integrated approach to therapy?
3. Why is it important to appreciate a client's spirituality?
4. Can you find evidence in Scripture for the major approaches to therapy?

CHAPTER 3

How Therapy Works

> "Surely he has borne our griefs and carried our sorrows."
>
> —Isaiah 53:4

Chapter Preview and Learning Objectives

Chapter 3 explains the value of talk therapy in a person-centered approach as well as the uses of cognitive behavioral therapy, existential therapy, and family systems therapy. The chapter illustrates the importance of expressing emotions and the problems associated with mental health when emotions are neglected. The relationship between memory and emotion is explored as well as the way that memory is triggered to create various types of psychological defenses, including PTSD. Therapy includes at various times and in various ways the three tasks of healing, holding, and helping. The chapter discusses how and when to apply each.

Learning Objectives

Students will do the following in this chapter:

- Learn how talk therapy leads to neural integration and the relief of symptoms.
- Review each of the primary forms of psychotherapy.
- Understand the relationship between emotion, memory, defenses, and symptoms.
- Appreciate when and how to apply the treatment benefits of healing, holding, and helping.

I have often heard people ask, what good does it do to just talk about your problems? In fact, some people think that talking about problems only makes them worse. A better idea, many people say, is to stay positive; that is a true sign of faith. The apostle Paul wrote to the church in Philippi, "Finally, brothers and sisters, whatever is true, whatever is noble, whatever is right, whatever is pure, whatever is lovely, whatever is admirable—if anything is excellent or praiseworthy—think about such things" (Philippians 4:8). That is excellent advice. Paul is using "cognitive therapy." He is encouraging folks to stay positive and trust in the Holy Spirit.

I think it was on my 13th birthday that my parents gave me a copy of Norman Vincent Peal's *The Power of Positive Thinking* (1952). Years later, I returned the favor and gave my mom Robert Schuller's book *Living Positively One Day at a Time* (1988). Life is difficult, and it is difficult to remain positive. Joyce Myers, Sarah Young, and so many other Christian speakers and authors remind us of how important it is to hold on to our faith in Jesus Christ and to hold onto God's promises in Scripture to stay positive.

The idea of staying positive can be taken to an extreme, however. I have heard people warn others not to have a "negative confession" and, following Paul's advice in Ephesians, not to let any corrupt conversation proceed out of your mouth. Some Christians feel that it may be a sin or a lack of faith to talk about problems. There are clearly many passages in the Old and New Testaments about being careful about what you think and what you say. Again, Scripture has given us much valuable information and some important cautions about the things we say.

Why Talk About Problems?

Why talk about problems? The answer is because it often helps. I think Paul's admonition about corrupt communication is about fruitless complaining and grumbling. We know what happened to grumblers from the book of Exodus. The danger of a negative confession may be placing your faith in the wrong outcome. "We're not going to get through this!" could be an example of a negative confession. When someone says that talking about a problem will only make it worse, they may be right. But the thing that gets worse is not the problem; it is the emotions about the problem. That is the bad news. But it is also the good news.

It is bad news when a person is stuck with guilt or shame and cannot seem to recover from feeling horrible. The last thing they want to do is to talk about how bad they feel. Regret, remorse, and rage are three emotions that a person would rather not go near. Talking about feelings will likely intensify them or, at least, bring them to the surface when you would prefer to keep them buried.

Does it work to bury feelings? Sometimes. When you have prayed, when you have asked God to forgive you or to forgive someone else, and when you are trusting God to help you move forward, sometimes it is good not to continue to return to the past. "Let go and let God" is the popular saying. Usually that is easier said than done. It is hard to know why some emotions stubbornly refuse to let go. It is hard to know what feelings to leave alone and what feelings cannot be left alone. This is where talking about those feelings can be a good idea.

Reinhold Niebuhr wrote out a prayer for a sermon he delivered in 1943. The prayer reads: "God, grant me the serenity to accept the things I cannot change, courage to change the things I can, and wisdom to know the difference." Those famous words ought to be the central consideration in dealing with emotions. When it comes to expressing painful feelings, we need wisdom and courage. When we are searching for serenity, we need to have faith and trust in God.

For me, Niebuhr is repeating the wisdom of Jesus. Turning the other cheek is very hard for human beings. We are wired for fight or flight. When someone attacks us, we instinctively want to attack back or walk or run away. Jesus is telling us to do neither. Turn into the pain, He is saying. Turning the other cheek means not reacting on impulse. It means taking a breath, offering up a prayer for wisdom, and allowing time for the Holy Spirit to give some direction. Sometimes we know immediately that we are better off keeping our mouth shut. Other times we know that we need to speak up. The vitally important difference between a human reaction and a Spirit-filled response is taking the time to breathe and ask for wisdom.

You know from your own experience how difficult that is to do. When I have a couple in my office for marital counseling, I can tell immediately when the problem is the process. He speaks up, and she clams up. He attacks, and she withdraws, or she attacks, and he withdraws, or they both attack, and heaven help us. Niebuhr's serenity prayer is the right solution, but emotions and defenses get in the way.

Many people do not realize that marriage counseling has very little to do with giving advice. When people are afraid of going to a counselor, it may be because they are fearful of what the counselor is going to say: telling them who is right and who is not or what they should or should not do. People usually know what they should or should not do. The main problem is that they have trouble talking to each other without getting into an argument. They have trouble controlling their emotions and their fight-flight reactions.

What people need is to learn and rehearse skills—when and how to share feelings. They need to practice not doing what comes naturally. They need to practice doing what Jesus told us to do, learn to tolerate uncomfortable emotions, breathe, and ask for direction. In the majority of cases, when people do not get along, the process *is* the problem. What that means is that they do not know how to deal with their emotions. In the majority of cases, when I have gotten a call from a couple wanting marital counseling, they tell me that they cannot talk to each other. They cannot address any problems because they have a hard time talking with each other. Whatever the problem, if you cannot discuss it safely and skillfully—to use a term we used in the Navy—you're dead in the water.

I recall, growing up in the 1950s and 1960s, that many people were encouraged to keep their feelings to themselves, not to feel sorry for themselves, not be complainers, and if you can't say something nice, don't say anything at all. Probably many people who grew up in that era recall that slogan. It was the rule of living in "polite society." Unfortunately, there were consequences to that rule and to the mandate to always be polite. It turns out that stuffing feelings down can be bad for your health, impacting your physical, emotional, and relational well-being.

Like many men, I do not like talking about my feelings. This was reinforced by aspects of the American culture that have historically admired the lure of the rugged individual and the stoic pioneer who faced countless hardships without a murmur. Growing up as a typical American boy, I watched lots of movies. I only remember one film in which my hero John Wayne shed a single tear. He portrayed a retiring Cavalry officer who had been given a gold watch by his troopers. As he read the engraved inscription inside the watch, he self-consciously wiped away a tear and steeled himself for his brief remarks. That was my cultural model for manhood: emotional restriction and stoicism.

I am very fortunate, however, in having other role models. My father was born in Italy. Like me, he prizes the United States as a country and culture that offers the greatest opportunities for individual self-determination. But Dad held on to a bit of his old-world habits so that at the same time I was watching John Wayne movies, my father was offering another role model for manliness: vulnerability and genuine affection. Parents from cultures that do not overrate stoicism, and emotionally intelligent parents from any culture, will appreciate that emotional maturity requires both expressiveness as well as containment and the ability to recognize when which is appropriate. The old advice about children being seen and not heard does not work. Children need to be taught to express how they feel, but they also need to learn when and how to express themselves appropriately.

A new generation has been born, and I am watching many dads and moms make better parenting decisions than their own parents. But many people are still very emotionally immature, and therapists are dealing daily with the physical, psychological, and relational consequences. So I have had plenty of business. In fact, the profession of marriage and family therapy has exploded in the past 40 years. Hundreds of new therapists are licensed annually to deal with the outdated and deplorable consequences to individuals and families of this cultural habit of emotional stoicism.

Why Talk About Feelings?

Why talk about feelings? It is the same answer as talking about problems: Sometimes it helps. It is important to consider how and when and to whom to express your feelings. Ideally, good friends and family members would be your first choice. When you can count on being listened to by a gracious and loving person, it truly does feel better to get things off your chest. Ideally, good friends and family members would be those gracious and loving people. But there can be a problem with talking with friends and family: They have a lot at stake, which means that they may be too quick to give advice or too easily hurt or scared by what they hear. If you want advice, there is no problem in asking for it. But sometimes you just need to vent or share feelings. We tend to be protective of the people we love. If we know that our feelings will likely cause them pain, we typically choose to keep our feelings to ourselves. We do not want to "burden" our loved ones or contaminate them with our own negative thoughts and feelings. Often, pastors can do a good job of listening to feelings. Some problems are too embarrassing to confess to family or friends. Priests and pastors listen to confessions all the time. It is very unlikely that you will feel judged when you talk to your pastor. Thank God for them. You can also thank God for counselors. Counselors have the advantage of anonymity. In some cases, it is nice to talk to someone other than someone you know. This way no one you know will know what you do not want them to know.

Christians appreciate the value of confession. The apostle John tells us that "if we confess our sins, He is faithful and just to forgive us our sins, and to cleanse us from all unrighteousness" (John 1:9). It feels wonderful to know that God has forgiven you. Moreover, when you truly know the truth of that Scripture in your mind and spirit, it is a tremendous emotional release. God's advice and directives are transformative even when we do not grasp the wonderous neurological processes at work. Psychologists use the word "catharsis" to describe that emotional release. Catharsis can be an intense release of emotion. It may feel like "breaking down." Actually, it is "breaking through" all of the barriers that keep uncomfortable emotions tucked away. But catharsis does not have to be an intense experience. It can simply be a deep sigh of letting go. In any case, there are wonderful neurological processes at work to help promote healing and feeling better. Confession is good for the soul.

Emotion and Memory

When someone is talking about their feelings, confessing to something they have done wrong or telling a story about something unpleasant, the brain is actively connecting the story to the emotions involved. Emotional memory has been activated. People often think of a memory as an image, a picture in your brain about something you experienced (e.g., the image of children ripping open their presents at Christmas time). But memory is much more than that. Sometimes there is an image, like the wonderful time you had visiting friends or relatives. You can see their faces, hear their voices, and picture where you were and what you did. But another part of that memory may be the fragrance of turkey and pumpkin pie. You may recall laughter and seem to "hear" familiar voices. So more than an image, memory can also be physical sensations and often emotions.

Here is another interesting thing about memory. It is possible to feel feelings with no conscious connection to an event. For example, you are walking through your favorite grocery store in early November. Suddenly, you are in the best mood. You are completely unaware of the fragrance of a pumpkin spice candle on the shelf nearby. You just know that you feel happy ... or not. That innocent pumpkin spice candle may have triggered emotional memory of Thanksgiving dinners with people who are hard to get along with, are loud, or drink too much. The TV is blaring a loud football game, and no one is actually having a pleasant conversation. As a result, many any people simply hate the holidays.

Memory can be an image or emotion triggered by a sensation, such as a scent, a song, or even the temperature of an evening outdoors. Some of these triggered emotional memories can be pleasant and some not so much. Posttraumatic stress disorder (PTSD), for example, usually involves all three: image, emotion, and sensation. And when someone drops for cover following a loud bang, memory can also trigger behavior. People suffering from PTSD say that it does not feel like there is any "psychic distance"—that is, the past experience and associated memory feels like it is happening right now.

The potential behavioral response to a triggered memory is interesting. I was talking with a client years ago when his cell phone began to ring. His ringtone was the old fashion "briiing" that I was used to growing up. As soon as his phone rang, I began to get up out of my chair, just like I did for the first 60 years of my life. I laughed and sat back down. The imprinted memory had triggered a physical response.

Psychologists call certain triggered behaviors "regression." A female client once presented for therapy with feelings of depression after a breakup with her boyfriend. Part of her depression was related to being unhappy in her place of employment. She was the office manager in a small company run by a husband-and-wife team. Their constant bickering reminded her of her homelife as a child. She was telling me about that experience when she began to cry. Her quiet tears soon turned into to sobs. You can usually tell the difference between a sad feeling and the racking sobs of an ancient pain. She grabbed a sofa pillow and huddled in the corner of the sofa rocking and sobbing. That is what regression sometimes looks like. Regression is a childlike behavioral response to a present emotion connected to emotions from the past. Sometimes it is very painful to watch someone behaving like they did when they were little. However, regression may not always be especially dramatic. Sometimes it can be fairly benign. In fact, I think that most people have times when the feel the need to symbolically hide out under the covers. When stress mounts up, people may feel the need to zone out with an old movie or take comfort from Dr. Ben and Dr. Jerry.

Part of being a therapist cannot be learned. There is an intuitive component to knowing what to say and when to say it, what to ask and when to ask it. Whether it is intuition or accumulated experience, therapists need to know how to be present with their clients in ways that *support* the client's work, not *remove* it. After about 5 minutes, my client began to compose herself. "I'd like to ask you a strange question," I said. She nodded okay. "How old do you feel?" I asked. She looked puzzled. "How old do I feel?" she mused. "Oh, maybe around 5. Oh my goodness!" she exclaimed. "That's how old I was after my mom and dad broke up and my dad left. My mom worked in the evenings, and I would sometimes wake up and she wasn't there. I would sit at the front door and rock back and forth and cry." When someone is in the grip of regression and acting like a little kid, it is often useful to find out how old they feel. That is sometimes a clue to when and how the traumatic experience was imprinted. The key (and the "art") of therapy is timing.

Telling a story may lead to feeling feelings. Much of the time when someone tears up in the midst of telling a story, they apologize and sometimes change the subject. The social convention is that we do not want to burden people with our emotions. But in therapy, that is exactly what you want to do. Telling a story to a therapist usually brings emotion to the surface. Instead of choosing to avoid the emotions, in therapy you are encouraged to express them. That is how healing happens.

The psychological name for that healing process is *neural integration*. Neural integration is how the brain metabolizes strong emotion, redistributing the energy of the emotion to other places in the brain. A crude illustration is adding base to neutralize acid. Once integration or catharsis has taken place, you feel lighter, feel better.

I once had a client who complained about chronic stomach aches. There was no medical explanation for her symptoms. Her doctor suggested seeing a therapist for what she thought could be problems with how she managed stress. It turned out, in talking about the things that happened in her life, that she had been raped as a young child. Her tummy hurt, and she would sometimes remember the feeling. Memory, it turns out, can also be of physical sensations. When the brain *re*-members, it is able to put together an image, emotions, or physical sensations that can sometimes trigger behaviors and the physical echo from old hurts. A "complete" memory may consist of all four of these qualities of memory. *The Body Remembers: The Psychophysiology of Trauma and Trauma Treatment* by Babette Rothschild (2000) is a good source for understanding this phenomenon.

A flashback has been described as a complete memory with no psychic distance. "No psychic distance" means that it feels like it is happening right now: the gunfire, the traffic accident, the attack. A flashback is memory overload. Much of the healing process for post-traumatic stress requires reliving the horror. Therapy for PTSD is often a lengthy, painful process for both the helper and the helped. A saying in the language of recovery is, "You survived the trauma, you can survive the healing."

Why is healing for PTSD frequently a lengthy process? Because the brain has a lot of work to do to access and rewire emotional memory. God protects us from suffering the effects of too much stimuli and emotional overload by making it hard to alter the brain's wiring. Our fragile hold on sanity and emotional stability relies on the brain's preference for consistency—a tendency to hold on to what is familiar and defend against unpleasant thoughts and feelings. Thank God for that. However, those same innate protective defenses make it difficult and time consuming to heal memories of trauma.

A complete memory does not have to feel awful. When you listen to a favorite song and feel like dancing, you may recall the image of dancing with a loved one outdoors on a warm summer evening and the intoxicating feelings of being in love. It may bring back memories of dancing with your friends at a wedding. Or you may feel like lifting your hands in praise and worship, singing extatically and joyfully, remembering the image of an exhilarating time of worship.

So memories can be intoxicatingly wonderful or debilitatingly awful. Some memories are invited, and others are shunned. The term *suppression* describes a reluctance to talk about some things or think about some things and avoid places or people that may trigger unpleasant memory and emotion. "I don't want to talk about that!" and "Why do we have to talk about that again?!" are things people say when they want to suppress painful memories. I watched a movie recently where one of the characters said, "Talking about it will only make it worse." How many times have I heard that line?

Sometimes it is a good idea to avoid certain topics and suppress certain memories. As a therapist I pay close attention to that. When someone is insistent about not wanting to talk about certain feelings or memories, it may be because they are not ready to deal with them. A saying in the profession is that sometimes one needs to "honor the resistance." People are not always prepared to recall certain things. When therapists work with clients to set outcome goals for therapy, an important consideration is "What will be the outcome of the outcome?" In other words, is the person in therapy able to manage the difficult, sometimes overwhelming emotions and images that surface during therapy? In what ways might the person be changed? What might be the changes in relationships or lifestyle? And are the significant people in their life able to deal with those changes?

This is one of the reasons that therapy can sometimes take time. Trust is huge. The person in therapy will need time to develop trust in the therapist, trust in the process, and trust that they can manage the process and the outcome. Jeffery Kottler wrote the book *On Being a Therapist* (2010). He reports that at the termination of therapy with a client, she told Jeff that she had appreciated their talks together, appreciated his interest and interventions. And then she went on to say that what really helped was that he believed in her and she believed in him, and as a result, she was eventually able to believe in herself. Faith, it turned out, was the catalyst for healing.

This is why trust in your counselor, trust in God, and trust in yourself is so vitally important. You need to believe that the process of growth and change, while sometimes painful, is worth the work. There is a saying in the language of recovery—whether recovery from addictions or emotional injuries—that "you have to feel it to heal it." That is a big part of how therapy works. A person begins to tell a story about what happened or what is happening, and emotions are triggered. In the safety and acceptance of a therapist's office, people give themselves permission to be vulnerable. As the story continues, repressed or suppressed emotions are allowed to surface into awareness, where the process of neural integration can begin. But being vulnerable is not easy. It takes time to develop trust, especially when someone has had their trust betrayed. Over time, a client will begin to feel safe enough to practice being vulnerable. Leaning to tolerate the anxiety of being vulnerable is one of the goals of therapy. It is also an important quality for a therapist. The ability to tolerate vulnerability means that you are able to sit with suffering.

Vulnerability is a double-edged sword. If someone has good defenses against being vulnerable, that person may be better equipped to deal with ugly traffic accidents, emergency room trauma, and being on a battlefield. Thank goodness. But sometimes, folks who have good defenses against being vulnerable may also have a hard time feeling deeply. It takes being vulnerable to say, "I love you," to be overjoyed at the birth of a baby, or to be overwhelmed by the beauty of a sunset. You cannot have it both ways. The ability to protect yourself against intense emotion is a good thing (when it does not get in the way of being able to feel deeply).

How Does Talk Therapy Work?

Talk therapy is a carefully guided access to troubling, often buried, emotion. In his book *The Neuroscience of Psychotherapy*, Louis Cozolino (2002) describes the process:

> The combination of a goal-oriented and linear storyline, with verbal and nonverbal expressions of emotion, activates and utilizes processing of both left and right hemispheres, as well as cortical and subcortical processing. This simultaneous activation may be what is required for wiring and rewiring though the simultaneous or alternating

> activation of feelings, thoughts, behaviors, and sensations. The imprecision of stories may be a key to their success in the integration of neural systems with such diverse processing strategies. (p. 170)

Cozolino is describing the process of "neural integration." Emotion surfaces during talk therapy. Once surfaced, emotion can be felt, expressed, and integrated into other parts of the brain, lessening the intensity of the feeling. In *The Making of a Therapist*, Cozolino (2004) goes on to explain:

> In most cases, the primary focus of psychotherapy is the integration of affect and cognition through the alternating activation of emotional and cognitive process, the brain is able to interconnect neural networks responsible for those two functions. The various schools of therapy differ primarily in the emphasis they place on each of the human functions and the techniques they employ to regulate and integrate them. (p. 32)

Talk therapy is not just talking. It is talking about what has to be talked about in a way that allows the brain to do the healing work that God has equipped it to do. Recall from our discussion above that the ability to repress the memory of trauma is a coping mechanism that God has designed to help people, especially children, compartmentalize and dissociate the emotional consequences of trauma. In this way kids get to grow up without having to face the intense anxiety and pain that could compromise their ability to do well in school, make friends, and have the kind of growing up experiences that most kids get to have. *Dissociation* is the term used to describe the brain's ability to maintain memory or present experience out of conscious awareness.

This ability to repress and disassociate the memory of horrific experiences is truly a gift from God. Therapists routinely treat clients in early to later midlife for the reemergence of memories of trauma. These memories are sometimes triggered by current life experiences that are, in some ways, associated with memories from the past. The brain is not especially concerned about what day of the week it is. However, the brain is very interested in making connections between similar experiences. The brain remembers by the process of recollection, associating one experience with another. This is very useful for survival. The brain's ability to access associations between what is going on now and what happened then can save time, embarrassment, and injury. God designed our brains with an effective warning light. It is good to remember where the cliff is and where the lion lives.

Over time, adults acquire many more successful coping strategies than children. Adults can access perspective, positive self-talk, life experiences, and a stronger faith in God. Kids cannot. For that reason, God has given young children the ability to repress and disassociate trauma. God has wired our brains with the ability to quickly dissociate (block out) the memory of traumatic experience. This defense is a Godsend for children. Freed from the horrific emotions that attend trauma, kids are better able to function somewhat normally with less feelings of insecurity and poor self-worth. But while repression and disassociation is a Godsend, it can also be a burden, especially in later life.

A woman once contacted me because she was experiencing symptoms of depression. She did not understand why she would feel depressed. Her marriage was okay, she enjoyed her work, and she had friends at church. As we explored the possible origins of her depression, she began to have flashback-style memories of being molested as a child. More and more intrusive memories surfaced, each worse than the last. It seemed as if the amnesia barrier that had protected her from the memory of the trauma was dissolving. During one session, she reported missing time—not remembering lengthy segments of her previous week. In her therapy sessions, when she would sometimes switch from a kindly, passive person into a more hostile and aggressive personality, it became clear that she was suffering from dissociative identity disorder (DID). DID is a more accurate description than the former "multiple personality disorder." The focus of DID is on the process of dissociation as a valuable defense against horrific, often repetitive trauma. Shifts in styles of personalities or "alters" are caused by alternating aspects of consciousness. Certain "alters" become activated when necessary for protection. Again, thank God for His miracle of protection. When the diabolical intent of some to repeatedly abuse children could shatter a child's soul, God provides the means to hide parts of the self that are being victimized so that there is enough protection for the main personality to function without the debilitating horror of the ongoing awareness of being traumatized. As a result of this complex defensive structure, a child can learn in school, make friends, and have a fairly normal life while unconscious of parts of their life that are being victimized. My client, unfettered by her past trauma, graduated from college with high grades, got married, and had children. It was not until later, when her life was fairly stable, that she began to feel the early warning signs of the difficult task of the healing that lay ahead.

It is not hard to understand the mild form of disassociation that all of us may experience at times. Reading the same paragraph over again because while you were reading you were thinking about something else is a mild form of disassociation; so is missing a freeway offramp or daydreaming in class. More sever disassociation is often accompanied by losing time (e.g., walking out of a shopping mall and forgetting where you parked your car and what is in your shopping bag).

It is in traumatic situations where the gift of automatically repressing (removing from awareness) the memory of a horrific event is such an effective psychological protection. A tiny splinter in your hand or stepping on a small piece of glass may not hurt at first, but soon the redness and swelling will signal that it has to come out. It may be that increased anxiety, depression, or other forms of emotional sensitivity signal the brain's wanting to let go of painful memory so that healing can happen. The process of healing, itself, is typically a lengthy and painful process. Who wants to remember the images and physical sensations of being physically or emotionally abused? The most important prerequisite for healing is trust. A hurting person needs to trust the therapist, trust the healing process itself, and, hopefully, trust god.

Suppression is different from repression in that suppression is volitional, while repression is not. The defense of suppression, as I pointed out above, is consciously avoiding emotion. When people ask, "Why do I have to talk about the past?" it may be because they do not want to deal with the emotions that are likely to surface. And sometimes people are not even aware that the reason they feel uncomfortable with certain topics, certain people, or certain places is because they are locations of repressed, sometimes traumatic memory. These are unconscious "boulders in the road" that people have to keep detouring around. These detours compromise freedom of functioning, as conversations, circumstances, and relationships are all affected by the existence of repressed emotional memory.

Later in life, once our adult coping skills have matured, we are better prepared for the reemergence of traumatic memory. As with my client above, adults may experience unexplained times of anxiety or depression, moodiness, irritability, flashbacks, nightmares, and even loss of time as bits of memory being to surface. People try to deal with these experiences in various ways. But when they persist and when family members are affected, people may seek a therapist's help. Probably a quarter of my practice had been helping people heal from childhood trauma. It would not surprise me if other therapists would cite the same percentage. So, even though people would typically wish to avoid or suppress reliving painful memories, the memories need to surface in talk therapy in order to be processed and healed. The authors of *A General Theory of Love* explain the process:

> The mind-body clash has disguised the truth the psychotherapy is physiology. When a person starts therapy, he isn't beginning a pale conversation; he is stepping into a somatic state of relatedness. Evolution has sculpted mammals into their present form: they become attuned to one another's evocative signals and alter the structure of one another's nervous systems. Psychotherapy's transformative power comes from engaging and directing these ancient mechanisms. Therapy is a living embodiment of limbic processes as corporeal as digestion or respiration. Without the psychologic unity limbic operations provide, therapy would indeed be the vapid banter some people suppose it to be. (Lewis et al., 2000, p. 168)

Talk therapy is not vapid banter. When someone is telling a story and emotions begin to surface, the usual social convention is to apologize for "getting emotional" and changing the topic. But in therapy, people are encouraged to access rather than avoid troubling emotions. Once accessed, the tears, the anger, and the emotion is able to express itself in catharsis. Through the miracle of neural integration, as discussed above, the brain can remove the emotional boulders from the path of one's life. Talk therapy, when it is a genuinely vulnerable admission of pain, works. It sounds simple and simplistic, but it is actually how healing happens. When someone goes to their priest, minister, rabbi, or close friend and confesses a wrong committed or suffered, healing happens. When someone prays, earnestly and sincerely, perhaps with tears, and confesses according to that ancient and powerful prayer in the Episcopal Book of Confessions that "I have sinned against you in thought, word, and deed, by what I have done, and by what I have left undone. I have not loved you with my whole heart; I have not loved my neighbor as myself. I am truly sorry and humbly repent," healing happens. Healing happens, not because of any ritualized prayer in any denominal context but because of a sincere and heartfelt acknowledgment of the pain of doing wrong.

Forgiveness is extremely powerful. When offered with sincerity and an open heart, God works to relieve burdens. From the beginning, Christians discovered that confessing to one another was both liberating and restorative. Without understanding the neurological mechanisms at work, the emphasis of *sincere* repentance enabled supplicants to access the brain's healing capacity. Experiencing communion and community becomes more refreshing and joyful when liberated from the weight of unaccessed pain or unforgiveness.

I have frequently recommended various exercises of forgiveness to clients. Often, writing letters to people that have caused you suffering can be an effective form of healing, whether or not the letter is actually mailed and whether or not its recipient is living or dead. The exercise does help to access and create new neural pathways. The neurological dynamics of Gestalt therapy work similarly. Using various exercises (the empty chair exercise is very common), a client will do the unfinished work of closing the emotional loop, accessing the undealt-with emotions that have been in the way of experiencing or offering forgiveness.

An Episcopal priest once demonstrated an effective form of Gestalt therapy by inviting a seated client to imagine an overpowering image in the chair opposite. The client could imagine a raging forest fire, a flood, a horrific monster. From the perspective of the client, the image could be terrifying. The client was then asked to stand up between the two chairs, looking down at where they previously sat and looking down at the threatening image. The client was asked to imagine that they were now looking down from the perspective of God's omnipotence and overpowering love. From standing in the place of God's love and forgiveness, it was possible to access the deep emotions and barriers that stood in the way of forgiving and being forgiven.

Healing, Holding, and Helping

My wife and I have three types of hugs. We have everyday hugs accompanied by "love you" as we are off in different directions. The second kind of hug may be more of a romantic nature. The third type of hug is when the world crashes in on us and we hold on to each other for dear life. That hug is often accompanied by prayer. Everyone needs to be held at times. It is wonderful when it is a physical hug from a spouse, relative, or close friend. One of the many tragedies of the COVID-19 pandemic was not being able to hug or even shake hands. I miss a nice handshake from a friend. We have family in Italy where kissing on both cheeks is commonplace. How the Italians must have missed that. Human beings and others of the sixth day of creation need to be touched and feel a connection. Recall the research on baby primates (Harlow et al., 1965). The infant Rhesus preferred to cling to the wire mesh "mother" that was covered in terrycloth as opposed to the plain wire mesh mom complete with a bottle of nourishment. Online platforms overflow with evidence of the mammalian need for connection and touch. Why is that?

Certainly, staying close to mom is instinctive, both for food and safety. But you also find adult mammals curled up with each other or just hanging out together. We have two ducks frequently visiting our backyard and pool. They gorge themselves on the food we put out for the birds, swim around a bit, and warm up on the pool deck. The same pair are always together. Scientists talk about "seasonal bonding" for purposes of procreation and safety. My wife and I just think that they like each other. Oh, that reminds me of another psychological term you should know: It is called "projection."

I discussed how healing happens above. But interestingly, therapy is mostly about *holding*. It would be inappropriate for professional counselors to physically hold their clients. Although, when an autistic child is out of control, holding them may help. But the type of holding I am referring to is the holding "environment" provided by the therapist and the context of therapy. A holding environment is the reliable stability, acceptance, and ongoing compassion that a client comes to expect from therapy. Therapist's "hold" their clients with the quality of their attention and care. It is not commonplace for anyone to have another's full attention and interest for an extended period of time. That act, in itself, is tremendously healing. When someone becomes accustomed to the consistency of caring, over time trust is built, and with trust, a client may be open to feeling valued and feeling important. Once again, the authors of *A General Theory of Love* attest: "People do come to therapy unable to love and leave with that skill restored. But love is not only an end for therapy; it is also the means whereby every end is reached" (Lewis et al., 2000, p. 169).

Providing a holding environment is especially valuable when someone is grieving a loss. When someone has lost a loved one, one of the best forms of therapy is to provide a safe place to grieve. Among the most valuable forms of therapy for someone grieving the loss of a loved one is to encourage them to talk about how much they miss that person. That may seem counterintuitive, but in many cases, that is exactly what the grieving person needs to do. I recall an older man who had lost his wife of 50 years. "Tell me about her," I said. He spent the next couple of months telling story after story. We cried, laughed, and allowed the free range of emotions and processes necessary in those stages of grieving described by Elizabeth Kubler Ross.

My wife worked with a Vietnam War veteran suffering from delayed PTSD. She asked him if he had ever talked about his experiences with anyone. He replied "no." "You can share them with me," she said and spent many months "holding" the space for this person to revisit the horror of incident after incident of that terrible war that needed to be dislodged from his soul.

In the healing process of neural integration described above, the more intense or complex the memories, the more time it takes to process them. Wonderfully, therapy can move quickly at times—but often not. It is not uncommon for a therapist to join a hurting person on a long path to freedom from trauma. The journey may be horrifying and agonizing for both client and therapist, but with God's help, healing can happen.

The third part of "healing, holding, and helping" is the helping. Hopefully, all therapy is helping in some way. But there are times when people are stuck with an unresolved conflict or a difficult decision. Therapists can sometimes help by providing direction or a safe place for a person, couple, or family to discuss and discover options. A pastor or elder is often the first person contacted and probably the one providing help much of the time. But in some cases, a pastor or elder may decide to refer to professional help. People will sometimes need to talk over a decision about how to break bad news to a family member or whether to make a move to a new city, to find another job, to set boundaries with relatives, or how to manage a 34-year-old son living in the basement.

I have often provided help to business partners: sisters who co-owned a business, a father and son arguing about business practices, and former friends trying to work out who was supposed to be doing what in the company. Sometimes helping is quick and easy, and sometimes it involves a referral to a professional mediator. The point is that therapy may be a lengthy and arduous process, but sometimes it is simply helping folks decide on the best choice or direction to take in order to move forward.

Questions for Review, Reflection, and Discussion

1. What are typical symptoms of posttraumatic stress disorder?
2. What are some of the triggers for emotional memory?
3. Describe dissociation.
4. How does repression differ from suppression?
5. How can talk therapy be effective in therapy?
6. Describe the process of neural integration.

CHAPTER 4

The Therapist and the Therapy

> "Now to each one the manifestation of the Spirit is given for the common good."
>
> —1 Corinthians 12:7

Chapter Preview and Learning Objectives

Of the seven major categories of human problems (emotional, relational, cognitive, behavioral, spiritual, physical, and crisis), there may be as many as 30 therapeutic approaches. A psychotherapist must be familiar with these problem areas and skillful in applying the most effective therapeutic approach(es). The most important factor in successful therapy is the quality of care offered by the therapist. A Christian approach to therapy may be unique in providing an additional spiritual resource and perspective in the task of helping people heal. The best way to survive the stress of the profession is to feel called to do the work. Like the spiritual discipline of walking a labyrinth, the journey to become a therapist and doing the work of therapy requires both patience and faith.

Learning Objectives

Students will do the following in this chapter:

- Become familiar with problem areas and therapeutic approaches.
- Understand the value of the therapeutic alliance.
- Appreciate the benefits of a Christian approach to doing therapy.
- Explore the student's spiritual calling to the work of therapy.

Different Problems, Different Approaches

Talk therapy is the most common form of therapy. It is the center of the wheel from which all other forms of therapy are the spokes. When discussing how counseling works, it is important to identify the reasons a person makes an appointment. There are seven large categories of problems: emotional, relational, cognitive, behavioral, spiritual, physical, and crisis. Within these categories, Dr. Barbara Ingram, in her book *Clinical Case Formulations* (2006), lists 30 specific life problems and suggests therapeutic approaches that would be appropriate in addressing these problems. I recommend this book to anyone who wants a clear outline of the problems people face and the many therapeutic approaches to help them.

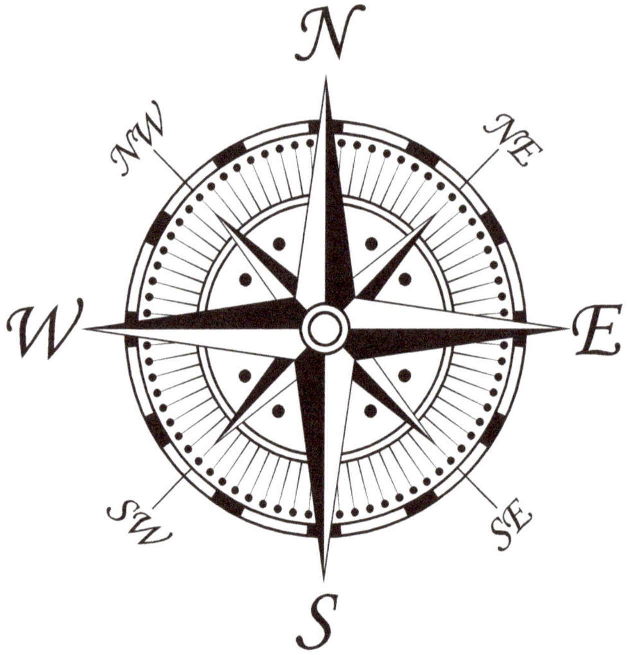

FIGURE 4.1 *Compass Card*

When teaching students about the different approaches to therapy, I often refer to the mariners' compass. A ship's helmsman steers his course guided by the ship's compass. The therapist steers the course of therapy guided by an internal compass: their ability to match a treatment plan to the presenting problem of the client. Clearly, the ability to steer the right course depends on the ability to navigate the many potential directions a course of treatment may take. The navigator's skill is tested by the strong and varied currents of conversations present in a typical hour of therapy.

While there are four main points of the mariner's compass (north, south, east, and west), the therapist's compass must include a fifth point. The five main compass directions (psychodynamic, humanistic/existential, cognitive/behavioral, systemic, and medical/biological), as discussed above, share many similar goals and strategies for healing and growth. In navigating treatment, it is important for the therapist to be very familiar with each of these compass points and directions.

When a therapist is considering a psychodynamic approach to therapy, the therapist is interested in what happened in a person's life that has contributed to their developmental challenges. What attachment issues or significant relationships were at work in the client's early life? What were the dynamics of social and familial conditioning that may have contributed to the problems the client is facing today? What types of life experiences or traumas might have occurred? A psychodynamic approach provides not only insight into these issues but also an opportunity to work through or heal these developmental conflicts.

The therapist must understand how to navigate in a humanistic/existential direction (i.e., what is important) by offering unconditional positive regard, empathic listening, and genuineness. Carl Rogers (1951) was confident that when a therapist offers these qualities, the client will be able to overcome the all-to-common conditions of worth that limit their potential. That potential is fully realized when, according to Abraham Maslow (1954), a person has managed to meet basic survival needs, has experienced belongness and love, and has reached a quality of self-esteem that opens to the possibility of *self-actualization*—a confluence of doing with being.

Striving to be an authentic self, facing life and death courageously, and embracing the freedom that comes with the responsibility of being fully alive describes the "existential" goal of creating meaning and striving for what is truly important in life. The core competencies for a therapist doing the work of existential therapy are patience and empathy. Finding the right path through the pain of loss, searching for how to make sense of tragedy, and establishing a sense of meaning and personal value in the midst of challenging life experiences takes time and the willingness to compassionately "suffer with."

Changing behavior and ways of thinking frequently requires practice. The "cognitive and behavioral" direction on the clinician's therapeutic compass (i.e., what is needed) helps a client to acquire the insights and behaviors essential for mature living. A mature individual examines their thoughts and beliefs in the light of reality and healthy decision making. Mature decisions are made in spite of or in the face of difficult emotions. Growth in maturity requires learning and rehearsing these skills. As I pointed out above, the core competency of mature living is being aware of and making realistic, adaptive life-enhancing decisions. The therapist encourages the client to explore alternative ways of thinking, feeling, and behaving with a view to creating the habit of examining the core beliefs and automatic thoughts that interfere with mature decision making.

It has been said that culture is the sea in which we swim. We are continually influenced by familial, cultural, and philosophical systems. Consequently, the therapist's compass must also point in a *systemic* direction. A systems perspective (i.e., what is involved) helps the client to successfully deal with the complex challenges of being human. No current textbook in the field of clinical training fails to review the important steps to being culturally sensitive. It is also essential to have a thorough understanding of how families influence thoughts, beliefs, and behavior. The rules, roles, and rituals that we grow up with condition our worldview, values, and perceptions. Because of this, each new client interviewed, regardless of apparent similarities, represents a cross-cultural encounter requiring curiosity and genuine respect for different family experiences. I have included an exercise in the Appendix for the reader to explore their own family's rules, roles, and rituals. So much of our current behavior and ways of thinking are set down in a script-like fashion as children. It is interesting and useful to take a close look at the family rules that may still be influencing us unconsciously. Becoming aware if this early scripting frees us to make wise choices for our life today.

Offering a systemic approach to therapy requires a thorough understanding of the myriad dynamics and complexities of a system. A family systems therapist must recognize the operation of homeostasis, scapegoating, circular causality, emotional cutoff, multigenerational transmission, and so forth. Working with an entire family presents unique challenges to grasp the family dynamics at work and work to "unbalance" the system sufficiently to create new patterns of interaction. I have included a visual, displaying various approaches to family therapy, in the Appendix.

The fifth direction in therapy is the need to consider physical and biological issues. Issues such as sleep problems, chronic pain, physical injury, and other health problems certainly influence the process and outcome of therapy. A common concern for therapists is the need to refer a client to a physician for medication. Serious problems, such as depression, anxiety, sleep disorders, and other types of psychological disorders, should not be treated with talk therapy alone. As always, people suffering with physical illness are encouraged to contact the elders of the church for prayer. There should be no conflict or contest between faith and science. God has given us many and various tools and talented people with which to carry out His work of healing.

A skilled psychotherapist speaks many psychological languages. People present with a variety of problems that call for a variety of theoretical perspectives and approaches. It is good when a therapist can quickly and intuitively grasp the best direction and intervention to use with a patient. Sometimes the focus will be on present problems, sometimes on past effects. The focus may be on disruptive thoughts, feelings, or behaviors. Whatever the focus, that intuitive approach must arise from a solid foundation of clinical training. To that end, I agree with the authors of *A General Theory of Love*:

> Strip away a therapist's orientation, the journals he reads, the books on his shelves, the meeting he attends—the cognitive framework his rational mind demands—and what is left to define the psychotherapy he conducts? Himself ... The dispensable trappings of dogma may determine what a therapist thinks he is doing, what he talks about when he talks about therapy, but the agent of change is who he is. (Lewis et al., 2000, p. 186)

The affirmation above is repeated again and again in psychological literature. Current textbooks on counseling techniques all agree that the therapist themselves are the catalyst of change. Carl Rogers, with his research into the healing properties of psychotherapy, was possibly the most articulate on this point. But while I agree with the quote from the authors above, I am fairly sure that they take for granted that the agent of change, the therapist, has thoroughly learned their craft. An accomplished artist has mastered technique so thoroughly that the brush seems to be directing itself. I have an artist friend who, at various shows, is frequently asked the question, "How long did it take you to paint this?" He always enjoys answering, "40 years."

Much the same, a competent therapist has skillfully and intelligently integrated and refined their theoretical insights. And those insights find their common roots in the fundamental truths and stories about what people feel and need. They may have a preference for a specific theoretical approach, but ideally, that approach has been carefully selected from a clear understanding of its advantages and disadvantages relative to other approaches and against the backdrop of the therapist's own unique personality, style, and clinical strengths. Clearly, the most valuable clinical strength, along with training and experience, is a person's relationship with Jesus Christ.

What Makes Counseling Christian Counseling?

The answer to that question, of course, is Christ. Scripture says that if a person is truly a follower of Jesus Christ and committed to the guidance and direction of the Holy Spirt, that person has access to an extraordinary source of compassion and insight. The Christian counselors I have talked with have confirmed my experience that, at times, what occurs in a counseling session is nothing less than miraculous. Sudden flashes of insight, words of knowledge and wisdom, and the sense of God's presence lift a typical therapy hour into an experience of the sacred. There have been times over the years that I have strongly felt the desire to remove my shoes.

Having had those experiences, it is hard for me to imagine how anyone would be able to successfully survive the profession without God's help. God's help, of course, is present and active, whether or not we are aware of it, but there is clearly an extra measure of confidence and faith in a successful outcome of therapy when one believes in and actively seeks God's provision and direction. Sharing a journey with a client who has been physically and emotionally abused, who has been raped, betrayed, abandoned, or is desperately unhappy with life, is frequently traumatic and exhausting. I could not do it unless I knew that I was called to this very difficult path.

Interestingly, therapeutic techniques can be a way to avoid being on that journey with a client. It is possible to hide (and probably many do) behind techniques. "Case management" is a term that is often used in the profession. There is nothing wrong with the term. It signifies an intelligent approach to clearly understanding and identifying the problems a client is facing, developing a set of appropriate outcome goals, and defining the process goals that a clinician will follow in order to provide effective treatment. There is nothing wrong with the term, but one needs to be cautious. "Desacralization" is a term that has been used to describe the temptation to shrink back from the enormity of the significance of being on a healing journey with another human being. If therapists reduce injured people to "cases" and become stuck in treatment modalities, they risk missing the awesomeness and opportunities of their calling.

The Therapeutic Person

There are many gifted people in the body of Christ. In 1 Corinthians 12:7–11, the apostle Paul tells us that God's wisdom, knowledge, and healing is at work in the body and that the Spirit of God has been given for the benefit of all of us. Healing, restoration, and transformation are available in Christ's Body, the church. So why do we need psychiatrists, psychologists, and counselors?

The *therapeutic person*, whether psychotherapist, social worker, religious leader, or gifted lay person, is able to find what is needed from God to extend His healing work to a struggling human being. That person may also be *called* to do the work of healing and is frequently used by God to touch lives. That gifted, therapeutic person, called to work of healing, will likely be even more effective, more frequently successful, and less likely to make costly mistakes, when they have had formal psychological training.

That training, depending on the therapeutic focus and geographical region, will include years of formal education; many hundreds, sometimes thousands, of hours of supervised experience; a rigid licensing procedure; and confirmation by a state licensing board. Granting an individual a license to practice psychotherapy, a state board of consumer affairs attests to an applicant's qualifications to practice in that state. But it cannot attest to that person's effectiveness. There are many outstanding therapists and some less so. The therapist's experience, scope of practice, and familiarity with the presenting problem will be a factor in any successful treatment. Why do we need psychology? If you, your spouse, children, relatives, friends, or parishioners need mental, emotional, or relational help, you are safest and more likely to have a successful outcome when you see a trained professional. Why is that?

Gifts and Calling

There is no question that the Spirit of God is able to work effectively through God's people. The Holy Spirit is able to provide a word of knowledge, a word of wisdom, and a healing experience through any committed believer. But most often, God equips His people with special gifts for particular aspects of ministry. He also equips His people with a special calling: a prompting to get the additional training and experience necessary to be especially effective in the pursuit of that calling.

God calls people to many different types of work. One can feel called to a particular work or called to be a type of person whom God can use to touch lives regardless of the type of work. I have often heard people report that they love their work and would not want to do anything else. I have heard that from firefighters, plumbers, nurses, cabinet makers, composers, and even street food vendors.

When Abraham Maslow coined the term "self-actualization," it was because he believed that it was possible for a thoughtful and tenacious person to discover what they are meant to do. Carl Rogers believed similarly and used the term "actualizing tendency" to describe the process of biological organisms growing to reach their full potential. The church did not need Maslow or Rogers to tell us what we knew already: that God enables people to discover their gifts and calling. What Maslow and Rogers did accomplish was to give us a host of valuable insights about that growth process and a great deal of additional language to help us gain a clearer understanding of what that process looks like and what it is able to achieve.

Science is in the service of God. Scientists may not know where their industry and inspiration come from. Perhaps those who do know may find additional motivation and meaning in their work. Or perhaps not. God is the author of industry and inspiration whether or not one realizes it. But it has been my experience that people who acknowledge that their gifts and insights come from God find a greater sense of joy, purposefulness, and endurance in their work.

It has been said that when one is doing the right work, the energy for the work is *in* the work. I have been tired at the end of a long day working with clients—tired, but not depleted. There were mornings, even after coffee, when I was not quite ready to face the day. But as the work began, I felt God's presence and felt energized by the Holy Spirit to do the work

He has given me. There is no greater joy than doing the work God has called you to. More than 50 years later, I still enjoy and am inspired to do the work God has called me to.

Without God's grace and gifts, we would be in a great deal of trouble. We are fearfully and wonderfully made, which includes His provision: our psychological defenses against our enemies of debilitating anxiety and paralyzing imagination. God has also provided gifted people to help us. These included physicians, psychiatrists, psychotherapists, social workers, pastors, and a host of compassionate individuals who are inspired by the Spirit of God to care for others. I have often asked students in my graduate courses how many of them felt called to become counselors at a young age. Typically, well over half the class raised their hands. God has called men and women into his service, often as early as they are able to hear His voice. God's spirit, like a flame, is infinitely available to every willing heart.

In 1996 James Hillman wrote *The Soul's Code.* He initially wanted to entitle his book *The Acorn Theory* because of the idea that everything that causes an acorn to become an oak is resident within the acorn. The book is an interesting accumulation of illustrations about people who sensed their calling, the trajectory of their soul's code, at a young age. As a young person, I had a vague idea about wanting to help people. I started down a path that led to another path, and another path, until I finally discovered what God had already planned for my life. When people allow God to lead, He is able to enhance their innate talents and abilities and give them additional gifts and motivation to be of service in His kingdom. As the illustration of the labyrinth in Figure 4.2 portrays, often the path God has chosen for us is circuitous.

Read Chris Vogler's *The Writer's Journey* (2007). The book is not just for writers; it is for anyone interested in the story arc of successful films featuring a hero's or heroine's journey. Life is a journey, and we are all heroes and heroines in our own story. Vogler makes the point that all meaningful journeys consist of archetypical patterns: leaving the familiar, facing the unknown, dealing with allies and enemies, finding mentors, crossing thresholds, ordeals and challenges, and coming to the end of the journey, hopefully, having attained something of value. You will find connections from your own story in Vogler's work. He also provides an interesting critique of many films as illustrations of archetypical patterns alive in stories.

The Journey

Figure 4.2 is the plan for the labyrinth at Chartres Cathedral in France. What is the difference between a labyrinth and a maze? People often confuse the two. A typical maze is designed for entertainment. With all of the possible wrong turns and dead ends, one can spend a lot of time trying to get to the center of the maze and a lot of time trying to get back out again. A maze is usually built of a hedge material tall enough to keep you from seeing where you are going. A labyrinth, on the other hand, is very different.

A labyrinth is typically laid out in tile on the floor of a cathedral or from rocks or plants in a garden. It is not for entertainment. It is for growth. Walking the labyrinth is a spiritual exercise. There are no dead ends or wrong turns. You will arrive at the center—just not in a linear way or in a way you can control. Walking the labyrinth requires patience. While there are no wrong turns, you will spend much of the time (apparently) going the wrong way, and

FIGURE 4.2 *Chartres Cathedral Labyrinth*

much of the time you will be going around in circles—a little like life.

The lesson of the labyrinth is a lesson about life. Life requires patience, obedience, and faith that with God's help and leadership, you will arrive at a good place, the place that God has prepared for you. You will not know the outcome of your journey until you arrive, not at a location, but at an understanding. The labyrinth teaches us that our job is to walk, trusting that God is leading.

As a young Christian, still on active duty, I was given a book that helped me on my journey. In 1957, Watchman Nee, a Christian church leader in China, published *Sit, Walk, Stand*, a commentary on the progress of the Christian journey from the book of Ephesians. Nee (1957) pointed out that the first task of a Christian is to fully grasp that we are *seated* with Christ in heavenly places (Ephesians 2:6). From this confidence we can *walk* in those ways that He has prepared for us (Ephesians 2:10) and are thus able to firmly stand against the wiles of the devil (Ephesians 6:11).

The idea of sitting and walking before standing made sense to me. It also made sense to George Herbert, a 16th-century English cleric, who wrote the poem, "Love" (Herbert, 1983, p. 141)

> LOVE bade me welcome; yet my soul drew back, Guilty of dust and sin.
>
> But quick-eyed Love, observing me grow slack from my first entrance in,
>
> Drew nearer to me, sweetly questioning If I lack'd anything.
>
> "A guest," I answer'd, "worthy to be here:" Love said, "You shall be he."
>
> "I, the unkind, ungrateful? Ah, my dear, I cannot look on Thee."
>
> Love took my hand and smiling did reply, "Who made the eyes but I?"
>
> "Truth, Lord; but I have marr'd them: let my shame Go where it doth deserve."
>
> "And know you not," says Love, "Who bore the blame?" "My dear, then I will serve."
>
> "You must sit down," says Love, "and taste my meat." So I did sit and eat.

In his argument with Christ, Herbert realized that he was not the one in charge. He learned that we are not ready to serve until we have spent time sitting at Christ's feet, discovering who we are and Whose we are. We may not feel worthy; Love says we are. In

George Herbert, "Love (III)," *The Temple: Sacred Poems and Private Ejaculations*, 1633.

gratitude we may want to jump into walking and even standing. Love says, "First, you must sit, learn about me, learn to trust me, and learn to savor our relationship."

In a class in systematic theology at Fuller Seminary, Ray Anderson reminded the class that God is not the *object* of our investigation but the *subject* of His self-disclosure. In those early days of my faith renewal, I also read *New Creation Realities* by E. W. Kenyon. In illustration after illustration, Kenyon hammered home the truth and power of those amazing words by the apostle Paul in his second letter to the church at Corinth: "Therefore, if anyone is in Christ, the new creation has come: The old has gone, the new is here!" (2 Corinthians 5:17). After I finished the final chapter of *New Creation Realities*, I closed the book, closed my eyes, and whispered a heartfelt "Thank you, God." To this day, I cannot imagine a more powerful affirmation of the value of each of God's children.

It often takes time for the truths in Scripture to penetrate. One walks the labyrinth as a reminder. You walk slowly, patiently, prayerfully, confident that life is purposeful and that God is leading. The psychologist Albert Ellis, who founded an approach to therapy called "rational emotive behavioral therapy," is one of the pioneers of the cognitive behavioral approach to therapy. Ellis (1961) is best known for his ABC approach to therapy, stressing the importance of belief. In Ellis's equation, C (an emotional consequence) is not directly related to A (an activating event). It is A plus B, the *belief* about the event, that creates C. That formula is at the core of most self-help books and many sermons. Cognitive behavioral therapy along with the heart of Christian doctrine affirms that it is what you believe that drives your emotions and behaviors. It is important to look carefully at what you believe.

I have not thought about the relationship between Albert Ellis and Charters Cathedral, but of course, the connection is that it takes time, patience, and faith to change, to step out on what you believe. When the apostle Paul talks about the renewal of your mind and Albert Ellis reinforces the value of belief, both describe the power of faith. Faith in the Gospel of Jesus Christ is acquired by sitting and strengthened by walking. We sit at the Master's feet as we attend to His Word as it is ministered to us in Scripture, sermon, and the counsel of Christian brothers and sisters. I am reminded of the awesome opportunity I have as an elder and teacher. Like all students, I have spent many hours *sitting* and studying. I have *walked* with the Lord for many years. And now I am able to *stand*, believing that God is helping me to be a capable instructor.

Questions for Review, Reflection, and Discussion

1. What is the value of the therapeutic alliance?
2. What is valuable about a Christian approach to counseling?
3. What value is there to feeling called to do the work of therapy?
4. Have you felt a calling to do a certain type of work?
5. If you do not have a labyrinth nearby, what can you do to apply its lessons?

Credits

CHAPTER 5

Denial and the Mechanics of Escape

> "He prepares a table before us in the presence of our enemies."
>
> —Psalm 23:5

Chapter Preview and Learning Objectives

This chapter addresses the benefits and liabilities of denial and other psychological defenses. God gifted us with an innate ability to cushion ourselves against trauma. In addition to our psychological defenses, the Christian faith encourages us to know that God will help us through life's difficulties. The philosopher Søren Kierkegaard stated that everyone has to deal with existential anxiety. The choices people make in relation to that anxiety comprises much of human behavior, both healthy and dysfunctional. Other psychological defenses, such as repression, suppression, displacement, sublimation, and dissociation, are discussed in the chapter as well as the most common fight-flight defenses. Our most effective life skill is to cultivate faith in God.

Learning Objectives

Students will do the following in this chapter:

- Recognize the nature, benefits, and liabilities of psychological defenses.
- Appreciate the extent and pervasive effects of existential anxiety.
- Explore individual defensive history and preferred fight-flight mechanisms.
- Understand the benefits of leaning on God in difficult times.

I grew up in the 1950s. For me, it seemed like a very innocent and wonder-filled time to grow up. My parents took my brother and me to Disneyland the year it opened, and like many other boys, I later wore a Davy Crockett coonskin cap. In 1959 seven astronauts were chosen to participate in the Mercury space program and the U.S. economy was doing very well. Everything seemed happy and positive. Oh, except for the threat of imminent nuclear annihilation! Those of us who were children in the 1950s recall drop drills in school and periodic testing of air raid sirens. Someone in our classroom would be selected to close all of the window blinds to prevent glass from being blown into the classroom from the atomic blast. Building fallout shelters and stockpiling emergency food and other essentials, many people were preparing for a nuclear attack. Thank God for denial. If it was not for God's gracious gift of this built-in cushion against terror and trauma, all of us kids of the 1950s would have become nervous wrecks.

Denial—The Good Kind

God has given us three formidable cushions against the wear and tear of daily anxiety and fear. These three cushions are faith, caring people, and our psychological defenses. We know about the power of faith and of the love and care of others. But for many people, the workings of denial and others of our psychological defenses are still pretty mysterious. Denial is the brain's ability to screen out some of the horrible things we might imagine could happen to us. For example, can you imagine not being able to ride in a car, go on an airplane, or even leave the house for fear that something awful could happen? God has blessed us with the ability not to dwell on or be paralyzed by everything that could possibly go wrong in our lives.

Good denial is feeling confident that you can drive on the freeway, board an airplane, or visit your friends in another state and probably not have any serious problems. On the other hand, bad denial is thinking that bad things will never happen to you or that God will protect you from ever having an accident or getting sick. When the Lord is our shepherd, we can be confident that He will prepare a table before us in the presence of our enemies, not that we will never have enemies. Our enemies are our fears and worries, our bad habits, and, sometimes, hurtful things done to us by others. The table that God has set for us are His provisions for times that we are fearful, discouraged, and injured by life or by other people. Good denial allows us to wake up in the morning without a terrible sense of sadness and foreboding about the condition of the world. The world's problems can wait a bit while we have our morning coffee. Again, denial is a cushion that allows us to be in the present moment without having to deal with a flood of "what ifs."

Denial is different from pretending. Pretending is volitional; denial is fairly automatic. Pretending that we can go to sleep at night and not be burgled does not work very well. We are too aware that we are trying to trick ourselves. Not locking our door at night, believing that no one would be interested in breaking in, does not work very well either. Denial is simply the brain's ability to be fairly certain that we are safe at night—but it is probably wise to lock the front door.

Denial—The Bad Kind

Bad denial is thinking that we are immune from life's difficulties, that life should be fair, that everything will work out the way we want. This kind of denial gets in the way of growth and reasonable precautions; it also gets in the way of trusting God. M. Scott Peck began his book *The Road Less Traveled* (1978) with three words: "Life is difficult" (p. 1). According to Peck, people must choose to come to grips with that fact or live in denial, trying to avoid the unpleasant truths about life's difficulties. The Bible does not lie about reality. Jesus said, "In this life you will have tribulation" (John 16:33). What is his remedy for life's tribulation? It is not denial. It is not a healthy financial plan or daily vitamins. "Be comforted," Jesus said, "I have overcome the world" (John 16:33). What gave the apostle Paul the strength to endure his tribulation? His answer: "For to me, to live is Christ" (Philippians 1:21).

Too much denial is dangerous. Bad things happen, often with tragic results. Too much denial (the "It won't happen to me" type) means that people suffer from the results of senseless risks. Too little denial is also dangerous. People with obsessive compulsive disorders, anxiety disorders, and agoraphobia live with debilitating fear that controls their lives. What is an optimal amount of denial, denial that is protective but not overly restrictive? How does one acquire an optimal amount of denial?

Christians have to be particularly wise not to confuse faith with denial. It is hard to do. It is important to have faith and to believe that God answers prayer. It is also important to use common sense. Automobiles need fuel. People sometimes require medicine. God gave us a sound mind as well as the promptings and conviction of the Holy Spirt. They ought to work together. Optimal denial is a balance of faith and common sense that comes with time, maturity, and practice.

Existential Denial

In a class on theological anthropology at Fuller Seminary, I was assigned a book by Ernest Becker, *The Denial of Death*. Interesting, I thought, that my professor is assigning a book by a cultural anthropologist from a Jewish background. What does this book have to do with a biblical understanding of human nature? Becker wrote his Pulitzer Prize–winning book in 1973 one year before he died of cancer at age 49. It has turned out to be one of the most important books in my library.

The Denial of Death is mainly focused on understanding human behavior, especially as it relates to the problem of managing anxiety. Reading the book, you are presented with two important existential questions: How should I live, and in what should I believe? The psychologist Eric Fromm said that one of our fundamental human needs was what he called a "frame of orientation": a map of reality to help us make sense of the world and goals to move us forward (quoted in Feist et al., 2017, p. 191). From his expansive scope of philosophy, theology, psychology, and literature, Becker concluded that the best frame of orientation was the Christian faith. Toward the end of the book, Becker (1973) makes this astonishing statement: "Christianity, on all the things we have listed, stands high, perhaps even highest in some vital ways, as people like Kierkegaard, Chesterton, the Niebuhr's, and so many others have compellingly argued" (p. 204). After reading this strange quote from a cultural anthropologist with a Jewish background, I was able to grasp why my professor had assigned it.

The existential philosopher Søren Kierkegaard used the term "angst" (translated as "dread") to describe the background emotion of pervasive anxiety that all human beings share in common. In his book *The Concept of Dread* (1844), Kierkegaard explained that angst lies at a low level of awareness, which, at times, surfaces into consciousness revealing our finite nature: that we will one day die. Human beings are conscious that they are finite. They may choose not to think about that fact, but the fact will not go away. Each human being is unique, valuable, and potentially very creative. Human beings typically believe that their life has meaning, that they matter, that they have something to give or leave behind for the next generation. It is painful to consider that life is short and may end without one having lived a truly meaningful life. Physical and emotional symptoms originate not only from toxic relationships but also from this pervasive and deep-seated type of anxiety.

Psychology is tasked with dealing with these physical and emotional symptoms, but according to Kierkegaard (1844), only faith in God can successfully manage angst. Kierkegaard argued that allowing ourselves to face the reality of being finite creatures is what will eventually lead us to faith. Psychology can help but it cannot save. In *The Concept of Dread*, Kierkegaard (1844) states, "So soon as psychology has finished with dread, it has nothing to do but to deliver it over to dogmatics" (p. 145). He used the term "dogmatics" where we would use terms such as "theology" or "faith."

Existential therapy is an extension of existential philosophy. The reason that so many Christian therapists embrace this approach to treatment is because existential philosophy, along with the Christian faith, is interested in the relationship between both our physical and our spiritual existence. Existentialists describe human beings as having a "dual ontological" nature. That means that human beings live constantly in a tension between two diverse natures: our creative potential (possibility) and our daily struggles (necessity) between our finite life and our infinite spiritual existence. Existential philosophy asserts that living daily in that impossible tension is what creates existential anxiety (as well as the potential for growth), and much of human behavior, for better or worse, revolves around managing that anxiety.

Three Paths

There are three ways to manage existential anxiety. You can avoid possibility, avoid necessity, or understand God's purpose for your life. People avoid possibility when they preoccupy themselves with staying safe, keeping their world small and manageable, avoiding taking risks, settling for a two-week vacation at the same location every year, and, if they are well off, retiring near a golf course. Kierkegaard called this being "tranquilized in trivia."

People avoid necessity when they put off seeing doctors, do not take care of themselves physically, develop an uncritical "God will provide" or "It will all work out" attitude, and take unnecessary risks. Recall that the term "suppression" means "I don't want to think about it. I don't want to talk about it." Suppression and avoidance are psychological defense mechanisms but are different from denial in that people typically do not choose to be in denial, but they do choose suppression and avoidance.

The best way to deal with existential anxiety is to face it. Rollo May wrote *The Courage to Create* in 1975. An existential psychologist, May encourages people to find the courage to come to terms with death. Life is finite. Peter reminds us in 1 Peter 2:24 that like grass, we soon wither and die. With courage and prayer, one can find a creative way to contribute, to make a difference in the time we have on Earth. Becker (1973) concludes *The Denial of Death* with this quote: "The most that any one of us can seem to do is to fashion something—an object or ourselves—and drop it into the confusion, make an offering of it, so to speak, to the life force" (p. 28). Life is difficult. How do we respond to that? Becker says we need to make something, to create. He was right. That's exactly what we were created to do. In Genesis 1:28, God commissioned us to be cocreators. In using existential language, Becker had the right idea, but lacking a strong faith in Jesus Christ, his directive is not very helpful.

When God spoke to the first humans and to all humans in Genesis, He instructed us to be fruitful, multiply, replenish the earth, subdue it, and have dominion over the fish of the sea and the birds of the air. In this, God is speaking to the human race, but what if He were speaking to you? How would you make sense of this verse if it was God's commission to you personally? Thinking about that question, I concluded that God meant us to be lovers and gardeners. We are to deeply love God's creation, each other, and to take care of the Earth. There are many ways to do this. It is up to each one of us to discover the best way to be cocreators with God. I could write a great deal about the psychological value of finding one's purpose, the work that God has given us to do. But Rick Warren has already done that.

So I will ask the question again. What is an optimal amount of denial, and how do we achieve it? Scripture gives us more insight: We must face the truth. The truth of living this life is that we will soon die. That fact cannot be avoided. Nothing can be achieved if we stay in denial about how soon our life will be over. If facing that truth causes anxiety and dread ... good. Kierkegaard said that dread is our "schoolmaster" leading us to Christ. Finding our purpose in the brief time we have, participating in God's work, to the best of our ability, and learning how to live wisely from the pages of Scripture will help us to find the best way to live effectively. Optimal denial is facing life honestly, dealing wisely with daily necessity, and staying open to God's possibilities.

Defense Mechanisms

Most people probably understand the concept of "defense mechanisms" and could give you a few examples. Sigmund Freud was not the first person to notice the clever ways human beings have of defending against unpleasant experience. Psychological defenses, like denial, are typically instinctive methods the brain uses to manage intense unpleasant emotions. In some cases, people also use defense mechanisms to hide from vulnerable positive emotions. It is hard for some people to say, "I love you" or "I'm happy that we are such good friends." People who are too well defended against intense emotion miss out on being overwhelmed by a spectacular sunset, the sight of their lover's face, or a baby's laugh. Hiding one's true feelings can be useful at times, but there is no great benefit in practicing stoicism.

Many people cushion themselves from ever becoming vulnerable. That is often because of physical or psychological trauma. I have treated hundreds of people for the effects of childhood abuse. Sometimes the abuse was physical, sometimes sexual, and very often the abuse was emotional. The psychological injuries inflicted on children remain (to use a metaphor) as pieces of jagged shrapnel buried deep inside. Much of the time, people may be unaware of this "shrapnel" until it is touched. A word, a memory, a location, or person from the past may touch the wound and trigger a strong emotional reaction.

People who have had these traumatic experiences know that it often is not until later in life that the memories of abuse begin to surface into awareness. Either something or someone has triggered the memories, or the person is in a stable enough place in life where the reassociation of memory can be tolerated. Recovery from abuse can be painful and destabilizing, but God has gifted our psyche with the ability to heal. A saying in the language of recovery is, "You survived the abuse; you can survive the recovery."

Mild dissociation is pretty commonplace. Do you ever find yourself reading a chapter for school or work and realizing that you have not a clue about what you just read? Where were you while you were reading? People with attention deficit disorder know what it is like to read the same paragraph two or three times. Let's just say, I am glad my car knows its way home. I have missed freeway offramps working on lesson plans for class in my head. The popular term for mild dissociation is "zoning out." Part of your brain may be trying to pay attention, but another part is daydreaming or thinking about something else.

Profound dissociation resulting in dissociative disorders is much less common. Dissociation is a bit like repression. Repression is the brain going into shock. Another of God's gracious gifts against trauma, repression is an automatic shutting away and forgetting of traumatic experience. As in dissociation, repressed memory seems to surface into consciousness much later after a traumatic experience, which is why PTSD takes time to heal. PTSD can be severe or moderate. If you witness a terrible traffic accident, you may not have been directly involved—but actually you were. The brain tends to hold on to shocking experiences and replays them again and again until the memory of the event is more fully metabolized. If you actually were *in* the traffic accident, it will take a much longer time before you are able to recover emotionally.

God has given us cushions against horror. Dissociation, repression, and denial are automatic and not volitional. Other psychological defenses, such as projection, displacement, and sublimation, are easier to understand. *Projection* is seeing your own disowned and unacceptable behavior in someone else. For example, I try not to be competitive on the highway, but I get angry at other drivers who are. What does that tell me? *Displacement* is typically being irritated by someone who does not deserve it (i.e., taking out angry feelings on someone or something that happens to be handy). *Sublimation* is a choice to distract yourself. The difference between sublimation and denial is that one chooses to sublimate: "I don't want to think about this, so I'll get busy doing something else." Sublimation is useful if it does not become a lifestyle. Healthy psychological defenses include anticipation, rehearsal, and prayer. I have included a quiz on the different types of psychological defenses in the Appendix. See how many you already know before looking them up.

In very simplistic terms, psychological defenses seem to come in two broad categories: fight and flight (freeze, in my mind, falls under the flight category). Blaming, scolding, interrupting, yelling, controlling, or trying to browbeat with "logic" are examples of fight defenses. Avoiding, evading, complying, withdrawing, and emotional coldness are examples of flight defenses. Certainly, flight defenses can have their own particular ways of attacking and controlling another person. When someone storms out of a room, slams the door, and shouts an obscenity, that behavior looks and feels more like fight than flight. And the manner in which one fights, if it is simply intellectually sparring, is probably just disguised flight. So it can be unclear which defense is which. The important thing to know is that defenses, whether the fight or flight type, exist to minimize the threat of harm or pain. Unfortunately, getting defensive can cause harm or pain to someone else. Whether one is being overtly controlling by scolding and criticizing or covertly controlling by avoiding the person or situation, the effect is still the same. People are hurt and scared when they are attacked or abandoned. In fact, abandoning someone may actually feel like an attack.

A typical argument is characteristically carried on by defenses. The humans behind those defenses are powerless, for a time, to manage their runaway emotions. I frequently refer to this as a "tennis match." You know you are being defensive when you are intent on winning your point. You are not being curious about what the other person is trying to say, you cannot wait for your turn, you are tempted to interrupt, your body feels tense, and you feel like raising your voice or leaving the room. When you are able to remain calm and successfully manage your defenses, conversations and even arguments will feel more like playing catch than playing tennis. Talking together will be more cooperative and less competitive. The goal will be less about winning one's point and more about allowing both people in the room to feel heard, understood, and accepted. I'm not saying that "tennis" cannot be fun. Arguments can be enjoyable forms of intellectual sparring and may be very illuminating when done respectfully with openness and good will. But people need to be very careful to end the "fun" when tension mounts and feelings are being hurt.

If you are with a group of people—when it is not a debating society—it is best not to argue at all. You already know how to do that, and you do not need more practice. Instead, practice sharing "I" messages. Practice being curious and interested in others' opinions. Practice being patient and allowing differences. There are plenty of things to practice that do not involve arguing. We cannot do away with defenses altogether; they are too important to us. We can, however, learn to control our defenses better. We can manage to suspend them when we need to carefully listen to someone and hear what they are feeling and trying to say. The point of effective communication is learning to manage one's defenses in order to successfully hear and be heard. In her book *Just Listen*, Sarah Dessen (2008) points out the challenges of talking to someone who is actually a good listener:

> This is the problem with dealing with someone who is actually a good listener. They don't jump in on your sentences, saving you from actually finishing them, or talk over

> you, allowing what you do manage to get out to be lost or altered in transit. Instead, they wait, so you have to keep going. (p. 298)

Finding someone who is truly a good listener is rare. It takes practice. You need to suspend the tendency to analyze, categorize, and judge. You need to become aware of your particular favorite fight-flight defenses and attend to the meaning of the words and the underlying emotional content. I have more to say about the art of listening in Chapter 11. Below is a list of typical fight-flight defenses. Look them over and check the ones you tend to use most often.

You will find as you look through the list that you tend to have more defenses on one side than the other. There is a reason for this. Physiologies are wired differently. It is hard for some people to step back and not have to confront a situation. It is hard for others to step up and deal with the challenge.

Fight Defenses	**Flight Defenses**
accusing	withdrawing
threatening	ignoring
parenting	silence
scolding/lecturing	insincere complying/agreeing
name-calling	doing "poor me"
insinuating	stonewalling
labeling	passivity
problem solving	coldness
analyzing	justifying
sarcasm	passing the buck
filibustering	forgetting
dumping	being too "reasonable"
attacking	leaving/avoiding
gender bashing	changing the subject
dredging up the past	inappropriate humor
passive-aggressive	staying busy
needing to be right	intellectualizing
raising your voice	minimizing
acting out behaviors	hiding true feelings
physical abuse	placating

Looking at the list above, which are your favorite defenses? There are certainly many other forms of psychological defensiveness, of evading the difficulty of feeling feelings. Above are just a few examples. Drug or alcohol addiction; compulsive house cleaning; romantic affairs; and preoccupation with any activity, such as video games, golf, romance novels, TV, sports, shopping, politics, money, exercise, and one' physical appearance, can all be forms of medicating or avoiding difficult emotions and the work of creating deep and meaningful relationships.

Any activity can be pushed to preoccupying extremes that distract one from what is truly important. But the difference between an OCD personality disorder and the need to be preoccupied with house cleaning or organizing one's workspace is that OCD folks have less choice in their compulsivity, whereas most of the rest of us can learn to do a better job at managing our defenses.

Keep in mind that psychological defenses do not fall into neat lists, as illustrated above. Human beings are complex, and so are their means of coping. I encourage clients to memorize the 23rd Psalm. Memorizing this Psalm keeps it readily available when you are feeling anxious or depressed. It is not simply a defense against those unwanted emotions; often it is the cure. When you are upset, sit down, take some deep breaths, close your eyes, and walk through the Psalm. Picture yourself lying down in green pastures and walking along still waters, knowing that God will lead you in the right path, His path. Even when you feel overwhelmed, He is there with his provision and protection. According to Proverbs 4:22, God's word is medicine. I saw a client recently who has been affected by OCD most of his adult life. Like the rest of us, he would like Scripture to be the only medicine he ever needed. I reminded him that doctors and psychiatric medication are also from God.

Psychology helps us to understand ourselves and the people around us. It helps us to understand our emotions, our psychological defenses, and, ideally, how best to manage the frustrations and challenges of life. Psychology does not replace Scripture. It amplifies it. God has told us how to live, how to stay healthy, and how to have a good relationship with others. He has also inspired poets, writers, philosophers, artists, and those who study psychology to give us fresh vision and illumination of His inexhaustible wisdom.

Questions for Review, Reflection, and Discussion

1. What are the main purposes of psychological defenses?
2. Describe existential anxiety.
3. What are your most common psychological defenses?
4. Which do you tend to do more, fight or flight?
5. What are good spiritual defenses for unwelcome emotions or situations?

CHAPTER 6

Problems and Promise

> "Although they claimed to be wise, they became fools."
>
> —Romans 1:22

Chapter Preview and Learning Objectives

The chapter explores the kinds of challenges and problems extent in psychology. A formidable challenge to psychology is whether to view it as an art or a science. The solution to the confusion and competition between psychology as science or art is language. Psychology is an accumulation of useful stories—narrative systems. The therapist's grasp of the genre of their profession and the application of the right stories in treatment is where the integration of art and science takes place. The promise of psychology is its increasing openness to faith practices for both therapist and client. Among the most successful integration of faith practices into treatment is the increasing numbers of therapists who embrace a Christian perspective in the work of healing.

Learning Objectives

Students will do the following in this chapter:

- Appreciate the most complex problem in psychology: forgetting its name.
- Understand the challenge of viewing psychology as a science or as an art.

- Explore the integrating promise of realizing psychology as language and story.
- Grasp that the field of psychological integration is the heart of the therapist.
- Describe the contribution of a faith-based approach to treatment.

Problems with Psychology

Psychology has problems when it ignores its name and forgets its history. There is good news and other news in every major evolution in human thinking. The good news of the period of the Enlightenment in the 17th and 18th century was to allow freedom in the exploration of the three philosophical disciplines of goodness, truth, and beauty. Established systems of religion or politics no longer had the final word on what could be thought of as true or good or what could be considered beautiful. The zeal to explore truth, unhindered by dogma or mysticism, gave rise to the empirical method. According to the empirical method, truth, to be true, had to be proven—subject to the laws of testing and prediction. That tradition is alive today in the concern for evidence-based psychotherapy. An evidence-based approach to treatment is a check against a host of possible treatment models not grounded in adequate research, tested hypotheses, or best practice experience.

Problems arise in psychology when it forgets its name, the *study of the soul*, and its historical roots as the care of the soul. Forgetting its name and its history, one dimension of modern psychology is reduced to an empirical study of the mind and of behavior—a small percentage of what it is to be human. Another dimension of psychology might be characterized more as art than science. There is an art to being with another human being with a quality of rapport and attunement that is transformative. As in the study of the arts, writing, painting, music, and so forth, there are certain fundamentals of the craft that cannot be ignored, but the person of the artist is the central factor in the work. The authors of *A General Theory of Love* have this to say about that:

> Strip away a therapist's orientation, the journals he reads, the books on his shelves, the meeting he attends—the cognitive framework his rational mind demands—and what is left to define the psychotherapy he conducts? Himself. The person of the therapist is the converting catalyst. Not his order or credo. (Lewis et al., 2000, p. 186)

So is psychology schizophrenic, split between a scientific and artistic approach to treatment? It can be. The split occurs when the languages used to describe the mental health profession and the work of psychotherapy are not carefully defined and adequately integrated. Empirical languages alone are not adequate for the work of healing souls. The metaphorical languages of the arts, philosophy, and theology, by themselves, are not sufficiently grounded in the fundamentals of the behavioral sciences to be effective in clinical treatment. How does one integrate both empirical and metaphorical languages?

An empirical approach to the study of human problems and treatment must be evidenced based, or it would not be scientific. No one ought to have a problem with that, any more than they would have a problem with an evidence-based approach to medicine, infant care, or nutrition. Unfortunately, psychology, in the past, often ignored empirical science and, in the process, has inherited very bad press.

Sigmund Freud, for example, while thinking that he was appealing to the scientific method required in his day, went wide afield of the rigor of empirical testing. His theories, while useful at times, were largely conjecture and extrapolation from his limited research. When someone feels the urge to make fun of psychology, they frequently mention Freud and some of his more controversial theories. For example, an older gentleman was once referred to me for counseling by his pastor. I knew that the pastor led a very conservative church, so I was pleased that he entrusted me with one of his flock. The man walked into my office and before sitting down said, "Now I want to make one thing clear: I don't want any of this Freudian double-talk." I smiled and said, "Alright, then, no Freudian double-talk."

Freud, like so many psychiatrists of that period in history, were products of their training and culture. Even as recently as the child-rearing advice of Dr. Spock and the silly ideas of *Men Are from Mars, Women Are from Venus* have led to wrong ideas about human nature and the benefits of psychology. It is no wonder that so much of what has been proven to be culturally dated, wrong-headed, or even dangerous has given psychology a bad name. In addition, psychotherapists, immersed in evidence-based treatment and empirical procedures, may also scoff at the pop psychology and the metaphysical/metaphorical language of so much of what is labeled as "psychology."

Nonetheless, in spite of conflict and controversy from both within and without, psychology as both art and science is of tremendous value in understanding human nature, human problems, and human suffering. The application of psychological insight integrated with the teachings of Scripture and the application of faith based practice can be a powerful instrument in healing human hurts.

Integrating Psychological Languages

Empirical languages appeal to validation. Metaphorical languages appeal to conceptual usage. For example, there is no such thing as an ego; no amount of research and testing can find one. The term "ego" is a metaphor. A metaphor is a term used to access a concept. The metaphor of ego, for instance, has robust usage in describing maturity (a strong ego), immaturity (a weak ego), selfishness (egotistical), a self-serving nature (egocentric), and egoism.

Metaphorical language facilitates the conception of processes, states, and characteristics. "He is a hot-head," "She is tender hearted," and "They are joined at the hip" are some common metaphors. Psychology uses metaphorical language to communicate ideas such as ego, self-object, parentified child, and a host of other ways to conceptualize processes, states, and characteristics.

Students in training to become psychotherapists learn many psychological languages and techniques. Some of the languages and techniques are empirically grounded. For example, *The Diagnostic and Statistical Manuel of Mental Illness* (DSM), developed by the American Psychological Association, has been in use, with periodic refinements, since 1952. The DSM provides a standard in psychological practice for use among clinicians for diagnosis, treatment options, and communication with other clinicians, physicians, and insurance companies.

The DSM is an invaluable lexicon of terms that define and describe a vast array of human problems and is an essential sourcebook for communication with patients and other practitioners. The DSM is also a valuable sourcebook for assessing the criteria characteristics of a particular mental disorder.

Marriage and family therapists, clinical social workers, and clinical psychologists are all characteristically fluent in both the empirical and metaphorical languages of their profession. The languages of research and statistics, of biology and neuroscience, of psychopathology and treatment, of child and personality development, of family and relationship systems, as well as social and cultural languages are all metabolized and integrated into the psyche of the clinician. It is here, in the soul of the therapist, that the integration of empirical and metaphorical languages becomes both generative and effective.

Because psychology is such a vast area of study, it makes sense to distinguish which psychological language you are speaking. Are you speaking empirically, in the language of research, statistics, diagnosis, and evidence-based practice? Or are you speaking metaphorically using theoretical languages related to theories of treatment and approaches? Each theoretical approach employs its own distinctive language so that clinicians can conceptualize treatment methods and outcome goals.

Psychology, when it is understood in its fullest sense, is concerned with the health of body, soul, and spirit. It is able to integrate the languages of science, art, and ethical behavior—the confluence of the three philosophical concerns of truth, beauty, and goodness. Truth is honored when the psychotherapist works to ensure that the diagnosis is valid, the treatment plan is evidenced based, and the goals are observable and measurable. Beauty is honored when the quality of connection between two human beings, the rapport, attunement, acceptance, and caring, are palpable and transformative. Goodness is honored when strict adherence to moral and ethical guidelines and behavior promotes safety and respect.

An effective psychotherapist navigates a complexity of narrative systems—psychological languages selected to provide the best fit for their client. They have learned that everyone who comes in for therapy is telling a different story. As they listen to their client's story, they notice how the story reaches into the past for illustrations, circles around present problems, and anticipates challenges in the future. They will have to construct this format themselves, however, since stories told in therapy rarely follow a linear progression. Their client's brain searches for antecedents and consequences with which to create a narrative, an accumulation and representation of events and meaning selected to invite the therapist into their inner life and the challenges they face. The therapist is practiced at listening to client stories and finding the best way to move the story forward to a place of healing. Beyond the therapist's capacity to carefully listen and understand the client's story, however, is their capacity for heart-felt, empathic attunement. This is the core competency for effective therapy.

Promise

Psychology can only promise to continue to work to find the best ways to help people who are hurting. But there is promise for psychology. I have seen significant improvement in the 45 years that I have observed the field of psychology. There was a time when researchers and theorists in the field were extremely competitive with one another. I recall professors and fellow students identifying with particular schools of thought. This person was "Rogerian." This person was "family systems." This person was "Freudian" or "cognitive behavioral" or "existential" or "Gestalt."

I and others in my MFT classes in school wondered if we had to identify with a particular theoretical approach. Fortunately, we were trained in all of the various schools of thought and counseling skills so that we had a good basis of understanding of what might work best in what context. As a result, many of us resisted labeling ourselves. Instead, "eclectic" was the word used in those days to describe a counselor who was open to using a variety of skills and strategies, depending on the needs of the client. Even the term "client" is fairly new, replacing the customary term "patient" used by previous clinicians. Dr. Carl Rogers emphasized a more equalitarian approach to therapy. So "patients" became "clients." And the majority of therapists today are "working with clients" instead of "treating patients."

Two additional improvements in the practice of psychology have occurred in the past 30 years. The first is changing the term "eclectic" to "integrative." Eclectic had meant that a therapist was competent in applying different therapeutic approaches to different client needs. The term "integrative" has come to mean that a therapist has mastered the skills and strategies of each of the various potential therapeutic approaches and, as result, is able to intelligently integrate them. Dr. Barbara Ingram's 2006 text *Clinical Case Formulations: Matching the Integrative Treatment Plan to the Client* is an excellent illustration of this up-to-date approach to mastering multiple treatment modalities and applying an integrative approach to treat specific client problems. I highly recommend her work.

Another example comes from Andrew Christenson, a researcher at UCLA who has identified the most common and most successful therapeutic approaches used in marriage counseling and found five overlapping strategies (he called them "unifying protocols") in each of those approaches. You can read more about his research and find those five unifying protocols in the 2010 book *Enhancing Couples* as well as in Chapter 11 of this book.

The second significant improvement is an updated understanding of the importance of faith in the work of helping and healing. There has been a great deal of brain research reported in medical and scientific journals as well as in popular magazines, such as Emmons (2009), Gunter Brown (2012), Vance (2016), and many online articles reinforcing the importance of prayer, meditation, mindfulness training, and other spiritual practices. The terms "mindfulness" and "meditation" may alarm many Christians who consider godless meditation and other spiritual practices as harmful diversions and dangerously seductive paths leading people away from the true path in Jesus Christ. There are many different forms of meditating on Scripture, however, that can be very useful.

For example, as I mentioned, I frequently recommend to clients that they memorize the 23rd Psalm. I then encourage them to recite the Psalm daily until it becomes a part of their daily practice. When anxieties arise and life feels bleak or hopeless, David's Psalm is close within, ready to restore the soul and encourage renewed faith. I often find time to close my eyes and "lie down in green pastures or stroll by still waters," confident that there is a table set for me when I need God's provisions.

Historically, psychotherapists were skeptical about the importance of prayer and the power of faith. Today, however, most clinicians not only accept the value of a person's faith but also encourage it. And since the work of Carl Rogers, therapists understand the value of a "person-centered" approach, which means that unconditional positive regard, empathic attunement, and genuine acceptance are (or should be) the core consideration in any therapeutic alliance. Jesus Christ is in favor of improving the welfare of human beings. Therefore, honoring the client's believe system, when it leads to greater well-being, and even improving it, is (and ought to be) of value in the helping profession.

An elderly Jewish man once asked me to help him grieve the loss of his wife of many years. A former client of mine referred him. "Is he Jewish?" the elderly man asked his friend. "He knows what he's doing," his friend replied. The many hours I spent with this wise, elderly Jewish man are among my sweetest memories. He told me story after story, sometimes weeping, sometimes laughing—stories about the loving partnership he had with "the most wonderful woman in the world!" "Is this what I'm supposed to do?" he asked. "Just tell stories?" "It's exactly what you're supposed to do," I replied. "But there's one thing more, you need to go back to temple." "That's hard for me," he said. "I'm still mad at God for taking my dear wife." "Even though I walk through the shadow of the valley of death," I mused. "Thou art with me," he replied, and smiled.

As psychology continues to learn and grow and improve its understanding of how best to help people, so too has the application of psychological knowledges among the clergy. There was a time when uninformed pastors actively preached against members of their flock seeking "secular" counseling. That may still be true among some pastors. But in the past 45 years, I have observed significant changes. Not only are Bible colleges and seminaries providing courses in pastoral counseling but some schools are also providing degrees in both pastoral ministry as well as clinical psychology. Informed pastors know, and may have been taught, to respect their own lack of training and refer difficult problems to trained Christian counselors. In the ideal, a pastor, priest, or rabbi may work conjointly to offer the best of both psychological and pastoral care.

Given that psychologists in the past were often skeptical of the value of religion and some even hostile to it, it is understandable that the clergy have felt very protective of their flocks. I have heard, firsthand, of pastors preaching against professional counseling. Certainly, the fear is based on the suspicion that therapists might undermine Christian values and could possibly damage a Christian's faith. In fact, I once shared that fear. As a pastor in the mid-1970s, I did not know very much about what went on in a therapist's office. But I was wise enough to know that there were some problems I was not equipped to handle. In those days I only knew of one Christian counselor in my community. I interviewed him and decided that I could trust him with referrals. Today there are dozens of faith-filled therapists in my community, just as there are many more Christian people and pastors who are comfortable acknowledging that they have benefited from professional counseling. It seems that more therapists are accepting of the benefits of prayer and faith in the work of healing souls. It also seems that more Christians are accepting of the benefits of professional therapy when necessary.

The Rise of Christian Counseling

There are two approaches to Christian counseling. One type is a counselor who offers "biblical" or "faith-based" counseling. That form of counseling often resembles pastoral counseling, in that the focus of therapy is the counselor and client working together to discover how best to apply Scripture to address the presenting problem(s). The biblical or faith-based counselor may be a trained and licensed psychotherapist, pastor, or lay-person. The Stephen's Ministry is an illustration of a well-run and effective program for training and equipping lay counselors to help extend the pastoral ministry of the church. I discuss the Stephens Ministry in more detail in Chapter 14.

In 1978 I was an associate pastor at Emmanuel Presbyterian Church in Thousand Oaks, California. The elders of the church decided to poll the entire congregation to determine goals for the next few years. I thought they did a cleaver job of having everyone write out 10 goals. We added all of the goals together, looking for overlapping themes and ideas. At the end of the process, we had the final 10 goals, one of which was to create a counseling center. It struck me that the congregation had realized that the mission of the church could include a mental health contribution to its outreach to the congregation as well as to the community. The congregation was advocating what, in my mind, was a better understanding and acceptance of the need for trained mental health professionals in the work of Christ—that it was possible to integrate science and faith.

The second type of Christian counseling is offered by trained and licensed therapists who, as Christians, are well-versed and supportive of Christian values and encourage clients in the practice of faith and prayer. The value of seeing this counselor is their application of sound therapeutic practice and experience combined, ideally, with a thorough understanding of the benefits of biblical guidance. An effective Christian therapist may also be accepting of clients who are not Christian but, nonetheless, appreciate the value of supporting a spiritual foundation of faith and care for others.

Questions for Review, Reflection, and Discussion

1. What does it mean when I say that psychology can sometimes forget its name?
2. Is psychotherapy a science or an art? Explain your answer.
3. In what way is clinical practice benefited by understanding therapy as language and story?
4. Explain the difference between "electric" and "integrative."
5. Are you a biblical counselor or a Christian psychotherapist? What is the difference?
6. How might you respond to a pastor who asks the above question?

CHAPTER 7

On Being Human

> “So God created mankind in his own image, in the image of God He created them; male and female He created them. God blessed them and said to them …”
>
> —Genesis 1:27–28

Chapter Preview and Learning Objectives

What defines a human being is “response-ability.” While God spoke creation into existence, He spoke directly *to* humans. God endowed humans with the ability to respond to Him, to each other, and to the Earth. Not to be responsible with our ability to respond is a contradiction of human nature and the origin of sin (dysfunctional behavior). The image of God is fulfilled in our connection with God, the connection between men and women, our connection with others, and our impulse to create. Our divine commission from the first chapter in Genesis is to be lovers and gardeners. We humans have a hard time dealing with our dual ontological nature: both dirty and divine. Psyche (soul) connects those two disparate and often antagonistic aspects of being human.

Learning Objectives

Students will do the following in this chapter:

- Understand human nature (the image of God) as the “ability to respond” and responsibility to our creative commission.
- Explore the nature and consequences of our dual ontological nature.

- Appreciate the complexity of living cooperatively as Spirt, soul, and body.
- Grasp the nature of psyche.
- Appreciate that the human story is a story about vital relatedness.

What makes us human and different from other creations of the sixth day? It is not just our superior intellect, our ability to make and use tools, or our ability to imagine and achieve flying to the moon. What makes us human is that God has created us in "His own image" and has spoken *to* us: "And God blessed them and said to them" (Genesis 1:28). God spoke creation into existence. But he tenderly crafted us with his loving hands and then spoke directly to us. Does God speak to all of His creation of the sixth day? Perhaps. Perhaps an important difference between animals and humans is that animals do not have that particular form of soul (the image of God) that allows them to have a personal relationship with their creator. In speaking to us, God endowed us with the ability to respond. That is what makes us human: the ability to respond to God, to each other, and to our planet. And with the ability to respond comes responsibility. Not being responsible with our ability to respond is a contradiction of human nature, of our divine commission, and is the origin of sin and psychopathology. People are less human, less than God created them to be, when they do not fully realize their divine creation and potential.

> God blessed them and said to them, "Be fruitful and increase in number; fill the earth and subdue it. Rule over the fish in the sea and the birds in the sky and over every living creature that moves on the ground." (Genesis 1:28)

According to our commission in Genesis, God has assigned us the task of being lovers and gardeners: to create new life and to take care of the planet. How are we doing so far?

The answer to that question is glaringly obvious. On our own, we have not done a good job with our responsibility, with baring the image of God. The Episcopal prayer book has, for ages, led God's people in a collective confession of our failure: "We have left undone those things which we ought to have done; and we have done those things which we ought not to have done; and there is no health in us" (Protestant Episcopal Church, 1842, p. 30).

In 1536, John Calvin wrote the *Institutes of the Christian Religion*. In chapter one, Calvin states:

> Without knowledge of God there is no knowledge of self. Again, it is certain that man never achieves a clear knowledge of himself unless he has first looked upon God's face, and then descends from contemplating him to scrutinize himself for we always seem to ourselves righteous and upright and wise and holy—this pride is innate in all of us—unless by clear proofs we stand convinced of our own unrighteousness, foulness, folly, and impurity. Moreover, we are not thus convinced if we look merely to ourselves

> and not also to the Lord, who is the sole standard by which this judgment must be measured. (McNeill, 1975, p. 37)

The first thing we need to know about being a human being is that we need help. God created us out of dirt. We are biological beings. We are reminded of that fact every day. And every day, as we get older and begin to decline, we are reminded that our biology will go back to being dirt. There is never a day that we do not need help. Our life begins and ends dependent on others. Thank God there is more to us than just our biology.

Another thing we need to know about being a human being is that we are not simply biology. Genesis tells us that God breathed his Spirit into the dirt. Now we have a real problem. Being human means having to live daily with our dual nature: biology and spirit. It seems that human beings are a complex and competitive admixture of transcendent spirit and dusty biology. Existentialists call that admixture the tension between possibility and necessity, between being, at once, both finite and infinite. No wonder we need help. We need help to understand who we are and how to live with this dual ontological nature that God has given to us. How, in Heaven's name, do we manage that?

There is much that psychology can offer, but it cannot tell us who we are or why we exist. Those answers must be found in Scripture. To know who we are and why we exist, we must first know our origin and the reason for our creation, and second, we must allow ourselves to be measured and defined by God's standards.

It may be that the closest that secular psychology has come to understanding the indispensable role that faith plays in human health was voiced by Carl Jung in his 1933 book, *Modern Man in Search of a Soul*:

> During the past thirty years, people from all the civilized countries on earth have consulted me ... Among all my patients in the second half of life—that is to say, over thirty-five—there has not been one whose problem in the last resort was not that of finding a religious outlook on life. It is safe to say that every one of them fell ill because he had lost that which the living religions of every age have given to their followers, and none of them has really healed who did not retain his religious outlook. (p. 229)

The problem for human beings is, having been made in the image of God, we are the children of God. We have response-ability; and we are responsible to that ability. It simply does not work for us to try to live life independently of Him. Obviously, having been invited into relationship with God, we must be given the same freedom that all children have: the freedom to go our own way and choose not to have a relationship with Him. When we make that fateful choice, we become less human.

This is exactly the problem facing the human race. When people separate themselves from a relationship with God in Christ, they cannot be who they truly are and could be. As we saw in in Chapter 4, Maslow (1954) described the concept of self-actualization as integrating one's doing with one's being. Carl Jung used the term "individuation" to describe much the same idea. These are wonderful ideas, and the best ideas that psychology can offer. But neither of these psychologists described the surpassing joy of knowing the fullest truth of one's value and the experience of being deeply and eternally loved. That knowledge comes only be being in the presence of almighty God, made possible through Jesus Christ.

A Living Spirit

All human beings share the Spirit (breath) of God, (Ruach Elohim) which animates earth (Adama). But for that Spirit to be fully alive, it needs to be in relationship to God. It is in that relationship that human beings have Soul (Nepesh). Jesus warned us that if we pay too much attention to the things of this world, we would be in peril of losing our Soul, our *relationship* with God.

Carl Jung wisely entitled his book *Modern Man in Search of a Soul*. Jung used the term "Self" to describe what theologians refer to as "spirit." The human spirit is that particularization of God's Sprit that contains the blueprint of God's plan for each human being and an endowment of the potential for relationship with Him ("and God *spoke* to them"). Psychology can help us with discovering and living that blueprint, but it can only point us in the direction of that vital relationship.

The term "Self," as Jung described it, belongs to the language of psychology. In theological language, the Self could be thought of as one's spirit. The Quaker's concept of "Inner Light" is one way to think of Self or spirit. The Quakers believe that there is something of God in everyone. Because illumination—access to that inner light—is available to all, according to Quaker doctrine, everyone has value and is deserving of respect. I use the term "Self" when thinking psychologically and "spirit" when thinking theologically. The common denominator between those terms is *transcendence*, the ability to see beyond the finite into the infinite. In theological language, one's spirit is both immanent and transcendent, which is what Jung meant when he thought of the Self as an archetype: the personal experience of a transpersonal dynamic. In other words, each of us is endowed with the capacity for self-awareness on the one hand and transcendent experience on the other.

Whether or not that idea is of any use to anyone and in what context the concept is understood is a matter of choice. And clearly, it is a very important choice. The most important choice we make in life is how we view our life. For optimal mental and physical health, it is imperative to locate the core of one's value not in accumulations or accomplishments but in one's spiritual endowment and commission. That endowment and commission is living our life connected to the life of God and from the life of God, connected to the lives of others. To have a living soul (to be healthy psychology) requires a relationship with God and with others since the nature of God is love.

Fully Human

In Volume 3 of Karl Barth's *Church Dogmatics* (1948), Barth explains that "God's transcending choosing, which has chosen man to be God's covenant partner, is reflected in the choice immanent to human nature in which man willingly chooses to live as one human being among others, as an I relating to a Thou" (p. 216). Commenting on Barth's thoughts, Ray

Anderson, in a lecture at Fuller Theological Seminary on the *Theology of Personhood* (1976), affirms that human beings experience freedom "only insofar as this freedom allows itself to be taken captive in God's true freedom. Again, repeating the words of Calvin "to will his human, to will rightly of God." Anderson confirms that the freedom to be fully human is grounded in the freedom of God. God has patterned our life to a be life in Him. We are fully human when we embrace that intimate relatedness.

We were not created to choose alternatives. The tree in the garden may look good: good for food, a delight to the eyes, and able to make one wise. But the goodness, truth, and beauty that the tree offers is outside of God's will. A choice to choose against the will of God is a choice to be less human. In Deuteronomy 30:19, Moses says to God's people, "This day I call the heavens and the earth as witnesses against you that I have set before your life and death, blessings and curses. Now choose life, so that you and your children may live." Choosing to follow God is a choice for life. Other choices are not.

To be fully human is to be full-filled. The exciting thing about the infilling of the Holy Spirt is experiencing the transformation of our appetites. We are surrounded by temptations and adversity. The Holy Spirit fills us with the strength and wisdom that we need to stay close to the Father, to know His path for us and to stay on it. To be fully human is to experience the joy of fellowship with God. When we are walking in God's ongoing love, we require little else of life. We have what we need.

Because we have what we need we are free to see our priorities more clearly, we do not need to compete with others to feel significant; we are significant. We do not have to strive for acceptance; we are accepted. We do not need to worry about losing love; love dwells deeply within us.

Here is the intersection of psyche with spirit. The theme common to both psychology and Christianity is the primacy of love. To quote, again, from Lewis et al. (2000) in a *General Theory of Love*: "Love is not only an end for therapy, it is also the means whereby every end is reached" (p. 169). A healthy individual for Freud is a person who is able to love and work. Jung (1977) said, "Sooner or later it will be found that nothing really new happens in history. There could be talk of something really novel only if the unimaginable happened: if reason, humanity and love won a lasting victory" (para. 1356). In his bestselling *The Art of Loving*, Eric Fromm (2013) said, "Love is a decision, it is a judgment, it is a promise. If love were only a feeling, there would be no basis for the promise to love each other forever. A feeling comes and it may go. How can I judge that it will stay forever, when my act does not involve judgment and decision?" (p. 63). I could continue to quote psychologists about the primacy of love in mental health, but to fast-forward to the most up-to-date understanding of psychological well-being, I will quote the Surgeon General of the United States. Vivek Murthy, in his 2020 book *The Healing Power of Human Connection in a Sometimes Lonely World*, affirmed that human beings are hard-wired for connection: "We know we are attending to those connections when we feel 'at home' with a closely knit group or family. We are wired to associate belong with the sharing of stories, feelings, memories, and concerns. That's why our bodies relax and our spirits lift when we connect in genuine friendship and love" (p. 32).

When our spirits lift it is because, in that instance, we are free. We are free from the push and pull of fears. Scripture confirms that love casts out fear. When we are in our family, with our brothers and sisters in Christ, we feel at home where we are safe and loved. Love frees us. We can relax and know ourselves to be accepted and valued. We are free from fear and isolation when we participate in God's family. Murthy (2020), whose job it is to track the nation's health, states that there is an epidemic of loneliness in this country: an epidemic that leads directly to a degrading of mental health, increased physical illnesses, and suicides. All of this can be prevented.

When the apostle Paul states that it is for freedom that Christ has set us free, the freedom he is describing is the freedom to set our human needs and fears to one side and to reach out to the lonely, to the hurting. Our freedom is *in dependence.* We were created to be dependent on God and others. That is our nature. That is what makes us fully human. We are fully human only insofar as the freedom we have in Jesus Christ allows us to be taken captive in God's true freedom.

Psyche

When I was in seminary, reading the *Denial of Death*, I was awakened to a deeper appreciation of the connection between theology and psychology in the word "psyche." Psyche, the Greek term for soul, is of interest to both disciplines. An enlightened minister, priest, or rabbi is just as concerned for the care of the soul as is the psychotherapist. They may approach their work from differing perspectives, but their common goal is the welfare of a human being. Soul is best understood as relational. Soul connects our spirit to our biology and connects our life to the lives around us. My thoughts about the relationship between Spirit and soul are inspired by the text of Genesis 2:7, which describes the meeting of the finite with the infinite. Living daily in that impossible tension creates the existential concept of dread, with all of the defensive strategies necessary to manage the tradeoff between the intoxicating pull of possibility while living with the repetitive necessity of one's biology. So how does the idea of "soul" fit into this complex mix?

Soul is profoundly relational. It is a connection, a conversation, a wrestling match between sprit and biology, between breath and dust. Psychology, the study of the psyche (soul), is the study of relationships: the relationship one has with one's own life, with one's Self or spirit, and the relationship one has with other people. It is the study of our wrestling and relating, both within ourselves and with others.

The work we do in life is the work of accessing and strengthening soul—enlivening the relationship we have with God, with ourselves and others, and with the world around us. We join with other believers in order to affirm our need for community and to extend God's gifts to others. We join a group not just to experience being safe at home in the family of Christ but also to experience the golden moments of sublime connection and the peak experiences that remind us of life's possibilities.

Increasingly, psychologists look for an "evidence-based" approach to theories of personality and theories of counseling. Psychology, from this perspective, is a rigorous empirical science involving measurement, testing, and prediction. This is an important and valuable story. Testing truth is an essential human endeavor. The problem, of course, is that a statistical approach to understanding human behavior is limited. Psychology has been forced to find other stories to explain human behavior—stories that can exist on a continuum between measurement and metaphor. The language of psychology is replete with shared metaphors. Ego, personality, self-object, identified patient, and self-actualization are all useful metaphors. Stories, not statistics, it turns out is a much more interesting and useful language form with which to grasp human nature and potential.

Relatedness

The central story of the human experience is the story of relatedness. It is impossible to know exactly when a human's story begins. Each of us is the product of the stories that went before. Practically speaking, I can think of no better introduction to an individual's story than that found in Dan Siegel's *The Developing Mind*. The subtitle of his book says it all: *How Relationships and the Brain Interact to Shape Who We Are*. Siegel (1999) beautifully explains the interdependence of both nature and nurture:

> Therefore, caregivers are the architects of the way in which experience influences the unfolding of genetically preprogrammed but experience-dependent brain development. Genetic potential is expressed within the setting of social experiences, which directly influence how neurons connect to one another. Human connections create neuronal connections. (p. 85)

In the quote above, Siegel describes the first story of life: the story of parent and child. The parent contributes the DNA, which sets the stage for the genetic unfolding. But it is the system of relatedness between parent and child, the "epigenetics," that drives the preprogrammed potential into actual neuronal connections. The temperament of the infant interacting with the temperament of the caregivers co-create the experience-dependent brain development. This cooperation of infant and maternal-paternal interaction has been termed *attachment*. And the nature of the story of attachment significantly influences the development of the individual's story for the rest of their life.

John Bowlby's trilogy, *Attachment* (1969), *Separation* (1973), and *Loss* (1980) revolutionized the study of human personality with his focus on the nature of maternal attachment and relatedness as the most significant influence on human development. Mary Ainsworth, strongly influenced by Bowlby's work, developed the "strange situation," identifying four categories of attachment styles that substantially influence an individual's story. Initially, classic psychoanalysts objected to Bowlby's work, but the story of attachment is now the most influential understanding of the developmental history of an individual. The significance of early attachments is recognized in other fields beyond psychology as well. Dan McAdams wrote The *Stories We Live By* in 1993. The subtitle is *Personal Myths and the Making of the Self.* In this fascinating book, McAdams creatively relates personality development to literary genre:

> Secure attachment may nudge us in the direction of comedy and romance, insecure attachment, in the direction of tragedy and irony. By the time each of us reaches adolescence and adulthood, we are ready to create stores of a certain quality or type.
>
> By the time we think seriously about the meaning of our own lives, we may already be predisposed to create that meaning through the filtering glass of tragedy, comedy, irony, or romance. (p. 53)

Before Bowlby and Ainsworth told their stories, Melanie Klein talked about the relation of infant and mother in yet another story. Because of her background as a psychoanalyst, Klein used the familiar psychodynamic language of the ego and its objects (other people). Her "object relations" theory tells an imaginative story of how an infant might try to make sense of their world when they do not yet possess the cognitive history with which to create a map of their experiences. The "object" in this case is the mother's breast, hand, or face. As the infant develops, they will acquire primitive emotions of affection or hostility based on the availability of the breast when they are hungry, the hand when they need soothing, and the face. They will also create the means to manage the anxiety and confusion of being separated from their caregiver. From our first attachments onward, human beings are wired for connection and the multifaceted challenges of maintaining connections.

So from the early days of psychology to the present, the central focus of understanding human nature has been inseparably connected to the idea of relatedness. That is not news to Christians. Christians understand that the human story is a story of needing to be in a loving response-able relationship with God and with others. We are fully human only in that relationship. When God placed the tree in the garden and said "no" to Adam and Eve, God set a boundary. Without boundaries, there is no relating. That boundary gave humankind the possibility of not relating: of choosing away from God, of choosing not to be human, of choosing death. Every day we have many choices. Each choice is a choice toward life or death, to embrace our creation and commission to be responsible to our inheritance of response-ability or to choose to be less human, less that we were created to be.

Questions for Review, Reflection, and Discussion

1. What does it mean to be created in the image of God?
2. What is our divine commission? What does that mean in psychological terms?
3. Explain the concept of human beings' "dual ontological nature."
4. What psychological problems does that dual nature create?
5. What is "psyche"?
6. What is required to be "fully human"?
7. What does it mean that we live inside of stories?

CHAPTER 8

Depression, Anxiety, and Other Troubling Emotions

> "Save me, O God! For the waters have come up to my neck. I sink in deep mire, where there is no standing; I have come into deep waters, where the floods overflow me. I am weary with my crying; my throat is dry; my eyes fail while I wait for my God."
>
> —Psalm 69: 1-3

Chapter Preview and Learning Objectives

This chapter introduces the epidemic of depression in the United States: 18.5% of Americans have reported times of depression. Historically, the church has not understood depression and, at times, has seen it as a lack of faith. Consequently, many Christians have been unwilling to understand or acknowledge feelings of depression both to themselves and to others. However, there are many causes for depression that are not about a lack of faith. Christians should not be judgmental or reluctant to discuss depression. This is true of other troubling emotions, such as the many varieties of anxiety, shame, and guilt. This chapter reviews the most common approaches to treating depression, anxiety, and other unwelcome emotions.

Learning Objectives

Students will do the following in this chapter:

- Review the many causes and types of depression.
- Evaluate the Christian church's view of depression.

- Understand the spiritual and existential origins of depression.
- Explore the causes and treatment options for panic and anxiety disorders.
- Consider the causes of shame and guilt and how to apply Scripture in treatment.

Someone said to me recently, "I have faith in God. I know He can and does heal. Why can't I get over this depression?" Many of God's people ask themselves that question, whether it is about depression or bouts of fear, anger, or anxiety. The answer to that question can be extremely complicated because there are so many different types of depression and different causes for troubling emotions. The Centers for Disease Control and Prevention (CDC, 2020) reported that 18.5% of Americans reported symptoms of mild to severe depression in 2019.

Depression

Being depressed is not something many Christians want to admit to or discuss. Often, depressed people blame themselves. They wonder if they lack faith or if they have done something wrong. They wonder why God seems so distant and uncaring. A difficulty in understanding the nature of depression is that there are so many different causes. Depression can be a state of mind or emotions, and it can also describe a physical problem in the body. Depression usually follows the experience of loss, and sometimes, depression is the result of the wear and tear of our emotions and chemical resilience over time. Regardless of the origin of someone's depression, they need understanding and compassion, certainly not judgement.

A great deal of research has been done into the causes of depression. One conclusion is that depression may be caused by chronic negative thinking. David Burns, following the cognitive therapy research of Aaron Beck, wrote *Feeling Good* in 1980 and the *Feeling Good Handbook* in 1989. Beck's depression inventory has been a standard instrument for assessing negative thought patterns and their relationship to mood disorders. Burns describes many types of typical thought disorders, such as "all or nothing thinking," "globalizing," "them vs. us thinking," "grandiose" and "persecutory" thinking, "catastrophizing," and so forth. In his handbook, he invites the reader to do some self-assessment with lists of helpful exercises. The reader is encouraged to discover underlying dysfunctional beliefs and automatic thoughts that create the "cognitive distortions" that can cause a depressed mood.

Cognitive Therapy for Depression

The central task of cognitive therapy is to help people identify and transform negative thought patterns. Scripture is an especially valuable resource in the cognitive approach to treating mood disturbances. No doubt, most pastors and Christian friends encourage using the powerful affirmations of Scripture to combat a thought life that tends to struggle with anxious and depressing thoughts. Christian counselors are very aware of the power of cognitive and behavioral therapy. In fact, I have often suggested that clients read the *Feeling Good Handbook* and do the exercises. Over the years I have suggested memorizing many of the Psalms and especially the 23rd Psalm. I have also encouraged clients to read other types of devotional literature that I knew, over time, would have a very beneficial effect on my clients' mental and emotional health. I especially stress that changing a person's habit of negative thinking and replacing it with more positive affirmations is often a lengthy process.

The difficulty with a purely cognitive approach—changing habits of thinking—is that it takes time and repetition. The brain seems to resist change. That is understandable, considering that the brain is responsible for our hold on sanity. In order to feel sane and secure, the brain needs a certain amount of continuity and consistency. The brain is not well equipped to deal with too much change at one time. So the brain develops habits of thinking and perceiving in order to make life seem to be consistent and manageable and to keep a firm grasp on sanity. To prepare Joshua for entering the promised land, for example, God instructed him to keep His Word continually on his lips and in his heart. The greatest of all cognitive behavioral therapists understood the importance of a daily diet of faith and positive thinking. Over time, rehearsing positive affirmations will help people think and feel better about their life.

In *The Mindful Brain*, Dan Siegel (2007) makes the interesting observations that over time, and with practice, a mental *trait* can be transformed into a permanent mental *state*. He backs up this observation from fMRI research that reveals increased cortical thickness from the practice of mindful meditation. In other words, the apostle Paul's statement about the renewing of your mind can actually take place at the cellular level. The key to this transformation is regular practice. God instructed Joshua to keep His Word in his thoughts day and night, promising success in the work he was commissioned to do. Aaron Beck correctly understood that a major cause of depression was the habit of negative thinking. The solution, as Brother Laurence (1967) pointed out was daily practicing the presence of God.

Existential Therapy for Depression

If one's thought life was the only source of depression, transforming one's thoughts would have a direct and positive effect on one's feelings. But another significant source of depression is loss. Losing a relative, a friend, one's job, or one's health are all accompanied by depression, the feelings of loss. The appropriate response to the feelings of loss is grieving. Well-meaning Christian friends say things like, "You'll see him again" and "She's in a better place." These are true, but frequently ill-timed, statements. People need time to grieve: to allow the emotions to work the way God intended them to work, to help people slowly adjust to someone or something that is gone. Physical pain is valuable in that it signals injury that requires care. The mental pain of loss also signals the need for care. The brain needs time to heal. Recall that the existence of significant attachments is essential for well-being. The brain needs time to adjust to the loss of that attachment.

It is inappropriate and ill advised to prematurely attempt to cheer someone up. Job's comforters have been given a negative review because they employed the time-worn belief that Job must have "earned" his suffering in some way. But do not forget that they sat with him for seven days without saying a word. American culture does not permit sitting silently with someone for seven days. We are too busy and have too many demands and often want a quick fix. What should we say when someone is grieving? What should we do?

Step 1 in helping someone to grieve is not to be afraid of grief. Jesus was not. God gave us this powerful emotion to help us along the path to accepting the loss and letting go. Sadness is the energy to let go of an attachment. It is a critically valuable emotion. Without the work of grief—allowing the tears and torment of deep sadness—one is likely to stay in a place of anger, resentment, or bitterness.

I have heard too many sayings that have crept into our culture that steer people in exactly the wrong direction. "Keep a stiff upper lip," "You need to keep going," and "Life goes on" are not the worst ones. The worst ones are the ones we used to tell our kids (e.g., "Big girls don't cry" and "Quit being a baby!"). This culture of wrongheaded stoicism goes way back. Maybe there was a time when men were thought to be weak if they shed a tear. But Jesus taught us that a true man or woman is not afraid of emotions.

Depression can also be caused by unrelenting stress, emotional exhaustion, or a breakdown of one's healthy brain chemistry. Whether by loss or compromised chemistry, depression will often require psychotherapy and sometimes medication. There have been numerous podcasts and lots of internet information during the COVID-19 pandemic on the emotional costs, not just of loss of life or income but also on the toll of constant stress and emotional exhaustion leading to depression. The brain wants to hold on to what is consistent and familiar, and nothing about 2020–2021 was consistent and familiar. My guess is that many more people last year sought help from physicians for medication for anxiety and depression.

A fourth reason, among many, for people getting depressed is midlife or other significant life transitions. Again, the brain wants to hold on to what is familiar. Facing an empty nest, a significant transition in geography or lifestyle, or getting older is stressful. It is a type of loss. But even if the transition is welcome, it is still an adjustment. What is next? What will be required? Do I have what I need to deal with change?

Anxiety

Anxiety is very useful. Except when it is not. Anxiety is the brain's ability to anticipate physical or emotional harm or challenges. Anxiety prompts us to prepare for a job interview, a speech, an exam, or asking someone out on a date. In those instances, anxiety acts like a psychological defense against the possibility of embarrassment or disappointment and energizes us to be prepared.

The date April 15 creates anxiety for many Americans. If too much denial eclipses a healthy amount of anxiety, Tax Day will suddenly arrive without being prepared for it. But with a sufficient amount of healthy anxiety, one can anticipate that day and will be able to pay one's taxes on time. But what happens if every day feels like April 15? What if whatever you tell yourself about how irrational it is to feel anxiety about something, you cannot seem to shake the feeling that something bad will happen? Anxiety is different from fear in that fear is typically related to a specific threat, while anxiety feels like fear but without a specific focus. The presence of persistent anxiety can be a serious problem. The *Diagnostic and Statistical Manuel of Mental Illness* (American Psychiatric Association, 2013) lists several types of anxiety. Among them are:

- specific phobia
- separation anxiety
- social anxiety disorder (social phobia)
- panic disorder
- agoraphobia
- generalized anxiety disorder

I once had a panic attack on an airplane. It was not because it was an airplane; I love to fly. It was a hot day, and I was sitting in a window seat with the sun streaming in. There was a luggage problem that delayed our flight. After 45 minutes of sitting in that cramped seat, I was starting to feel claustrophobic and suddenly felt the need to get out. My heart was racing. I broke out in a cold sweat and knew I was beginning to panic. Panic attacks are horrible. People report feeling like they are dying. They think they are having a heart attack or something is terribly wrong. From 1%–2% of the population experience panic attacks, and 5% of the population will suffer a panic episode in their lifetime. Panic attacks often occur when a situation feels both threatening and out of control. Sometimes the threat is the apprehension of having another panic attack. In other words, having one panic attack makes it that much easier to have another one.

On the airplane, I did what I recommend people do. I got out of my seat and moved around the cabin. I used the restroom to splash cold water on my face, I did some deep breathing, and, returning to my seat, I asked my wife to talk to me while I continued to do deep breathing. I was trying to distract myself and take my mind off of how anxious I was feeling. When people have a history of panic episodes, I recommend that they see their physician for medication to help with their anxiety. I also instruct them in ways to bring their anxiety levels down. Breathing exercises, reciting the 23rd Psalm, self-soothing talks, mindfulness training, and so forth are important for all of us to practice.

"I heard you in the garden and I was afraid" (Genesis 3:10). The Bible does not tell us what Adam felt after he sinned. It may have been shame: "because I was naked" (Genesis 3:10). He realized that he had broken God's commandment. It may also have been a profound feeling of loss. Whatever Adam was feeling, the first emotion we hear spoken from a human being in Scripture is fear. In my view, anxiety is the predominant emotion experienced by the human race. I know of two people (I am sure there are many) who agree with me, one who wrote recently and another not so recently: Murray Bowen and Søren Kierkegaard.

In 1985, Bowen wrote *Family Therapy in Clinical Practice.* In it, Bowen describes the problem of chronic anxiety that all human beings face. Søren Kierkegaard also wrote about chronic anxiety. Both Bowen and Kierkegaard understood the problem of pervasive anxiety: Both wrote about different causes and consequences, but both agreed that all human beings suffer from anxiety. Why is that important to know?

Existential Anxiety

Understanding this pervasive grip of anxiety is important in understanding the human condition. What do human beings do with the existential anxiety Kierkegaard termed "angst"? *Angst*, translated as dread in his book *The Concept of Dread* (1844), is a low-level awareness of life's apparent meaninglessness and the foreboding of inevitable death. How do we avoid this type of anxiety? Ernest Becker gave us some help in his Pulitzer Prize-winning book *The Denial of Death* (1976). Denial seems to be among the most successful means of escaping dread. It is easier for many of us in the 21st century to just not think about it. We have many too many distractions. So a large portion of the population is doing what Kierkegaard (1844) described as being "tranquilized in trivia." That may be especially true in the United States where we seem to be socialized to be competitive: to be more, do more, have more. It is difficult to step out of the blur of this fast-paced, competitive society. In the daily push and pull of busyness, the cost of this form of denial is avoiding authentic possibilities, avoiding our divine commission to be co-creators. Rollo May (1975) said that it takes courage to be an individual, one who does not hide from dread, does not escape into busyness or trivia, and finds *The Courage to Create* (the title of his book).

In a 2019 talk given by Jordan Peterson on the belief in God, Peterson says that our response-ability is to "act out the spark of divinity that is within you by confronting potentials with the Logos that is within to take the opportunities that are in front of you and to transform them into the present in the best possible way, using truth and courage and careful articulation as your guide." I love that idea. I am also aware that another possibility is to simply turn on the golf channel. The heart of an existential perspective and the heart of what makes us human in the image of God is that we are responsible. We have choices.

Each day we face the existential dilemma of possibility versus necessity. We can throw ourselves into all sorts of meaningful projects as a way to avoid existential anxiety. Or we can bury ourselves in tedium. Is there a balance? It is reported that Michelangelo worked consistently painting the Sistine Chapel. Eating and sleeping were an afterthought, as was changing his clothes. When he finally took off his boots, layers of skin came off as well. That may be a good illustration of ignoring necessity in the service of possibility. Many of us do not have that problem. If anything, most of us here in Southern California seem to be chasing after "necessities": the new car and the bigger house. Too often, our "possibilities" are in the service of these "necessities" and we end up running in the wrong direction.

It is precisely here that a belief in Jesus Christ makes a world of difference. If you are "all in" as a follower of Christ, you know that you have been called to a work in God's Kingdom. You have been gifted and commissioned. Your job is to discover that work and to do it, to the best of your ability, until you die. Affirming and living that truth, in a balanced life, by wisely meeting God's possibilities and wisely meeting daily necessities is the only good solution to existential anxiety.

The problem, of course, is that it takes people and practice to move the wonderful thought that you belong to God and have gifts to bring into the world into a sure and working confidence—a confidence that moves. People and practice help us to transition from thought to movement. God has put people in our lives for us to care for, to learn from, to support us, and to irritate us. We need all that God has provided to help us to move a thought into a conviction, and from a conviction to a sustaining emotional force. We need people to support us, people to learn from, and the inevitable and essential irritations that help us to practice patience and learn how to find God in the midst of emotional challenges.

Shame

After depression and anxiety, another troubling emotion encountered in therapy is shame. Shame is imprinted in our emotional life from bad parenting. In *Healing the Shame that Binds You*, John Bradshaw (1988) differentiated normal and healthy shame from what he termed "toxic shame." *Shame* is thought of as an inward feeling about oneself as contrasted with guilt, which is an awareness of how one's behavior impacts others. *Healthy shame* is the awareness of a failure of character followed, hopefully, by a decision to work on oneself. *Toxic shame* is a sense of despair that there is something fundamentally wrong with oneself: that "I am a bad person." A skillful parent will help a child understand the difference between making a bad choice and being a bad person. A parent who overutilizes shaming as punishment for bad behavior is creating a shame-based child, a child who will grow up to feel bad about themselves. We have seen too many shame-based family systems where an angry statement (e.g., "You should be ashamed of yourself!") is used to control not only behavior but thoughts and emotions as well. In a shame-based family system, parents indoctrinate children into a proscribed and well-regulated family functioning with comments like, "You should be ashamed to think that way" or "You should be ashamed to feel that way!"

Therapists often hear statements like, "I know I shouldn't feel this way" or "I shouldn't think this." Worse than this is the statement, "I hate myself. There is something really wrong with me!" Toxic shame can lead to suicide. When early childhood shaming is so substantially imprinted into a person's emotional life, it is easy to lose hope. In my therapeutic practice of 35 years, I would estimate that self-shaming has been the most difficult challenge for clients to overcome. Shame, like the food additive MSG, intensifies other conditions such as depression and anxiety by adding the additional burden of "I shouldn't feel this way." Self-shaming makes all of life a burden.

Healing

God can heal all troubling emotions. God can heal depression, anxiety, shame, envy, regret, and guilt. God created the process of healing. He created the brain's ability to quickly defend itself from trauma through the process of repression. Over time, bodies heal, and so do brains. In talk therapy the brain is able to recover repressed emotional memory and through the process of neural integration neutralize the intensity of the repressed emotional content. People leave the therapy session feeling lighter and are less likely to avoid people, places, and triggering memories.

God uses His Word as the foundation for replacing outdated cognitive schemas and unwanted behaviors. Over time, attending to the promises contained in Scripture creates a new brain. As Dan Siegel (2007) reminds us, practiced *states* can become enduring *traits*. When the Word is a lamp to your feet, when the Lord is your shepherd, it is easier to find and stay on the right path. With a renewed mind and the light of the Holy Spirit, life is transformed.

Questions for Review, Reflection, and Discussion

1. What are some of the major causes of depression?
2. Why is it difficult for Christians to talk about troubling emotions?
3. What may be spiritual and existential causes of depression?
4. When are you most like to experience anxiety?
5. What are some treatment approaches to depression and anxiety?
6. What is the difference between shame and guilt, and how does Scripture help in healing?

CHAPTER 9

The Helping Professions

Pastoral, Social, Psychological, and Medical

> "There are different kinds of gifts, but the same Spirit distributes them. There are different kinds of service, but the same Lord. There are different kinds of working, but in all of them and in everyone it is the same God at work."
>
> —1 Corinthians 12:4–6

Chapter Preview and Learning Objectives

God has gifted people with a heart for helping. Healing hurts can take place over coffee with a close friend or family member. Pastors, elders, and other laypersons are gifted by God to know how to listen compassionately and therapeutically. Healing originates with God. He has given his children the ability to heal physically, emotionally, and spiritually and to help others to heal. We are all called to love. We are called to be compassionate and available when needed and invited by the Holy Spirit to help someone in need. Psychologists, social workers, mental health nurses, marriage and family therapists, and psychiatrists are not only called but also trained to specialize in treating mental illness of various types and in various contexts. This chapter reviews the variety and specializations of mental health practitioners.

Learning Objectives

Students will do the following in this chapter:

- Acquire knowledge of a variety of mental health practitioners.
- Explore their individual sense of God's calling.
- Grasp the relationship of calling and effective treatment.

Different Professions for Different Needs

God has gifted people with a heart for helping. A kind word over coffee on the church patio can change a person's life. Taking soup to an elderly neighbor may be all that is needed to restore faith. In other words, a loving act does not need special training. But combine a heart for helping and a willingness to serve with training for specific service and God's work can be even more powerful. This chapter is about people whom God has called into the mental health profession. It is kind of a silly distinction, isn't it? We are all called into the mental health profession. There is nothing more valuable for anyone's mental health than to hear about and follow Jesus Christ. But it is good to know the differences in titles and training that exist within the mental health profession.

The first persons Christians ought to contact when they need help is their pastor or elder. Whatever the problem, pastors and elders should be sought out for prayer and support. In many cases, pastors have been trained in pastoral counseling and can be very effective in helping with personal and relationship problems. Similarly, elders, especially elderly elders, have accrued a great deal of wisdom over the years. It is sad that many people are too embarrassed to talk with their pastor or reach out to an elder. It is understandable, albeit unfortunate, that many people are hesitant to share their problems with people with whom they will be in regular contact. It may be that parishioners could be encouraged to be more open with each other. But that may be a stretch for some.

It is surprisingly helpful to talk with someone about your problems. I explained above how processing feelings works in the brain to lift burdens and transform emotions. The apostle John encourages us to confess our sins, knowing that God is faithful to forgive us. The saying is that confession is good for the soul. Confessing to a priest may seem like an empty and antiquated ritual, but offered in the right spirit, it can be surprisingly powerful. A great deal of professional therapy centers around the power of confession. The Catholic church permits both anonymous confession behind a screen as well as face-to-face confession in a place dedicated for that purpose. I would like to hope that when someone confesses to a priest or pastor, instead of being embarrassed about being human, that person would be able to celebrate not only relief but also a greater sense of connection.

Ideally, pastors know their limitations. Serious relationship problems, addictions, major depression, personality disorders, interpersonal violence, and panic episodes are some of the problems that require a referral to a professional. As a pastor in the late 1970s, I did not know of many Christian therapists in my area. I found one and interviewed him. He and I collaborated for many years. He provided the psychotherapy, and I assisted with prayer. Both are powerful in the work of healing. Because professional psychotherapists adhere to strict standards of confidentially, my colleague got permission from my parishioner before letting me know how things were going. Were you surprised that I used the term "colleague"? You shouldn't be. Christians, in whatever context, are in service to God.

Again, priests, pastors, and elders ought to be the first to be called upon for help. If the problem warrants professional care, those first responders can become the supportive team for referral, support, and prayer. We all need support and prayer, and at times, we need someone trained and skilled, a specialist to help us heal.

Licensed Clinical Social Workers

A licensed clinical social worker (LCSW) receives similar training as a marriage and family therapist (MFT). An LCSW can set up an office and see individuals, couples, and families in the same way as MFTs. The difference between the two is that LCSWs focus more on the environmental and social factors surrounding the person(s) seeking help. As such, LCSWs are likely to work in agencies such as child and adult services, where they are able make home visits and assess relevant social, environmental, and financial conditions. In California, LCSWs obtain 3,000 hours of supervised training and are required to pass an ethics exam as well as an Association of Social Work Boards clinical exam. You often find LCSWs working in hospital settings, especially hospitals focusing on treating problems of mental health. In whatever context, an LCSW will:

- observe client behavior, assess social contexts and needs, and create treatment strategies
- diagnose and treat psychological problems and emotional disorders
- work with psychologists and physicians to develop and implement treatment plans
- coordinate with social services to facilitate relevant care

Marriage and Family Therapists

MFTs treat individuals, couples, and families. Licensing, in most states, require a master's degree as well as many hours of supervised training. Where I worked in California, a candidate for licensure is required to obtain 3,000 hours of supervised work with clients. That work may include group therapy as well as individual, couple, and family therapy. In addition, licensure requires passing two exams, ethics and clinical. State licensing boards determine the numbers of training hours in required fields of study and exams that are consistent in all training institutions. As you might suspect, MFTs tend to specialize in relationships. Our training prepares us to work with individuals, but we are often called up to work with couples and families. As an instructor I taught courses in diagnosis and assessment, group therapy, couple therapy, family therapy, theories of personality, and theories and techniques of psychotherapy. The expectation of the schools where I taught were that graduates would be prepared to treat a wide variety of patient populations and problems. There was also a great deal of emphasis on cultural competency. Every course I taught had a segment of training that dealt specifically with the application of treatment in cross-cultural contexts.

Licensed Clinical Psychologists

A licensed clinical psychologist has a doctor of philosophy degree in clinical psychology or a Doctor of Psychology degree. These advanced degrees equip psychologists not only with the ability to apply expert therapy with many types of patient problems but also to specialize in areas such as pediatric psychology, forensic psychology, the treatment of posttraumatic stress, anxiety disorders, and major depression. Many psychologists are skilled research scientists and are frequently called upon to undertake careful diagnoses of mental disorders and to write up thorough psychological evaluations. This is often the case where the legal process requires information on the suitability for an individual to stand trial, the likelihood that an individual may have committed a crime, or the suitability of shared child custody.

Psychologists are frequently experts at using psychological tests and assessments to determine eligibility for certain areas of high-stress employment. These fields may include the FBI, the military, air traffic control, the medical profession, and others. As a candidate for the ministry and prior to attending seminary, I was under the care of the Presbytery of San Diego. The Presbytery required my being interviewed by a committee on ministry of the Presbyterian Church as well as a psychological evaluation. The pastors and elders of the presbytery knew, of course, that anyone desiring to take up the work of pastoral ministry needed to have their head shrunk. I passed the psych. eval.

Some of the questions that I seem to recall on the standard psych exam, the MMPI, that I was given caused me to pause. I think I recall that one question was something like, “Do you believe that you have a special relationship with God?” I wondered, if I answered correctly (that I did have a special relationship with God), would I be considered sane or insane? Fortunately, the 567 true-or-false questions on the MMPI are designed to evaluate, among other factors, the sanity, reliability, and consistency of the test taker. The test convinced the church elders that I was crazy enough to join their ranks.

I am being a bit silly here, but only a bit. Pastoral ministry is what an experienced psychologist would say is high-stress employment. Professor Ray Anderson of Fuller Seminary said in my ordination address that the profession is “impossible.” By that he meant, of course, impossible for any one individual to successfully meet all of the needs and expectations of a church community.

Psychiatric Nurses

A psychiatric nurse is a registered nurse with specialized training in working to provided diagnostic and mental health services to individuals, families, groups, and communities. The American Psychiatric Nurse Association describes psychiatric mental health nurses (PMHNs) as individuals who offer primary care services to psychiatric mental health populations with diagnoses and treatment of many types of psychiatric disorders. These professionals may work as independent practitioners or in concert with psychiatrists and in mental health facilities. They are also licensed and qualified to prescribe psychotropic medication.

For accreditation, The American Nurses Credentialing Center requires a candidate to have been licensed as a registered nurse with 2 years of full-time practice and 2,000 hours minimum of clinical practice in psychiatric mental health nursing within 3 years and an additional 30 hours of continuing education. Licensing may vary depending on one’s state requirements.

Psychiatrists

I took Dr. Anderson’s advice to heart. As a pastor I knew when a parishioner needed the help of a psychologist or psychiatrist, and I made a referral. As a medical doctor, psychiatrists specialize in knowing and utilizing psychotropic medications. These are medications that help to adjust levels of brain chemicals (i.e., neurotransmitters), such as dopamine, serotonin, and norepinephrine. The medications most often recommended by psychiatrists are antianxiety agents, antipsychotics, antidepressants, stimulants (e.g., Adderall), and mood stabilizers. Psychiatrists can also prepare psychological evaluations or work closely with a psychologist. This is especially true in psychiatric hospitals where a psych team may include a psychiatrist and psychologists and also LCSWs and psychiatric nurses.

In the days when I did intake evaluations, I asked my clients questions about the nature, history, and severity of their presenting problems. I also asked questions about their past; their family and social relationships; any troubling thoughts, emotions, and behaviors; any physical illnesses and injuries; and where they look for sources of faith and spiritual support. In other words, I went down a checklist of psychodynamic, systemic, cognitive and behavioral, and existential strengths and challenges. But I also asked the medical and biological questions that would help me to determine the client's need to see a physician or psychiatrist. I have often worked together with psychiatrists to assess problems, treatment strategies, and medication management. Referrals and consultations have gone both ways. Any enlightened mental health professional welcomes (or should welcome) consultation with other professionals and faith leaders.

Returning to the first paragraph of this chapter, God gives people a special calling to follow a particular path. He equips them with spiritual gifts, talents, and traits of personality to complement that calling. Accompanying that gift may be a prompting to receive the training and experience to work in specialized contexts. Frequently, circumstances prevent someone from having that training, and the demands of life may seem to create limitations. Nonetheless, God's calling on a person has not gone away. When a heart is open, opportunities present themselves. Circumstances may limit some paths and, at the same time, open others.

My pastor has been preaching about love recently. As he was preaching, it occurred to me that the ability to love is the great leveler. In Samuel 16:7, God said to Samuel, "Man looks at the outward appearance, but God looks at the heart." The joy that comes from experiencing the Holy Spirt working in you to touch a life is available to everyone. At the end of the day, that is all that matters.

My father was obnoxiously friendly—or, at least as a young person, he seemed that way to me. On a road trip with my family, Dad would pull into a gas station and begin to talk to the service attendant. Self-serve stations had not arrived yet. Dad would ask them about their town, good places to eat, the weather, and even ask sometimes-personal questions about their families and how long they had lived in the area. He was just such a friendly guy. I hated it. I would slump down with my brothers in the back seat, hiding in embarrassment. Dad was an engineer, not overly or even openly religious. He was just a friendly guy who was interested in people. Some people were probably annoyed, but I wonder how many people felt a little less insignificant because someone found them interesting.

When I think back to how God used my dad—just because he had an open heart—I realize how little is required to care about someone and help them to feel valued. We have all had the experience of having a doctor, a teacher, a neighbor, or a favorite relative who seemed to be genuinely interested in us and how that made us feel. Professional training and qualification are invaluable for specific types of service to God. But equally important is a heart that is open to people.

Physicians

If you are depressed or chronically anxious, consider seeing your family physician. If you have a family doctor who you frequently see and who knows you well, talk to that person. There are some good reasons for that. One reason is that your doctor may have your medical history and your family's medical history and may be able to connect your emotional challenges with a possible physical illness. Often, physicians are skilled and knowledgeable at prescribing medication for emotional problems. Jane, my doctor, is excellent at taking time and looking at many possible sources for medical problems. She is especially skilled at dealing with a wide range of issues related to women's health. I have frequently recommended her to both my male and female clients because of her success in treating emotional problems. If your doctor is not confident that they are the right person to see, you may get a referral to a psychiatrist whom your doctor has worked with and knows will do a good job.

I understand my clients' reluctance to seek medical attention. The most common reason is a mistaken idea that because they are a Christian, an emotional problem represents a lack of faith. Both Christian and non-Christian clients may be worried about the effects of the medication, the possibility of becoming addicted to some medications, and not wanting to believe that they need a "crutch" to get through their problems. Since I began my practice in 1985, I have seen greater acceptance of psychotropic medication. But those who are still distrustful of medication typically lack an understanding of how medications work. For that reason, I often find myself explaining basic brain chemistry or pointing them to relevant online tutorials.

Jesus Christ is the "great physician." All of us work for Him. In 1983, H. Newton Malony, a longtime professor of psychology in Fuller Seminary's School of Psychology, wrote *Wholeness and Holiness: Readings in the Psychology/Theology of Mental Health*. Dr. Mahoney skillfully connected the relationship of spiritual health with psychological health. This may have been a novel idea to many psychotherapists in 1983. From the wealth of psychological research published in books, articles, and podcasts in the decades since Dr. Mahoney's work, it seems to be common knowledge in the psychological community that a client's spiritual beliefs and resources are invaluable for maintaining and enhancing mental health.

Questions for Review, Reflection, and Discussion

1. Describe the focus of the major professions that deal with mental and emotional health.
2. Describe the various functions of the major professions that deal with mental and emotional health.
3. Who might be on a mental health care team?
4. What questions might you ask a mental health professional to decide whether to make a referral to that person?

CHAPTER 10

Mental Illness, Evil, and a Fallen World

> "Cursed is the ground because of you; through painful toil you will eat food from it all the days of your life. It will produce thorns and thistles for you, and you will eat the plants of the field. By the sweat of your brow you will eat your food until you return to the ground, since from it you were taken; for dust you are and to dust you will return."
>
> —Genesis 3:17–19

Chapter Preview and Learning Objectives

What does the Bible mean when it affirms that we live in a "fallen world"? What can be understood as "evil"? Is there a relationship between evil, a fallen world, and mental illness? This chapter delves into topics that are both unpleasant and controversial. However, those concepts exist in Scripture, so they are of interest to psychology as well as theology. One writer has described evil as "undermining." That word is an apt description of the world we live in and the many types of mental, behavioral, and emotional challenges humans face. The psychiatrist M. Scott Peck (1985) has provided another idea about the nature of evil and the difference between evil and mental illness. Peck even suggested DSM criteria for recognizing what might be thought of as evil.

Learning Objectives

Students will do the following in this chapter:

- Grapple with the concepts of a fallen world and evil in relation to mental health and the treatment of mental illness.
- Develop a personal understanding of a Christian approach to these topics.
- Appreciate the challenges and choices related to existential awareness.
- Explore how pride and narcissism can have terrible, undermining consequences.

Evil

Most people do not want to think about evil. I am one of them. I hate thinking that evil exists, that we are in a spiritual war with forces that are set upon destroying human happiness. It is pretty hard to wrap one's head around the reality that evil exists. And it takes courage to seriously think about what evil is and does. The best definition I have heard for the operation of evil is "undermining." I first heard that definition in a lecture by John Beebe of the Jung Institute in San Francisco. I think it perfectly describes the nature and agenda of evil. When someone undermines the faith of others—turns people against each other and creates chaos, conflict, and war—evil has succeeded. I cannot begin to fathom the degree of undermining of our nation's values, traditions, and political systems because certain individuals are intent on securing or maintaining power.

In his 1983 book *People of the Lie*, M. Scott Peck locates the origin of evil in the will. I am reminded of Lucifer's declaration in Isaiah 14, "I *will* be like the most-High." Erich Fromm and C. S. Lewis agree. In an article titled "Christianity and Culture," Lewis (1940) says, "There is no neutral ground in the universe: every square inch, every split second is claimed by God and counterclaimed by Satan" (p. 178). So yes, it comes down to the will. What will you choose? Jesus told us that the Kingdom of God is here. We are either servants of the King or we are enslaved to self, Satan, and to a fallen world. It comes down to a choice. In Romans 1:1, the apostle Paul made a good choice, calling himself a servant of Christ. He understood that giving oneself wholly to Christ was the only true freedom from the consequences of fear and selfishness. In his letter to a church in Galatia, Paul wrote, "It is for freedom that Christ has set us free" (Galatians 5:1).

Fear

It is interesting to me that fear is behind so much selfishness and evil. From the beginning, the enemies of God have used fear as a principal weapon. Satan tempted Eve with the fear that she was missing out on something that, to her, seemed good. And it is not just about missing out: human beings, who are not afraid of not having enough to eat or of being shot in the street, are afraid that they do not measure up or may not have quality of life and the things they think they are entitled to.

Fear is the cause of so much human misery and is one of the most pervasive characteristics in mental illness. In Kernberg's (1975) *Borderline Conditions and Pathological Narcissism*, he states: "Some narcissistic personalities present strong conscious feelings of insecurity and inferiority. ... They present a predominance of primitive defensive mechanisms such as splitting, denial, projective identification, omnipotence, and primitive idealization" (p. 229).

In *Escape from Freedom*, Erich Fromm (1941) also locates the extremes of neurosis in a choice (albeit an unconscious choice from the depths of fear, self-delusion, and denial) to avoid feelings of aloneness and powerlessness. In the worst cases, paranoia and the dread of insignificance pushes a person beyond benign evasions to the extremes of what Fromm (1964), in *The Heart of Man: Its Genius for Good and Evil*, termed "malignant narcissism" as a "severe mental sickness" representing "the quintessence of evil." He characterized the condition as "the most severe pathology and the root of the most vicious destructiveness and inhumanity" (p. 37). Peck (1983) quotes Fromm in *People of the Lie*: "Fromm saw the genesis of human evil as a developmental process: we are not created evil or forced to be evil, but we become evil slowly over time through a long series of *choices* [emphasis added]" (p. 82). We see the urgency of choice throughout Scripture. "Choose this day, whom you will serve," Joshua demanded of the people of Israel (Joshua 24:15). I will repeat again that we are created in the image of God, which means that we are able to respond. We are response-able. This is what makes us human.

However, we can also choose to be evil. Fromm (1964) said:

> Evilness is the attempt to transcend the realm of the human to the realm of the inhuman, yet it is profoundly human because man cannot become an animal as little as he can become "God." Evil is man's loss of himself in the tragic attempt to escape the burden of his humanity. (p. 192)

The burden Fromm spoke of is existential angst, the inevitable dread arising from our dual ontological nature. Our only true freedom comes from submission to God (our "higher power" in AA language). Otherwise, our efforts to be (in the poem, "Invictus" of William Henley 1888 the "master of my fate, the captain of my soul" may, with a narcissistic compass, follow the course of Captain Ahab and doom ourselves and others.

Pride

Herman Melville, like all true artists, looked ahead at what his generation was unable to clearly see. He predicted the evil to come. The term "monomaniacal" was used for Ahab's single-minded obsession with revenging the loss of his leg to the white whale, Moby Dick. In brilliant symbolism, Ahab got tangled up in the web of harpoon lines stuck to the back of the whale. He died tied to object of his hatred. His pride doomed him. Like Lucifer, pride was his downfall.

> You said in your heart, "I will ascend to the heavens; I will raise my throne above the stars of God; I will sit enthroned on the mount of assembly, on the utmost heights of Mount Zaphon ... I will climb to the highest heavens and be like the Most High." (Isaiah 14:13–14)

"I will be like the most-high" is the slogan of prideful narcissism. Melville understood this. There were plenty of examples from history. The pharaohs, caesars, and ancient kings and rulers gave Melville plenty of illustrations with which to model Ahab, a man who cared about no one and nothing except his hurt pride. The first mate, Starbuck, tried to reason with Ahab: "To be enraged with a dumb thing, Captain Ahab, seems blasphemous" (Melville, 1851/2002, Chapter 36). "Talk not to me of blasphemy, man; I'd strike the sun if it insulted me," was Ahab's reply (Melville, 1851/2002, Chapter 36).

"Not in America—this couldn't happen in America," people said after the capitol riots on January 6, 2021. "This couldn't happen in Germany," people reported having witnessed the death camps. "Could this be happening in Mother Russia? Surely not Stalin!" It should not surprise anyone how a power-hungry person, shrewd, charismatic, and intoxicated with pride, could successfully undermine a ship's crew or an entire nation. It certainly seemed that Melville could divine what lay ahead.

Peck showed a great deal of courage in writing *People of the Lie*. He knew that his reputation as a psychiatrist might well be undermined by the mental health community when he made the effort to discuss and diagnose evil. Nevertheless, he writes:

> The time is right, I believe, for psychiatry to recognize a distinct new type of personality disorder to encompass those I have named evil. In addition to the abrogation of responsibility that characterizes all personality disorders, this one (evil) would specially be distinguished by:
>
> a. consistent destructive, scapegoating behavior, which many often be quite subtle.
> b. excessive, albeit usually covert, intolerance to criticism and other forms of narcissistic injury.
> c. pronounced concern with a public image and self-image of respectability, contributing to a stability of lifestyle but also to pretentiousness and denial of hateful feelings or vengeful motives.
> d. intellectual deviousness with an increased likelihood of mild schizophrenic like disturbance of thinking at times of stress. (Peck, 1983, p. 129)

In view of these characteristics, does anyone come to mind?

In a counseling session, I once witness a church elder becoming drowsy in the middle of a heated argument with his wife. It looked as if at any moment he might fall asleep in the middle of their argument. I hate to have to suggest that he fit the criteria above. His scapegoating, intolerance to criticism, overconcern with his public image, and intellectual deviousness was blatant. Moreover, he was so well defended against criticism, he actually started to fall asleep—the ultimate flight defense. Clearly, I could have diagnosed him as a narcissist, but it might be worse.

Psychosis Versus Neurosis

Venkatakrishnan (2018) describes neurosis as referring to inner struggles and mental and physical disturbances, while psychosis is a major personality disorder marked by gross mental and emotional disturbances. Neurosis is a milder mental disorder, while psychosis refers to times or states of insanity (or mental imbalance). It seems that both Captain Ahab and the church elder may have had a psychosis. In 2006, Laura Sockol wrote a wonderful paper entitled "The Man Who Mistook a Whale for Pure Evil: A Diagnostic Assessment of Captain Ahab." It's an enjoyable case study based on interviewees (from the novel) who knew the captain. She lists some of the diagnostic criteria for narcissistic personality disorder, such as:

- irrational obsessions and dysfunctional cognitions
- delusions of grandeur
- maladaptive emotional responses
- impaired social functioning (Sockol, 2006, "Psychological Symptoms" section)

The church elder evidenced criteria for a narcissist but also fit some of the criteria for a Antisocial Personality Disorder as described in the Diagnostic and Statistical Manuel of Mental Disorders (DSM 5) (APA, 2013). Among the criteria for this disorder are:

- A pervasive pattern of disregard for the violation of the rights of others
- Deceitfulness
- Conning others
- Impulsivity
- Consistent irresponsibility
- Lack of remorse
- Failure to conform to social norms

I had not known this person for very long and I had not heard reports of his losing this temper or being violent, so I had not immediately thought of this diagnosis. I suppose I could have taken a cue from his wife who said that she thought her husband was "evil." I guessed she might have been exaggerating. But maybe not.

Do these diagnoses exist in the church? You bet. I once heard a professor say that he thought that most everyone was a little neurotic. We laughed. Then he went down a list of possibilities:

- anxiety
- depression
- addiction
- obsessiveness
- codependency
- controlling
- perfectionist

The list continued. We got his point. It is easy to say that everyone has challenges, because everyone does. I would like to think that the difference for Christians is that we are encouraged to be aware of those challenges and to seek God's help in dealing with them.

A Fallen World

Before I continue to tackle the problem of evil, I should tackle the problem of being human and the challenges of living in a fallen world. Recalling the quote from Calvin in Chapter 7, we cannot truly know ourselves without first knowing God. His nature and goodness are the standards of measurement for our own self-assessment. From God's perspective, according to Jeremiah 17:9, "The (human) heart is deceitful above all things, and desperately wicked: who can know it?" Both Calvin and Jeremiah have something to tell us about human nature. Here is where we begin our understanding of the origin of evil, by separating the vast majority of us who acknowledge our ability to sin from those few who do not and, perhaps, cannot.

What does it mean to live in a fallen world? Scripture tells us that the fall was due to disobedience—the *choice* to disregard the words and wisdom of God. The story of the first sin is brilliant in its accuracy and simplicity: "When the woman saw that the fruit of the tree was good for food and pleasing to the eye, and also desirable for gaining wisdom, she took some and ate it. She also gave some to her husband" (Genesis 3:6). The tree represents the three central concerns of philosophy: what is good, what is true, and what can be considered beautiful. Apparently, Eve thought that she must have misunderstood God's injunction. The serpent directed Eve's attention to the tree—that it was good for food, a delight to the eyes, and able to make one wise—so why, she thought, would a good God withhold a good thing from me? I must have gotten it wrong. What Eve got wrong is that she (and the rest of us) do not get to decide for ourselves what is good, true, and beautiful. Acting as an agent for oneself (autonomy) is a good thing—except when it isn't. How often do we make wrong choices because of the fear of missing out on something we have decided we should have?

Autonomy versus shame and doubt is Stage 2 in Erik Erikson's eight stages of the human life cycle. In this stage, from around 18 months to 2 or 3 years, a child learns self-awareness and self-control. Autonomy, from the Greek *auto nomos*, can have two meanings. The usually meaning of autonomy is self-regulation, but for the toddler, autonomy can also mean being a law until myself. The proverbial "terrible twos" is the little person's efforts to stretch autonomy from self-rule to ruling everyone else. "I get to do whatever I want!" says the tiny toddler. Skillful parents will help the child adjust to learning appropriate limits to their autonomy. Unskillful parents will shame a child into submission and create, potentially, a lifelong burden of shame and self-doubt.

John Bradshaw (1988) reminded us that while normal shame occurs as a result of transgressing a social norm, *toxic shame* is the conviction that something is terribly wrong with oneself. Narcistic personality disorder can often be traced to a genetic origin, but one wonders if toxic parents can also be responsible for contributing to the disorder. A typical defense against the burden of toxic shame, according to Alfred Adler (1979) and Karen Horney (1972) would be the chronic exercise of autonomy in the service of control and mastery over others. Erich Fromm (1964) believed that narcissism could be pushed to the extremes of malignancy—a "severe mental sickness"—as discussed above. He characterized the condition as "the most severe pathology and the root of the most vicious destructiveness and inhumanity" (Fromm, 1964, p. 37). It may be that this condition, this terrible ability to undermine others in the service of one's own narcissistic ends, comes close to what John Beebe described as evil (cited in Estés, 2003). In the 20th and, recently, in the 21st century, we have seen ample evidence of the undermining effects of malignant narcissism.

Before we go further in examining the nature of evil, it would be good to have a better understanding of human nature as it exists in the context of a world in which God does not rule, a world that has "fallen." What does it cost to live in a fallen world? Let's go back further to a time before the fall. This was a time, and will be again, when God's love was evident in every aspect of human experience. The clay of the earth, molded perfectly by the hand of God and inspired by His breath, created a perfect reflection of His nature and image as man and woman. Man and woman were companions with each other and with each of the creatures of the sixth day. The garden created for them was, and will be again, a timeless moment of provision and excruciating beauty. What happened?

Scripture tells us that Eve disobeyed because of an error in judgement. She is not God. She does not get to decide for herself what is good, true, and beautiful. Adam disobeyed, not because he was deceived but because he wanted what he wanted, and what he wanted was Eve. We do not get to have what we want just because we want it. Autonomy and narcissism destroyed the harmony between man and woman. The garden, the earth, locked away and in travail until the day of redemption, shattered God's perfect creation of all that was the sixth day. And so, we live in a fallen world.

Now, the dual ontological nature of human existence, clay and spirit, can no longer hold together. Paul understood this: "The flesh desires what is contrary to the Spirit, and the Spirit what is contrary to the flesh" (Galatians 5:17). This is where the existential problem of being human begins. When God scooped up dirt and breathed in His spirit and man and woman took it upon themselves to defy their creator, it set the stage for ongoing conflict. Now the question is, "Are we dirty, or are we divine, or are we both?" The wickedness that Jeremiah and Calvin spoke of stems from the impossibility of reconciling that ontological tension. Kierkegaard (1844) wrote about this problem in *The Concept of Dread* when he described the pervasive existential angst that we all live with. We cannot escape angst. In *The Denial of Death*, Ernst Becker (1973), following Kierkegaard, said that all of human behavior could be understood as the choices we make and the efforts we take to deal with dread.

We dress ourselves up, roll on deodorant, spray perfume or cologne, and try to be less muddy. It does not stop there. "That dress looked divine!" "She's a goddess." "He's an Adonis." "I want her to worship the ground I walk on." These are actually quotes I have heard in my clinical practice. And in this we want to blame God. He created us in His own image, to be like him. We are little gods. Of course we are; we are His kids. Like all kids, we want to be like Him. We want to be loving, kind, beautiful, generous, and good. But like all kids, we also want our own way. We want to feel special and valued. We want control over our lives and to feel powerful. Most of us want to be good, but we fall short, and we also want what we want. We are a mess. And like all kids, we blame Him: "Why did you make us this way?"

Fortunately, God is a great dad. She is also a great mom. Our tiny brain has a hard time with that, but that is not His/Her fault. God accommodates our tiny brain: Jesus called Him Father, and so do we. He *is* a great dad. He loves us even when we are muddy. He loves us when we try to pretend that we are as big and smart as He is. He loves us when we try to go our own way. He patiently waits for us to come home. And when we do, He hugs and kisses us and throws us a party. We cannot run away from his love. But we can run away from the gifts he has given us.

Existential Option 1: "I Hid Myself ... Because I Was Afraid."

How do we handle this dual ontological nature of mud and spirit? We have three choices: the same three choices that Kierkegaard outlined for us. Alfred Adler gave us three choices, and so did Karen Horney and Rollo May. In existential language, one choice is to hide. We can pretend that we are not muddy. We can be clean shaven, sweetly scented, and dress to impress. In the classroom, I was in the habit of asking the students (and instructing them not to raise their hands) how many of them put on deodorant that morning. Yes, it is a social convention, but the convention is a cultural collusion to try to hide our biology. And in many other unmentionable ways, we do not want to remind ourselves and others that we live in bodies, bodies that will decay and die.

But that is not the worst type of hiding. The worst type of hiding is hiding from who God made us to be. Marianne Williamson (1992) said it best in *A Return to Love*:

> Our deepest fear is not that we are inadequate. Our deepest fear is that we are powerful beyond measure. It is our light, not our darkness, that most frightens us. We ask ourselves, who am I to be brilliant, gorgeous, talented and fabulous? Actually, who are you not to be? You are a child of God. Your playing small doesn't serve this work. There is nothing enlightening about shrinking so that other people won't feel insecure around you. We were born to make manifest the glory of God that is within us. It is not just in some of us—it's in everyone! And as we let our own light shine, unconsciously we give other people permission to do the same. As we are liberated from our own fear, our presence automatically liberates others! (p. 165)

We hide from who God has created us to be, the existentialists tell us, because of the fear of possibility—the possibility of being or doing something outstanding. Consenting to possibility is an invitation to step out of the crowd, being exposed and vulnerable to criticism from self and others. It means facing the possibility of rejection and the terror of aloneness. This is why Rollo May (1975) wrote that it takes *Courage to Create*, to be an authentic individual.

Adler and Horney included a second way to hide. Adler used the term "excuses," and Horney used the term "compliance." Both of these "neurotic safeguards," or "neurotic trends," are ways to avoid possibility and responsibility by giving away one's power. We can abdicate our God-given potential by making excuses or by "going along with." This is the "immediate man" Kierkegaard (1849/1941) describes:

> For the immediate man does not recognize his self, he recognizes himself only by his dress. ... He has no self and a self he did not become, but he continues to live on with only the quality of immediacy. ... He now acquires some little understanding of life, he learns to imitate the other men, noting how they manage to live, and so he too lives after a sort. In Christendom he too is a Christian, goes to church every Sunday, hears and understands the parson, yea, they understand one another; he dies; the parson introduces him into eternity for the price of $10—but a self he was not, and a self he did not become. (p. 187)

We must not hide our light under a basket or make excuses. God's people must remember that we are all gifted. As Williamson (1992) says, we were born to make manifest the glory of God. We are given gifts to promote His work and His Kingdom on Earth. We actually do have value. We must not be afraid. Here again, Christianity provides the solution to one aspect of our existential dilemma. We do not need to hide. Because of God's unfailing love and generous gifts, He has made us special. In the words of Brené Brown (2014), "We are worthy of love and belonging."

Regardless of our efforts to hide from our ontological burden, the confusion and conflict of being both dirt and spirit, God seeks us out. We must live with the reality that we are, at the same time, finite and infinite. We cannot pretend that we are not finite and hide our biology, and we must not forget that we are gifted from God with infinite possibilities.

Existential Option 2: "I Will Be Like the Most-High!"

Some people think that they already are pretty special. They are God's gift to women, to men, to investment strategies, to the team, to the silver screen, to the nation. They are not muddy at all. The worst kind of sin is the illusion that you are too special to bother with God. You can put on a show of going to church, hold up a Bible, even become an elder. But be careful not to be like the Pharisee in Luke 18:11–14: "The Pharisee stood by himself and prayed: 'God, I thank you that I am not like other people—robbers, evildoers, adulterers—or even like this tax collector.'" Righteous in his own eyes, the Pharisee prevented himself from receiving grace. It turned out that it was the tax collector, very conscious of needing grace, that Jesus said was "justified before God" (Luke 18:14).

This second existential solution to dread is inflation. Inflation is still a method of hiding, but it is hiding from looking honestly at oneself. In the first half of life, the ego is tasked with developing a persona. One's persona is an effort to fit in, to look a certain way, to know how to behave socially. A healthy ego creates a healthy persona, one that sufficiently adapts to the demands of the other world without needing to be better than everyone else. Ideally, in the second half of life, one has met most of society's expectations and the ego turns its attention to looking within at one's Self. In the process, the ego must be willing to encounter the shadow: everything the ego would prefer to hide. Facing one's shadow, all that we dislike and disavow about ourselves, is painful. In 12-step language, Step 4 demands a fearless and rigorous moral self-inventory. Similarly, the third step in M. Scott Peck's four qualities of a mature individual is commitment to reality. Without a commitment to reality, to looking fearlessly at one's true self, including one's shadow, it may be tempting to hold onto and hide behind our persona.

Here we may want to review the difference between neurosis and psychosis. Neurosis, recall, is a type of mental disorder that creates chronic distress but does not include delusions or hallucinations. Psychosis is characteristically comprised of both delusions and/or hallucinations, which means that a person is in a state of imagination, such that they think that they are living inside that image rather than in actual reality. The neurotic person thinks there is too much wrong with them. The psychotic does not think there is anything wrong with themselves, only with everyone else. Research shows that underneath the narcissist's image and posturing is a very insecure individual. Again, we see the consequences of fear.

When Eric Fromm (1964) described malignant narcissism, he was describing a person who is so well defended against the reality of being a fallible human being that they attempt, and often succeed, in undermining reality, not just for themselves, but for everyone else. Certain charismatic individuals are so convincing in their self-deception that they are successful in casting a spell on their followers. I am not just thinking about Hitler, Kaddafi, Mao, Stalin, Jim Jones, or Captain Ahab. These are some of the standouts, but one does not have to look very far afield to know that there are plenty of narcissists in our own backyard. Like the Pharisee described by Jesus, there are plenty of folks who prefer pointing the finger at others.

Existential Option 3: "Blessed Are the Poor in Spirit."

Growth as an individual, whether you call it individuation (Jung), self-actualization (Maslow), or differentiation (Bowen), the road less traveled (Peck) requires the courage to face yourself in order to find your Self. The actualization tendency that Rogers described means that all of us have an instinct for growth. God gave us that instinct. We do not have to work at growing up physically, although we do have to work at staying healthy. God also gave us the gift of being able to respond to Him, to each other, and to the Earth. In the first chapter of Romans, Paul says that all of us are "able to respond" and that we have no excuse when we do not, because God's nature is evident, Paul says, plainly visible. Whether because of emotional wounding or pride, people repress the truth in unbelief. They hide, they make excuses, or they try to be superior to everyone else. God gave us the ability to respond. Not being responsible to our response-ability is a contradiction of human nature and the origin of all sin.

Jesus told us about the Pharisee and the tax collector. The mistake the Pharisee made (and all of us make from time to time) was comparing himself to others. Whether by looking up or looking down, comparing oneself to others is immature. It is immature because that was what we did when we were kids. It is not a grave sin when you are young. The process of ego development invites comparison. Adler talked about the "guiding fiction" that youngsters employ to imagine a future in which they will be heroic, special, significant in some way. The ego develops by evaluating one's strengths and talents in relation to others and selects an imagined course. But as I noted earlier, at some point in adult life, the ego must not continue to look outward in comparison with others but look inward at the unique gifts and path that God has chosen for us.

What is the third choice, the mature choice, with which to meet the existential challenge of living honestly in relation to the ontological pull of both possibility and necessity, of living in a fallen world in which evil contends with good? The mature choice is to strive toward both self-acceptance and authenticity. Maslow described the self-actualized person as self-accepting—not the inflated self-championing of the narcissist, but the sober, self-aware acceptance of a mature individual submitted to God. Self-awareness without self-acceptance would be unbearable. When I accept myself and do not compare myself to anyone, when I am okay with who I am and do not need anyone else's approval, I do not have to pretend or posture. I am free of the anxiety of approval, and so I am free to genuinely love. Maslow was right about self-acceptance but he did not tell us how to get there. The only way we can arrive at deep and lasting contentment with being human is to anchor our self-assessment in the conviction that God has made us and is with us.

Little Gods

It is wonderful to know that, like a child, we can approach our Heavenly Father for acceptance, forgiveness, comfort, encouragement, and direction. But children grow to become adolescents. They do not like being told what to do and often want to find their own way. Jesus told us about that in His story about the prodigal son. We can joke about how rebellious kids can be, but it is no joke when adults are determined to live life on their own terms, disregarding the needs and feelings of others.

History has given us far too many illustrations of the consequences of people flexing their little divinity. But you do not need to go back into history; simply drive the California freeways for up-to-date illustrations of someone living out the phrase "I will be like the most high"—doing whatever they choose. Reckless, inconsiderate driving used to trigger an angry and, sometimes, competitive response in me. I try to quiet my inner police officer by taking a deep breath and imagining that I am more mature. But then I am reminded about my own tendencies to rush through life and miss opportunities to care for or be courteous to others.

I do not do a very good job of being a god. I make mistakes. I disregard the needs of others. I injure myself. Thank God I am not God. More and more I appreciate the words of Paul, who called himself "the servant of Christ." Striving to be a captive to Christ is the surest way to escape being a slave to my own ego. I also relate to Paul when he laments in Romans 7:15, "For what I want to do I do not do, but what I hate I do." This is the very reason why it is so important to practice dying.

We have spent many years obeying the promptings of our egos, comparing ourselves to others, competing for successes, compromising values in the service of wants. We are very practiced at wanting what we want. That is not entirely bad of course. Things get done, goals are met, and some good may come from our strivings. In many ways, however, we miss the mark when we do not practice giving God control of our ways and our wants. "Unless the Lord builds the house, the builders labor in vain" (Psalm 127). How much more might be accomplished, how much more joy could we know and share with others, when we practice subjecting our "little divinity" to almighty God and trusting in Him?

The Ruler of This World

No chapter on evil and a fallen world would be complete without bringing up the one who Jesus called the "ruler of this world": Satan, the devil. In John 14:30, Jesus said, "I will no longer talk much with you, for the ruler of this world is coming, and he has nothing in Me." The English word "devil" is translated from the Greek *diabolos*, meaning slanderer, backbiter, false accuser. "Satan," from the Hebrew, also means slanderer but is most commonly referred to as the adversary, the one who opposes.

Jesus would not lie to us about the reality of Satan. And Jesus did not argue when Satan showed Jesus all the kingdoms of the world and said, "All this I will give you, if you will bow down and worship me" (Matthew 4:9). Why is this verse of the Bible important for our understanding of psychology? Because it is a key to grasping why human beings have a problem with God.

People have a problem with God because they think He is in charge. "Why, God, why?" has been asked countless times by people in pain. I asked that same question. Dealing with hurting human beings day after day, I became angry at God for not doing more to prevent human pain. Kneeling in an Episcopal church, with the choir singing softly on the side, I looked up at a very lifelike crucifix above the alter. It is hard to be angry at a man hanging on a cross. At that moment my anger left me, and I felt the pain underneath the anger: the pain of the human experience. We are the ones causing the pain. God is not the problem. He gave us His Word, He gave us His Spirit, He gave us his love, and He gave us His son. The rest is up to us.

But we have an opponent. The pain I have dealt with in my counseling ministry has been promoted by the father of lies, the thief who comes to steal, kill, and destroy, to undermine human happiness. The apostle Paul reminds us that our warfare is with principalities, powers, and the rulers of the world of this darkness. We live in a fallen world in which God is not in charge. C. S. Lewis has said, "God has landed on this enemy-occupied world in human form." Christ has commissioned us to occupy as much of this enemy held territory as we can.

This is where the ministry of Christian people, in all of our various roles, is so vital. Christians must take the problem of evil, a fallen world, and the devil very seriously. Lewis is right that we are in a war. In 1965, Donald Barnhouse, a Presbyterian pastor, wrote a terrific book: *The Invisible War.* Barnhouse does not gloss over the reality of Satan, demonic spirits, and our struggle with powers in heavenly places. Lewis (1942/2014) also said this about demonic spirits: "There are two equal and opposite errors into which our race can fall about the devils. One is to disbelieve in their existence. The other is to believe, and to feel an excessive and unhealthy interest in them. They themselves are equally pleased by both errors and hail a materialist or a magician with the same delight" (Preface). It is a mistake to imagine that the powers of darkness are only symbolic, that demonic forces that prey on human weakness are imaginary. Neither can we entirely blame human sin on Satan ("The devil made me do it"). A good understanding of psychology will help us to differentiate between authentic evil and organic disorders of the mind. While the enemy can slander, entice, and seduce, we are still responsible for our choices and our actions. Demons have been described as parasites.

They exist by feeding on bad choices. When resisted, they will flee.

The reason that the apostle Paul warned us about the nature of our enemies is because they cannot be defeated by normal human effort. Martin Luther (1529) wrote about this in *A Mighty Fortress Is Our God*:

> For still our ancient foe Doth seek to work his woe; His craft and power are great, and armed with cruel hate, On earth is not his equal. Did we in our own strength confide, Our striving would be losing; Were not the right Man on our side, The Man of God's own choosing. Dost ask who that may be? Christ Jesus, it is he.

I mentioned above that both Kierkegaard, the philosopher, and Jung, the psychiatrist, reinforced the fact that psychology can only do so much. There must be a transfusion of God's spirit for anything good to come from human effort. As Calvin (1975) said, "Therefore simply to will is of man; to will ill, of a corrupt nature; to will well, of grace" (p. 295). We Christians need to open our minds to God's word, our hearts to God's love, and, more than anything else, we need to open our lips in praise and prayer.

In his letter to the church at Ephesus, the apostle Paul told us about the weapons God has given to us for our warfare with the powers of darkness. If you think about Paul's teaching from a psychological perspective, you are reminded that the helmet Paul speaks of is a "cognitive intervention." So is the belt. Our shoes are both "behavioral and systemic." Our shield is both "cognitive and existential." These are defensive protection. Our offensive weapon is the sword of the spirit, the word of God. Knowing God's word sharpens our sword for the battles we face.

Our offensive weapon, prayer, brings us mental and emotional strength in the fight against what is not of God. Prayer changes everything. Prayer acknowledges our need for God. Prayer reminds us of our human limitations. Prayer readies us to see and hear God's provision and power. There is a great deal of psychological value in prayer. This has been demonstrated many times in laboratories and research facilities: that prayer quiets and focuses the mind and facilitates an overall sense of well-being. Prayer ministers hope and connects us with the faith we need to do the work that God has asked us to do. We live in a fallen world where God's enemies are all about. But we have a champion, Jesus, who fights with us and for us.

Questions for Review, Reflection, and Discussion

1. How do you understand the concept of a fallen world?
2. How are you effected by a fallen world?
3. Do you think you have ever encountered someone you thought could be evil?
4. Where do you think evil shows up? How would you recognize it?
5. Is there a relationship between a fallen world and mental illness?
6. How do you manage your dual ontological nature?
7. How might you describe sin psychologically?
8. Do you pray?

CHAPTER 11

The Psychology of Couple Relationships

> "That is why a man leaves his father and his mother and is united to with his wife, and they become one flesh."
>
> —Genesis 2:24

Chapter Preview and Learning Objectives

Two people becoming "one flesh" is not simply a metaphor. Couples become one in many symbolic ways, but there is also a physiological "oneness" that occurs in the limbic ties of an ongoing intimate relationship. *Limbic resonance* is the chemistry of falling in love. *Limbic regulation* is the physical stability created by the limbic tie. *Limbic revision* is God's mechanism of transformation. Love empowers partners to stretch. Stretching, for better or worse, creates growth. Marriage is a crucible of transformation where, by God's design, love is alchemically transformed into a life-enhancing and life-sustaining physical and psychological fact.

Learning Objectives

Students will do the following in this chapter:

- Come to appreciate God's design and goal for marriage.
- Understand the three phases of intimacy: limbic resonance, regulation, and revision.
- Appreciate how commitment opens to growth.
- Understand the role of pain in the strength training of love.
- Grasp that love requires death and that death can be redemptive or nonredemptive.

These Two Shall Become One Flesh

Is that a metaphor? Of course. Two people become one when they decide to live together. They become one when they make love, when they raise children together, when they share financial decisions. In so many ways, a decision to be together is a journey into oneness. But is it *just* a metaphor?

Lewis, Amini, and Lannon, the three psychiatrists who coauthored *A General Theory of Love* (2000) tell us that two becoming one flesh is much more than a metaphor. It is a physiological fact. Beginning with *limbic resonance*, the felt sense of oneness with another, *limbic regulation* is the quality of connection that ministers emotional and physical health to one's partner, and *limbic revision* is the miracle of two lovers altering each other's psychology, enhancing and sustaining the life of the other.

Limbic Resonance

Stage 1: Romance

What most people call chemistry, limbic resonance, is that wonderous feeling of connectedness that we feel when we feel that we have found the "right" person. This idea of the right person, the "soul mate," is partly a fantasy, partly a hope, and partly a possibility:

> Since time's beginning, romantic partners have searched for each other with exquisite but obscure deliberations. "In literature, as in love" wrote Andre Maurois, "we are astonished at what is chosen by others." And they are every bit as amazed at us. The very concept of compatibility discloses that a one-purpose template for loving predominates. Sexual attractiveness contributes only a minor filter to this selectivity. The number of couples who marry is a minuscule fraction of the many who find each other physically interesting. Not just any will do; in fact, to any one person looking for a mate, almost nobody will. (Lewis et al., 2000, p. 101)

God has designed us for limbic connection. Our limbic system is a set of structures in the brain that regulate emotion and memory. It also regulates the autonomic and endocrine functions that are triggered by emotional stimuli. Consequently, the limbic system is significantly involved in reinforcing behavior. Interestingly, that reinforcing behavior is partly responsible for who we fall in love with.

Melanie Klein (2002) was among the first to examine how an infant's brain develops in response to the child's interaction with significant people. Borrowing a concept from psychoanalysis, the ego and its objects, her ideas became the origin of object relations theory. Heinz Kohut (1977) termed these significant people "self-objects." A *self-object* is a person around whom the infant begins to model and create a sense of self. I frequently suggest that clients interested in this topic pick up a book by Harville Hendrix: *Getting the Love You Want* (1988). Hendrix (1988) provides a popular and user-friendly guide to object relations theory and how the theory relates to who you fall in love with. Hendrix developed *imago therapy*: the idea that we carry an image (imago) of an impactful relationship from our past, sometimes our mom or dad. This image may form the basis of who, for better or worse, we are attracted to (e.g., "Not just anyone will do"). Lovers tell each other, "I feel like I've known you all of my life!" Maybe they have.

So where does God fit into this idea? I like Hendrix's idea about the imago. It makes sense to me personally. In many ways, my wife reminds me of my mom. But she also reminds me of my dad. When I use the word "remind," I am not describing a physical resemblance (although Kathe and Mom share an uncanny physical resemblance). When I use the term "remind," I mean that in so many ways Kathe puts me in touch with familiar emotions from growing up. That is an important distinction. The brain holds on to memory and especially to emotional memory. So many wonderful and less wonderful emotions are triggered by many different types of stimuli, such as sounds, fragrances, the time of the day, or the time of the year. In this sense, memory is timeless. Is there a timelessness to our sense of eternity? More so than our brain, does our spirit recognize who God has chosen for us?

Object relations theory makes sense in the sense that at some level of awareness we are able to feel the rightness of the right choice. The central idea of imago therapy is that once we are conscious of the ways that our spouse is right for us, how, through the process of "reenactment," we access and potentially heal early attachment deficits, and how we ultimately marry our homework, once we are conscious of God's implanting this growth producing processes in us, we can relax a bit, be a bit more accepting and a bit wiser, and smile at God's genius.

Limbic Regulation

Stage 2: Connection

Scripture tells us that two people can become one flesh." Here is how:

> Limbic regulation affords lovers the ability to modulate each other's emotional, neurophysiology, hormonal status, immune function, sleep rhythms, and stability. If one leaves on a trip, the other may suffer insomnia, a delayed menstrual cycle, a cold that would have been fought off in the fortified state of togetherness. The neurally ingrained attractors of one lover warp the emotional virtuality of the other shifting emotional perceptions, what he feels, sees, knows. When somebody loses his partner and says a part of him is gone, he is more right than he thinks. A portion of his neural activity depends on the presence of the other living brain. Without it, the electric interplay that makes up him has changed. Lovers hold keys to the others' identities, and they write neurostructural alterations into each other's networks. Their limbic tie allows each to influence who the other is and becomes. (Lewis et al., 2000, p. 208)

But I think that there can be even more to this process of connecting. When two people love God, they fall more deeply in love with each other. It is inevitable. It makes sense that the depth of their felt sense of connection surely enhances their limbic tie.

Is it true that you should love God and not yourself? No. In fact, it is impossible. The more present God is in your life, the more you experience His love and the more love you have to give, and that includes yourself. How did a sinful woman find the temerity and courage to crash a dinner party for Pharisees, at the house of a Pharisee, in order to weep at the feet of Jesus? Jesus said that she had "great love." When you know Jesus, when you have great love, it is amazing what you will be willing to risk. And that is the point, isn't it? Self-acceptance and authenticity come from knowing the heart of the Lord. When you are authentic and self-accepting, and you have great love, you make an excellent partner. And when you are in God and know that He has given you the perfect person to be the arms and sweet voice of his love, loving that person is the greatest joy.

Limbic Revision

Stage 3: Becoming One

Living and loving someone for many years changes who you are. Of course it does. How could it not? Love stretches you. I had a class in Calvin's Institutes at Fuller Seminary. It was taught be a craggy old Dane. I recall his saying that Scripture is an anvil that has worn out many hammers. God's word will always stand up against any opposition: "Husbands love your wives" (Ephesians 5:25). "Wives be subject to your husbands" (Ephesians 5:22). Sometimes Scripture is hard on us. Can I love my wife the way Christ loved us? Can my wife maintain a spirit of respectfulness in spite of my bone-headedness? Scripture is hard on us.

Hard or not, that is what we are asked to do. And in the doing, we find great growth and great joy. And we change each other:

> In a relationship, one mind revises another; one heart changes its partner. This astounding legacy of our combined status as mammals and neural beings is *limbic revision*: the power to remodel the emotional parts of the people we love. (Lewis et al., 2000, p. 144)

Maybe some people take the idea of togetherness a bit too far. Being connected does not mean having to do everything together. There is no rule that you have to have the same checking account, sleep in the same bed, or wear matching outfits (unless you are in a bowling league). These are nice symbols of connectedness. But they are only symbols. When you have grown in your love for each other, you will grow as individuals. You have to. Love stretches you. You will do hard things because they are loving things. A loving relationship permits, encourages, and celebrates individual growth. Without that individual growth, marriage becomes boring, an acting out of a symbolic institution instead of a dynamic blending and revising of hearts, minds, and lives. When Jesus told us to love others as we love ourselves, it seems that he assumed that we do love ourselves. But does everyone love themselves?

Stretching

I suppose that, to a degree, everyone does love themselves. They would not survive otherwise. But for so many people, loving themselves is really hard. They may have grown up in a shame-based family where they were taught, directly or indirectly, that they were not loved. Worse, some people were taught that they were unwanted and had no value, which is why I sometimes hear clients say that they hate themselves. Can you imagine what you must have experienced in life to be able to make that statement?

Here is where God performs miracles. A person who has been betrayed, beaten, and brutalized by life can find healing and renewal. Sometimes miracles happen overnight. One day a person is without hope, and the next day hope has been restored. Overnight miracles do occur, but much of the time, miracles take time. And just because healing can take time does not make the results any less miraculous. For example, falling in love is a miracle. True, falling in love can be explained biologically and psychologically, but finding the right person to spend your life with feels miraculous. Who is the right person? The short answer is the right person is a person who makes you happy and, at the same time, a person who makes you stretch. People do not seem to be interested in people who are exactly like them. Neither are people interested in people who are totally opposite. It seems that God has designed human beings with an appetite for growth as well as for happiness. We seem to want challenges ... up to a point.

This appetite for growth takes place in all three areas of our being: physically, psychologically, and spiritually. Recall that Carl Rogers's term, the "actualizing tendency," applies to all living beings. This is the divine blueprint for reaching our biological potential. The wonderfully good news is that when Christ is in your life, you not only have a biological imperative for growth but also have an invitation by the Holy Spirit to grow spiritually: "Looking unto Jesus, the author and perfecter of our faith" (Hebrews 12:2).

How many ways does God stretch us? Make a list; the task will likely take the rest of your life. Since this chapter is about relationships, a good answer to that question is marriage. A good marriage is one in which you will be stretched. That does not sound like fun, and often, it isn't. But considering Hebrews 12:2 ("For the joy that was set before Him ..."), it is clear that God has a purpose for stretching us: joy.

It may seem counterintuitive that suffering brings joy, but of course it does. Hell week for my varsity football team in high school was aptly named. We started practicing for the season in late August 1965, in the hottest and smoggiest time of the year where I lived. Emission controls had just been mandated in Los Angeles, and it took many years to clean up our air pollution. So I vividly recall running around a football field with sweat in my eyes and lungs full of smog. We won our league championship that year. You can make a list of dozens of illustrations off the top of your head to show the relationship between pain and gain. Is marriage painful? If you do not know the answer, you have never been married.

Two Kinds of Pain

There seem to be two kinds of pain for Christians: redemptive and nonredemptive. Redemptive pain is pain that is good for you and helps you to grow; nonredemptive pain isn't. Redemptive pain happens when you choose a behavior or a path that will cause the suffering that leads to joy. Choosing to be patient or kind, even when it is uncomfortable, choosing to turn the other cheek when you would prefer to strike back, choosing to extinguish bad habits, and choosing to be better at loving your spouse are often painful choices that will stretch you, but they will ultimately lead to greater joy.

As a therapist I witnessed enough nonredemptive pain to last a lifetime. This type of pain comes from immaturity, selfishness, and evil. When, for whatever reason, a person decides to remain with a partner who abuses them, strips them of their value and dignity, and attempts to undermine their relationship with God, I think of this as nonredemptive pain.

Two Ways to Die

Jesus told us to take up our cross daily. The cross is an instrument of death. Why would Jesus invite us to take up a cross? The answer is because He loves us. Does that sound crazy? We human beings can be very selfish and shortsighted. In many ways, we are also very immature. In his letter to the church at Rome, Paul reminds us that "those who live according to the flesh have their minds set on what the flesh desires; but those who live in accordance with the Spirit have their minds set on what the Spirit desires. The mind governed by the flesh is death, but the mind governed by the Spirit is life and peace" (Romans 8:5–6). Apparently, what Paul is saying is that it takes death to defeat death. Picking up our cross means putting to death our propensity to only think about ourselves: what we want, regardless of whether or not it is good for us and whether or not it injures anyone else. This type of self-centeredness is deadly. There are two ways to die. We can die to ourselves in a way that invites growth and ultimately joy, or we can just die—slowly, over time, with no apparent redemptive value. We have choices.

Relationships that are meaningful and worth holding on to will stretch us and cause us pain. Love does that. We are not in heaven yet, and people are people. If we make the right choice of a spouse and friends, they will stretch us and cause us pain. Love does that. Love is the catalyst and fuel that initiates and drives the long journey of healing and growth. The next section is about how that happens: reenactment.

Reenactment

Among the reasons we are attracted to our spouse is the prospect of healing—not that we are necessarily aware of that. Of course, we may be physically attracted. That is the biological part. The spiritual part may be our sprit sensing God's direction for our life. Reenactment, however, has more to do with the psychological part, our need for healing deficits. In the film *Rocky*, Pauly asks Rocky about his relationship with Adrian. "We fill gaps," Rocky says. This is quite a sophisticated response, but Rocky has grasped the deeper attraction they have for one another. Gaps are filled in many interesting ways. Below, I will talk about the attraction of complementary personality types. But gaps are also filled by deep-seated psychological needs.

Reenactment is the process of activating emotional memory from previous experiences. It is an automatic process—largely unconscious—that God designed to help us become aware of buried hurts. Those hurts surface into awareness when we recognize familiar themes and patterns of relating. For instance, a wife may find herself responding—more accurately, reacting—to her husband's patterned drinking in the same way she did with her father. She may not have wanted to be conscious of her future husband's drinking habits, or perhaps she thought she could become successful in changing him, as she was not with her dad. If, albeit unlikely, he did become sober, this, for her, would be a corrective emotional experience.

But it may be more likely that in recognizing this reenactment of her childhood drama, she finds the courage to confront the situation. Whether successful or not, this would be another form of a corrective emotional experience: She found the courage she did not have as a little girl. Healing can come when the circumstances change or when we change to meet the circumstances. God's presence in the choosing enables change.

Frequently, the reenactment that facilitates healing old hurts and worn-out scripts can also be the brain's way of reliving and accessing pleasurable and familiar feelings from our past. Finding ourselves attracted to a particular someone sometimes triggers reenactment. It does not need to be a romantic attraction. We are simply drawn to someone who puts us in touch with familiar feelings.

"For better or worse" is the right way to think about reenactment. For example, research (Smith, 1998; Jones & Williams, 2015) has demonstrated that children growing up in a home where there was violence or addiction often find themselves, unknowingly, drawn to a romantic partner with a similar background (Office for National Statistics, 2017; Mikulincer & Goodman, 2006).

If that happens and both partners become aware of their backgrounds and make efforts to work on helping each other to heal and grow, they may be able to make things better. However, that is a huge "if." It is more likely that they will repeat familiar dynamics and resurrect a regressive cycle. In *Getting the Love You Want*, Harville Hendrix (1988) divides marriage into conscious and unconscious. In an *unconscious marriage*, the two partners recreate the dynamics that they grew up with. Nothing changes for the better, and because of the dynamic of a regressive cycle, things rapidly become worse. However, it is also possible that, with therapy, couples can become aware of their tendency to recreate the family dynamics of their past and work together to create a different emotional outcome. That is, they can become conscious of the choices they have to repeat old patterns or create new ones. This is a difficult task. It is hard to unlearn old emotional reactions and patterns of interaction. But with time and practice, different choices can lead to much better outcomes.

Hendrix created imago therapy, using object relations concepts, to underscore how frequently reenactment to an imago (image) of a significant person from the past is reenacted in the alchemy of attraction. I am using the term "image" in this sense to describe the internalized emotional memory of relationship dynamics with a significant person from the past—usually, a parent. Hendrix could see the concept of reenactment played out in many of the couples he worked with. The goal of imago therapy (to use a phrase from psychoanalysis) is to make the unconscious conscious. With increased awareness, partners can become more aware of behaviors and choices made from unconscious scripts and make different choices. Different choices can lead to becoming more skillful at loving each other.

Following Hendrix's lead, Woolley & Johnson (2005) focused on those troubling emotions that surface in relationships and the means to become more aware of how these emotions distort perceptions, intrude into conversations, and ultimately lead to conflict. Of course, all therapy needs to focus on emotions. Much of the time, that is where the majority of problems occur. The residue of emotional learning and emotional wounding takes its toll. All forms of therapy are needed depending on the types of client problems present, but no treatment approach should minimize the impact of life challenges on our emotions.

For me, the most useful approach to working with couples is based on the research of Andrew Christiansen (2010). Christiansen researched the most common approaches to working with couples and found commonalities—overlapping insights and techniques—with which to create what Christiansen terms "unifying protocols." These five beautifully integrated protocols address the most common problem areas in relationships. While Christensen uses technical terms to describe the protocols, I have paraphrased them below:

- Develop a clear understanding of each partner's contribution to problems in the relationship, exposing the "circular causality" that reinforces ongoing conflicts.
- Create guidelines and agreements for containing hurtful and defensive behaviors.
- Access and clarify emotionally charged issues and behaviors and encourage vulnerability, empathy, and mutual caring.
- Develop guidelines and strategies for constructive conflict and effective communication.
- Emphasize couple strengths and encourage positive, caring behaviors.

There is an art to working with couples. It is one thing to have an outline of strategies that work, but it is another to know how and when to apply those strategies. God has gifted people with a heart for working with couples. With training, insight, experience, and patience, God's gifted people can revive and restore marriages. I have often known times of discouragement when working with couples. Some seem entrenched in old regressive patterns, lack insight, and are resistant to change. Not all couples want to get better. For this reason, I pray before every session. The Holy Spirt has provided insights, stamina, and, most of all, patience. I could not do this work without God's help.

Christian couples will inquire about the concepts of submission and headship in marriage. I remind them that everything in relationships is about how to experience more of God's love and how to grow in love for one another. God asks us to grow to be more loving toward our spouse and children. Jesus commands all Christians to love one another, and in Ephesians 5:21, Paul requires all Christians to submit to one another. Love is made visible and becomes tangible by how we treat each other. Submission is mutual respect. We are submitting to one another in love, but actually, we are submitting to God so that His love may be more available for us to receive and to give to others.

In my experience as a therapist, it seems that men need more encouraging to step up than women. I wonder why that is? Who is more protective, the male lion or his mate? I do not have to ask that question about mother bears. Certainly, men have a strong protective instinct, but too many of us are willing to put in our 8 or so hours at work and let our wives be in charge of the children and the spiritual climate in the home. I wonder if it wasn't the same in Paul's day. Paul is asking guys not to be so passive, to take the lead in resourcing their families, not just by providing materially but, more importantly by being a model of love, assertive in leading the family's spiritual well-being. Headship is not about control. It is about leading in role-modeling Christ's love.

Questions for Review, Reflection, and Discussion

1. How would you describe God's plan for marriage?
2. Describe limbic resonance, limbic regulation, and limbic revision.
3. What is the relationship between commitment and growth?
4. What is the value of Christianson's unifying protocols?
5. What is meant by "two kinds of death"?

CHAPTER 12

The Psychology of Community and Connection

> "Not giving up our meeting together, as some are in the habit of doing, but encouraging one another—and all the more as you see the Day approaching."
>
> —Hebrews 10:25

Chapter Preview and Learning Objectives

The current Surgeon General of the United States, Vivek Murthy, states in his 2020 book, *Together: The Healing Power of Human Connection in a Sometimes Lonely World*, that human beings are "wired for connection." From studies of biology, anthropology, sociology, and Scripture, it is clear that he is right. There are huge physical and psychological benefits of being in community and experiencing connection. Murthy (2020) believes that one of the most pressing health problems in the United States is the "epidemic of loneliness." Historically, the Christian church has not been very helpful. For too many people over too many years, the church was viewed as a social gathering for qualified people only. Psychology and Scripture agree that human beings need each other. A community of faith *can* be a place of acceptance and healing and provide an invaluable sense of connection and belonging.

Learning Objectives

Students will do the following in this chapter:

- Explore the concept of "wired for connection."
- Understand the physical and psychological cost of isolation.
- Appreciate the many biological, psychological, and spiritual benefits of belonging to a community of faith.
- Consider how the Christian church can and should be more inclusive.

The Value of Community

People are healthier when they are part of a community. In 2021 I published a book entitled *Growing Groups: A Journey of Healing, Growth, and Renewal.* In that book I described Malcolm Gladwell's writing about the Miracle of Roseto:

> In his 2008 book *Outliers*, Malcom Gladwell wrote about the Mystery of Roseto, Pennsylvania. The mystery was why, between 1954 and 1961, Roseto had nearly no heart attacks among the otherwise high-risk group of men 55 to 65. In 1961, Dr. Stewart Wolf, the head of medicine at the University of Oklahoma, studied what has now become known as the "Roseto Effect." The doctor wondered why deaths from heart disease were so low. The men of this Italian American community ate poorly, drank wine in excess, smoked, and worked in dangerous conditions in a slate mine, just like they did in Italy. So, what was the reason? The reason, Dr. Wolf wrote in a 1963 paper on the Roseto effect, was community. Just like they did in Italy, the newly arrived Italian immigrants, mainly from the same village in Roseto, brought with them their extended families and their culture of connection. (Buckley, 2021, p. 156)

Connection and community, I am convinced, play a vital role in mental and physical well-being. It turns out that the "mystery" of Roseto is not a mystery. This Italian American community shared the common values and faith of the traditional Italian communities that gave them birth. This included a close-knit social structure, a structure with little competition for status, a willingness to help each other in times of need, and a value on people not based on acquisitions or accomplishments but because they *belonged*. In this illustration we see that the advice given in Scripture regarding not neglecting community turns out to have more than a just a spiritual application.

The best antidote for the stresses of normal living, the stresses that can kill you, such as financial worries, the drive to win approval, and the competition to get ahead, is knowing that you are not alone. In communities of faith, other people are there to help when you need them. Love is good for your health, not just for your spiritual wellbeing but for every aspect of your being. When a person feels valued, supported, and connected (the fruit of a close community), it is more likely that that person will live longer and enjoy a better quality of life.

Among the most successful therapeutic groups in the past 86 years is Alcoholics Anonymous. In my view, AA qualifies for the definition of a "community of faith"—not in the sense in which we typically think of a community of faith, but in some very real and powerful ways. AA works to help members draw on inner spiritual resources and the support of other group members for their healing and sobriety. AA can also function as a therapy group in that the principal task of the group is to take ownership for injuries received and inflicted. The searching and fearless moral inventory required of Step 4 (admitting wrongs), the willingness to correct defects of character in Steps 5 and 6, and the requesting of forgiveness and making amends in Step 9 are the foundational steps in any therapeutic process.

I mention AA because the central task, encouraged in meetings, is honest and vulnerable communication and a willingness to receive and offer forgiveness. I could wish that every Christian church evidenced similar qualities. I think that participants in AA would agree that in many ways AA is more church than church. They would say that the qualities of genuine connection and caring that they experience in meetings is what keeps them alive. I asked an AA member recently if members are allowed to socialize with one another. "Yes," he replied, "and it's much safer to socialize with other sober friends."

What works in AA, or any healthy church, is the willingness to be transparent, vulnerable, and rigorously honest. In this respect, AA may have an advantage. The 12 steps require members to honor and seek the qualities of character prescribed in the steps. Too much hiding happens in the Christian church where, frequently, the prime ethic is to look good.

I sometimes think of an AA meeting as similar to a Catholic Mass. Celebrating the Mass is reexperiencing the brokenness of Christ's body and the pouring out of His blood. Taken in the right spirit, one is invited to vicariously participate in Christ's suffering. So it is in an AA meeting. From one meeting to the next, members listen to painful confessions of bad choices. In so doing, they remember the suffering they experienced and inflicted upon others. The power of the Mass comes from the success of an open-hearted participation in suffering. The power of an AA meeting, enabling members to remain sober, comes from an open-hearted and vulnerable admission of being powerless over alcohol and the willingness to seek help from one's higher power.

The elephant in the room of an AA meeting, however, is there is no cross in the room. One can understand that, given that so many people have been injured by the church. AA is effective in creating sobriety and transforming lives—after all, it was a Christian group that began AA—and the concept of a "higher power" is certainly valuable; but the quality of connection that is possible with the person of Jesus Christ is the highest and, potentially, the most meaningful and empowering power.

The Costs of Isolation

In *Together* (2020), Dr. Murthy cites the costs of isolation:

> When you're chronically lonely—as a child or an adult—it seeps deeply into your state of mind. It colors how you think about nearly everything, especially your own character. You imagine that you're a misfit. You worry that you'll feel lonely even when you're with

> people. And most destructive of all, you question your self-worth, thinking that there might be something truly wrong with you that's causing this pain. (p. 27)

Murthy explains that at a basic biological level, being isolated from others (our protective group) may trigger an instinctive hypervigilance. Over time, episodes of hypervigilance may damage our physiology in addition to our psychology:

> Central to this stress response is a surge in hormones known as catecholamines, such as epinephrine. These course through the body, causing the pupils and airways to dilate and increasing heart rate and flood flow to the muscles, heart, and brain. The hypothalamic-pituitary-adrenal (HPA) axis is also activated. Starting from hypothalamus in the brain, signals cascade to the pituitary gland, then the adrenal glands, triggering the release of mineralocorticoids and cortisol which in turn raise our blood pressure and increase blood sugar levels so we have energy readily available. In this sense, our bodies read isolation, and often even the threat of isolation as an emergency. (p. 38)

Over time, the rollercoaster of emotions and corresponding stress hormones takes its toll on us physically. Physical illnesses can sometimes be traced to loneliness and isolation. Murthy quotes a study by Dr. Julianne Holt-Lunstad et al. that found that people with strong social relationships are 50% less likely to die prematurely than people with weak social relationships. (Holt-Lunstad et al., 2010; Murthy, 2020). Loneliness can kill. "In 2018, the US Centers for Disease Control and Prevention reported that 54 percent of those who have died by suicide have no diagnosis of mental illness" (Murthy, 2020, p. 125). When you watch the YouTube video "I Jumped Off the Golden Gate Bridge," you listen to the speaker, Kevin Hines, talk about his soul-killing loneliness (BuzzFeedVideo, 2015). Before deciding to jump, someone approached him smiling. For an instant, it seemed that someone cared. When that person simply asked Hines to take their photo, he became convinced that no one truly cared. Moments later he jumped. By God's grace, a Coast Guard vessel was nearby and rescued Hines from the icy water. Hines now does inspirational talks on suicide prevention. People need people who care.

Life Groups

Many churches are addressing the frequent lack of genuine community in their churches by creating "life groups." A *life group*—by whatever name—is a smaller gathering of church members, often in homes, where it is easier to form the close relationships necessary to develop trust and openness. There is frequently an understanding between life-group members not to gossip. I do not recall hearing that stated explicitly, but confidentially is crucial for trust, and trust is crucial for vulnerability, openness, and honesty. So perhaps life-group leaders ought to make keeping confidences explicit and remind members, from time to time, not to talk about the group outside of group.

Why have I frequently used the terms "vulnerability," "openness," "and honesty"? Because they are the essentials for authentic community. Those qualities are much more than beneficial social conventions; they are the requisite qualities for growth and healing.

Everyone understands the relationship between tolerating pain in the process of developing physical skills and strength. The same is true for emotional and spiritual strength. Learning to tolerate uncomfortable emotions builds emotional strength. A great benefit of being in a small group is the opportunity to build emotional and spiritual strength.

Being vulnerable is a wiliness to tolerate uncomfortable emotions: the very process needed to build emotional strength and ultimately spiritual strength. When a person pushes themselves through the vulnerability barrier and is willing to suffer discomfort and pain, that suffering creates a greater capacity for compassion (Latin for "suffering with"). I stated above that I do not know how I would be able to do the work of being with a terribly injured person without God's help. He gives me the necessary tolerance and compassion for being able to sit with someone who is suffering.

I sometimes have to ask a client to tell me what happened to them. I know very well that if a person wants to heal from past injuries, they will have to recall the painful incident(s) to memory. I remind myself of the many times I have had a scrape washed in urgent care or a bad cut stitched. I would rather the nurse or doctor simply bandage the wound. I know it does not work that way. I know it is going to hurt, but I also know that psychological wounds do not heal unless they are opened up and cleansed of painful emotions. The therapeutic process of neural integration is the cleansing remedy.

God created both the brain's ability to heal and the therapeutic support of a healing community. A successful life group is one in which members have practiced being vulnerable and have the capacity to "suffer with" people in pain. A life group can be a healing ER experience for a wounded person.

People in a life group and, ideally, in the larger community of faith can also be amazingly supportive and helpful. It is very encouraging to see how Christian brothers and sisters are able to reach out to each other and the surrounding community. Much of what the media presents can be negative, but often, we see food drives, homes being repaired, money made available, the homeless cared for, and a host of church outreach programs that bring the energy of the gospel to people in need. It is the connection among people of faith, however, that may be the most valuable asset in a church body. The feeling of being a part of a community, the support members give to one another, and the felt sense of belonging all have significant psychological benefits.

The Corrective Emotional Experience

I have talked with many female clients over the years who have reported to me that they did not trust other women. That has always puzzled me. I have not seen any differences between the reliability of men versus women. But then again, I am a man. My wife has told me that, as a man, I would not notice the subtle competition among women. She is right; I do not. I once had six female clients, all in midlife, all reporting symptoms of depression. They were alike in many ways: facing empty nests and unremarkable marriages and feeling unsure of how to face the future and find a sense of purpose and meaning. They shared one other thing in common. They did not trust other women.

I mentioned this to my wife, and she suggested that I invite them all into a women's support group. "I'm a man," I replied. "I've noticed," she said. "Take a risk." So I did, and it worked. Fortunately, the women had no difficulty accepting me as a group facilitator, and after a few sessions of getting acquainted, they connected in a way that was surprising and amazing. They told stories and found common challenges, they laughed and cried together, and they forged a healing bond. They learned to trust each other.

That is the "corrective emotional experience." It happens when you expect to experience the same things you have experienced so often in the past, but it is different this time. We write life scripts from what we know, what is familiar, what we have experienced. The brain loves the stability of familiarity. Yes, brains do crave novelty at times. But so much of the brain's job description is to hold on to what is familiar. The brain likes stability and consistency so that it is easier to understand, control, and predict—what the brain craves in order to safeguard sanity. But the brain can get stuck in the past, holding on to the comfort of the familiar at the expense of change and growth.

The women in the women's group had mainly negative experiences with other women, experiences that left them feeling vulnerable and threatened. It may simply have been the emotional memory of those experiences that caused them to feel guarded around other women. The group helped them to heal. They were very nervous to begin with, anticipating the emergence of similar uncomfortable emotions. To their surprise, the emotions did emerge, but with a different outcome. The other women in the group were very understanding and sympathetic. They did not judge. They did not abandon. Over time they even learned to trust each other.

I was a witness to this wonderful transformation in my clients. My wife was right. Put people together who have been wounded in similar ways and are hoping to heal, and by the grace of God, healing can happen. Once again, it was their willingness to be vulnerable with one another, their willingness to come alongside and to "suffer with," that made the difference. The support of others facing similar challenges, whether loss, betrayal, chronic pain, distrust, or depression, can be faced more courageously with the help of a loving community.

In many cases, a community committed to caring about each other can be even more effective than therapy. A significant benefit of being in a community is the opportunity to reexperience your family of origin. There will be group members who trigger emotional memories of your obnoxious uncle, your invasive mother, or your emotionally distant father. How will you deal with the unsettling internal turmoil of wanting to shut down, get angry, or quit the group? Below are some thoughts.

The Parent, Adult, Child Model

In 1961 Eric Berne wrote *Transactional Analysis in Psychotherapy*. In it, Berne introduced his parent, adult, child (PAC) model. In psychology, the idea of one's inner child probably originated with Berne. In the Christian faith, it originated with Jesus. The model is simple and very useful. Berne wrote that everyone has an inner parent, adult, and child. These "ego states" correspond to our internal message structure. We can *hear* from our inner "parent" advising us or scolding us. We can also inflict our inner parent onto someone else, advising or scolding them. The internal messages from our inner child typically involve wants and needs. It is up to our inner adult (the executive in the personality) to arbitrate between the "shoulds" of our parent and the "wants and needs" of our inner child.

A significant benefit of understanding Berne's (1961) model is its application in group work. In no other context are we as susceptible to reexperiencing our family of origin. For example, someone in the group will trigger a memory of an invasive mother, abandoning father, or irresponsible sibling. When we find ourselves being triggered, we can practice breathing and suspending our need to fix, heal, convert, or control—all of defensive strategies people use to avoid the discomfort of triggered emotions. Instead, we can invite the Holy Spirit to direct us to a loving response. We may decide to be curious about what emotions were triggered within. We may decide to simply accept the offensive behavior or remark of a group member. Or we may decide to wisely, lovingly confront the person. Whatever the choice, hopefully it will be a wise choice made in love.

The choice to make a spirit-filled response rather than a knee-jerk reaction is what makes someone an adult instead of a child. When I teach the PAC model, I frequently illustrate a time I went into a shop for coffee. My inner parent warned me that it might be a bad idea. Sure enough, waiting for my coffee, my inner child spotted the cookies and cakes. My inner parent and child began to argue. I tried not to make a scene. Fortunately, my inner adult finally showed up and negotiated a trade-off. The child got two donut holes and was satisfied. Life offers us many opportunities to negotiate trade-offs. Many if not most of those trade-offs occur within. Ideally, one's inner adult, the executive in the personality, will be wise and mature enough to make good decisions.

Unfortunately, one of the most common problems in therapy is a lazy or absentee inner adult. Another name for this absentee adult is "immaturity." A mature adult maintains a balance between the inner parent, adult, and child. The parent does not always run the show. If that were the case, life would only be work and responsibilities. The kid should not run the show: Nothing would be accomplished. A mature person has a healthy adult, with executive power to maintain a balance between energy out and energy in. One can easily spot an immature person when they always need to be the center of attention and get their way and throw a tantrum when they do not win.

You can see from these examples the corrective emotional experience at work. That dynamic can work in both directions. When a group member is intentionally or habitually offensive, expecting a reaction, and does not get one, they may see the behavior in a clearer light. Proverbs 25:21–22 uses the concept of "heaping burning coals." I take that to signify the discomfort someone (hopefully) feels when they have behaved badly and no one reacts. The opportunity to practice "turning the other cheek" and not reacting to an offender can be a corrective learning experience for all of us.

For those who want to read more on this topic, in addition to Eric Berne's *Transactional Analysis in Psychotherapy*, read Berne's *Games People Play* (1967). I also recommend reading *Born To Win* (1972) by Muriel James and Dorothy Jongeward. Muriel James provides a great illustration of the use of TA in *Born to Love: Transactional Analysis in the Church* (1973). James also wrote *Transactional Analysis for Moms and Dads* (1974). I also like *T.A. for Teens and Other Important People* by Alvyn Freed and Regina Faul-Jensen (1976). Transactional analysis may have been considered pop psychology at one time, but it is having a resurgence in clinical use.

Mean People

Most of the things that hurt us, that feel like slaps in the face, come from how people treat us. People can be nasty. Sometimes the nastiness is not intentional, but simply thoughtless. But when someone says something that is intentionally mean or nasty to your face or is gossiping behind your back, what do you feel like doing? I have not taken a poll. It would be interesting to find out. Possibly, half the people I poll might say, "I would ignore them" or "I would write them off and avoid them." Perhaps the other half would say, "I would confront them. Maybe I would take someone with me as Scripture suggests. But I certainly wouldn't just let it go!"

So there you have the two most common fight or flight defenses that I discussed earlier. When you looked over the list of fight or flight defenses, on which list did you check the greater number of defensive responses? The old saying about "sticks and stones" is pretty stupid. Words do hurt, and they hurt a great deal. What do you do when someone hurts you? You can strike back or run away. You can hurt them or hide from them. These are the options that most people practice, but in the words of Paul, "I will show you a more excellent way" (1 Corinthians 12:31).

Turning the Other Cheek

When it comes to relationships, whether marriage, family, or friends, what Jesus told us to do, as recorded in both Luke's and Matthew's gospel, is the most important advice in the Bible: "If someone strikes you on one cheek, offer him the other also" (Luke 6:29; Mathew 5:39). This might be interpreted as an illustration of the strategy of passive or nonviolent resistance. Both Gandhi and Martin Luther King Jr. advocated nonviolent resistance. And it was a very successful strategy in the service of obtaining their objectives. A Bible scholar might argue that this is the correct interpretation of what Jesus directed us to do when someone attacks us. I have no argument with that interpretation.

However, I would like to offer a different way of thinking about Jesus's words in the context of interpersonal relationships. If someone strikes me or, more likely, says something mean or untrue, I actually have three options. One option is to strike back. I could toss back an insulting reply or blast them in an email. Another option is to ignore the comment and let it go. Depending on what was said or done, I could see myself reacting in both of these ways. However, for me, turning the other cheek does not mean automatically laying down and doing nothing. For me, turning the other cheek is to avoid both of these fight or flight *reactions* in favor of a spirit-led and wise *response*.

I would take some deep breaths, take some time to pray, and take some time to consider the best (most loving and wisest) response. Notice I used the word "time." The difference between an immature reaction and a mature response is to take a few moments or a few weeks to ask God to help out with how best to respond. It does not take long to take a breath and take a moment to think before responding. Recall that the key to being mature is learning to tolerate pain. Turning the other cheek is staying in the discomfort long enough to get a clear sense of direction. For you, and perhaps for someone else, this is the corrective emotional experience that can transform the quality of connection in any relationship, small or large.

Questions for Review, Reflection, and Discussion

1. What is meant by "wired for connection"?
2. What are the costs of being isolated?
3. What are some of the benefits of belonging to a community?
4. What are some of the benefits of belonging to a community of faith in particular?
5. How might the church do a better job of encouraging community?
6. How does participating in a group facilitate a corrective emotional experience?

CHAPTER 13

Temperament, Gifts, and Calling

> "To equip his people for works of service, so that the body of Christ may be built up until we all reach unity in the faith and in the knowledge of the Son of God and become mature, attaining to the whole measure of the fullness of Christ."
>
> —Ephesians 4:12–14

Chapter Preview and Learning Objectives

This chapter confirms that God uses our talents and temperament, adding specific spiritual gifts, to empower you to do His work in the world. To this end, it is important to understand your innate temperament and to be open to finding your unique spiritual gifts and calling. The Myer-Briggs type indicator is a valuable resource in this process, as are the many resources available to help you discover your spiritual gifts.

Learning Objectives

Students will do the following in this chapter:

- Look at the relationship between innate talents, temperament, and spiritual gifts.
- Acquire an appreciation for the Myers-Briggs type indicator for assessing temperament.
- Discover one's own temperament.
- Consider one's spiritual gifts and calling.

How Do Gifts Differ from Talents and Temperaments?

Everyone is created in God's image. This means that all human beings are able to respond to God, and according to our commission in Genesis, we are called to be co-creators with Him. If God has called us to be His children and commissioned us for His work in the world, then all human beings bear His image and are gifted in some way. One of God's gifts is the blueprint for who we are and what He has placed in our heart to do in the world. God has also given us the freedom to choose to know who we are in Him and to follow our calling—or not. We have a choice. If we search for Him, He promises that we will find Him. If we look for it, we will find the path set before us.

Gifts differ from talents in that talents are innate abilities, while gifts are given. Genetic potential is responsible for a person's temperament and talents. In the ideal, we come to understand our innate temperament, and over time, we discover our talents. When God calls us to His work, the Holy Spirt acts upon our temperament, engages our talents, and transform our genetic potential into gifts for His service. For instance, a woman enjoys cooking and entertaining. She prefers small gatherings. God enters her life, equips her with the spiritual motivation for hospitality, and, the next thing we know, she is finding joy in the many ways of creating fellowship within the body. God inspires her innate temperament for His work.

Temperament

Psychology refers to *temperament* as consistent individual differences in behavior. Similarly, Lexico (n.d.-a) states that personality is "the combination of characteristics or qualities that form an individual's distinctive character." So temperament or personality can be understood as characteristics of behavior that are biologically based and relatively predictable of differences in personality.

There are many ways to assess an individual's temperament or personality. Some are sophisticated, well-researched, and empirically rigorous measures of factors that form a good predictor of how an individual may react to situations and behave in various contexts. Among the options available for understanding differences in temperament, my favorite, the one I use most often, is the Myers-Briggs type indicator (MBTI). The MBTI is not a rigorous test for assessing problems in personality and, unlike the MMPI, has no means to assess whether the tester is being candid and consistent. Rather, as a forced-choice instrument, it illuminates differences in preferences. The test is designed to reveal consistencies in preferences that indicate a personality style. I have found that the MBTI is a good predictor of personally styles, and my clients have frequently confirmed its accuracy and enjoyed having a clearer picture of themselves.

The Myers-Briggs type indicator is an easy and useful way to understand how people differ: why they see things differently, behave differently, and sometimes are in conflict with each other. The two most important uses of the MBTI are to facilitate understanding and acceptance. It is used in industry to help groups of people come to a better understanding of the people they work with. I once administered the MBTI to a small business of about 30 employees. I discussed the results of the inventory with each individual and again with all of the employees together over lunch. There were lots of "aha" moments and laughter when the sales team finally understood that engineers are not intentionally rude; they just did not like interruptions or socializing when they were focused on figuring out a problem. And the sales folks are not intentionally annoying; they simply thought that having relationships was important to moving a project forward.

I had my own aha moment in 1977 when I first took the MBTI. By then I knew I did not want to be an engineer like Dad. He was really good at what engineers are good at, and I certainly was not. I was more creative and artistic, like Mom. But I was frustrated that I could not do things or think of things the way Dad could. Dad was patient with me, but at times, I thought he may have been disappointed. However, when I realized that my temperament was very different than my dad's, with different interests and abilities, I was able to accept who I was. As I said, the value of the MBTI is understanding and acceptance.

Isabel Briggs-Myers and her mother Katherine Briggs used the personality concepts developed by Carl Jung to create a method of assessing differences in people's temperaments. The MBTI uses 160 questions to ask whether you tend to be more extraverted or introverted, whether you perceive things more concretely or symbolically, whether you tend to make decisions analytically or if you prefer to use more subjective values, and whether you prefer things to be decided and managed or more flexible and spontaneous. The MBTI has been refined over the years and may be obtained from Consulting Psychologist Press in Palo Alto, California. It is also available online.

After taking the MBTI in 1977, I began using it as a pastor in my marital and premarital counseling. I also used the Taylor-Johnson temperament analysis. They are both excellent instruments for helping couples prepare for marriage and provide understanding of potential conflict areas during marriage. Since then, I have scored hundreds of MBTIs. I have found it to be a very effective way of looking at differences between people and a way to understand the variety and complexity of their relationships. I especially appreciate the MBTI as a way to help people better understand themselves. Looking at results of the MBTI, couples have a better grasp of the ways they express and experience love, manage life, and deal with conflicts. Moreover, better understanding leads to increased acceptance of the differences, the reasons for attraction, and the inevitable irritations. If couples can accept the likelihood that God brought them to each other, it is possible to understand these irritations are essential for individual growth and healing, as I discussed in Chapter 11.

Over years of clinical use, I have noticed some regularly occurring patterns in interpersonal relationships. I have noticed, for example, that it is rare for people with identical temperaments to be attracted to each other. My guess is that that would be boring. Totally opposite temperaments do not seem to be attracted to each other either. That would require too much stretching. These types of relationships exist but they are certainly not the norm. It is more common for couples to share two of the four temperamental continua in common and have two that are different. People seem to be attracted to a balance of similarities and differences. This balance seems to provide couples with the benefits of familiarity sufficient to establish rapport and negotiate values and lifestyles, while also providing challenges for diversity and growth.

Apparently, an ideal relationship is neither too boring nor too challenging. People seem to be instinctively attracted to growth as much (if not more) as to happiness. If people simply wanted to be happy, they would probably look for someone with an identical temperament and, therefore, is easy to live with. But that virtually never happens. If people were too similar, there would be little work involved, little stretching, and little conflict—but also little growth.

So, whether consciously or unconsciously, people tend to be attracted to differences as much as to similarities. Hence, the existence of marriage counselors. As I stated above, I agree with those who warn that the MBTI, because it is self-administered and without any validity measurements, cannot be used to accurately diagnose psychopathology and should not be used for that purpose. Moreover, from my experience, an individual's responses to the 160 questions may vary somewhat depending on when and in what context the test is taken.

A consistent pattern of preferences typically points to consistent qualities of temperament. Temperament is inherited, but aspects of one's temperament and corresponding preferences can sometimes change over time. Preferences may also change from one context to another. For example, one may be more extroverted at home but less so in a group of people. Or, alternatively, someone can be quiet at home but very extroverted among friends. If one is "midline" between alternative preferences, it is possible to drift from one preference to another, again depending on the context. However, an extreme extrovert is unlikely to wake up one day and test as an introvert. Temperament preferences are flexible but not likely to vary radically over one's lifetime. In brief, the MBTI measures four continua of temperament: extroversion versus introversion, sensation versus intuition, thinking versus feeling, and judging versus perception. One may be extreme or mild on these continua, and people who are midline in some areas may drift slightly from one side to the other.

Figure 13.1 is a typical MBTI printout. This person scores mildly extraverted, highly sensing, moderately thinking, and mild to moderate judging. His type would be ESTJ. David Keirsey would describe his temperament as a "supervisor." If he were an ISTJ, Keirsey would call him an "inspector." While there are 16 possible types, there are many ranges within each type.

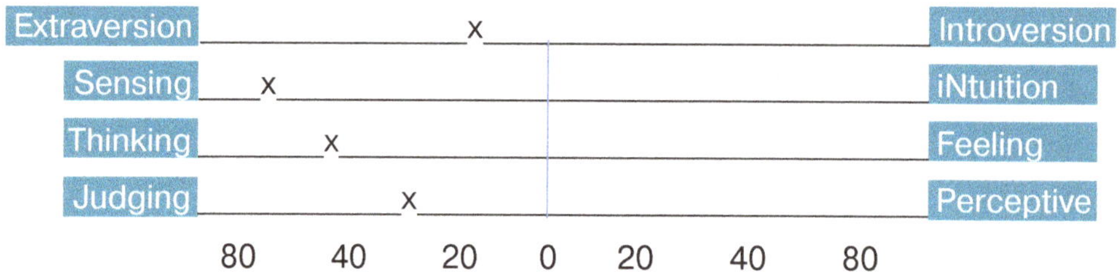

FIGURE 13.1 *Basic MBTI Printout*

MBTI Explained

Extroversion is an appetite for extensity: variety, involvement, and socializing. The further out one tests on that continuum, the greater the appetite. Introversion is an appetite for intensity: thoroughness, exactness, and intimacy. The sensing function is a preference for concrete sense data: What it is, what it does, and how it is made. Intuition is a preference for abstract or symbolic knowledge: what it means, what is behind it, and what is possible. The thinking function is more objective and analytical. The feeling function is more subjective and value driven. The "judging function" was Jung's (1971) term for a preference for making judgments (decisions), whether from thinking or feeling. The "perceptive function" is Jung's term for a preference to remain open to new information either from sensing or intuition. A person scoring high on the judging function prefers a "decided" approach to life, scheduled and organized. A person scoring high on perception prefers to keep things open and flexible. John Beebe a Jungian scholar and former president of the San Francisco Jung Institute, stated in a 2015 YouTube interview, "A Jungian Analyst Talks about Psychological Types"

> Jung said that we need a function to tell us what is, and that is sensation. We need a function to give it a name, and that's thinking. We need a function to tell us what it is worth, and that's feeling, and we need a function to tell us what its possibilities are, where it is headed, and that's intuition. He made it sound very simple.

Few people score in the extreme. Most score on a percentage—more one side than the other. Understanding someone's basic temperament and preferences is useful in being more tolerant, understanding, and accepting of differences.

Nonetheless, I resist thinking or talking about people in absolutes. I prefer to view people as complex and flexible and capable of cultivating temperamental qualities that may not be automatic. When Carl Jung wrote *Psychological Types* in 1921, he was addressing a question in his mind: How can two of his respected colleagues observe similar data and arrive at different conclusions? Jung (1921) determined that there was a "differentiation in their consciousness," which caused them to observe and respond to stimuli differently because of innate differences in their temperament. Jung's intention was to provide a vocabulary with which to understand and discuss those differences. It was clear to Jung that one's level of maturity, socialization, and social context would interact with and, at times, modify aspects of a person's temperament. In other words, in different contexts, extroverts might look more like introverts and introverts could look like extroverts. It is also important to know that Jung's principal concern was not putting labels on people but rather in understanding the different ways people process information and make decisions. Viewing the MBTI report form, for example, makes it clear that aspects of temperament lay on a continuum from very introverted, to mildly introverted, to extroverted, and so forth. So, as I mentioned above, all aspects of our temperaments exist in percentages.

When describing temperament, it is important to use terms like "sometimes," "usually," and "most often." It is also important not to imagine that a person who acts in a particular way this time will always act the same way next time or in a different context. I have learned that my impressions about someone's temperament may only be valid in a classroom, a counseling setting, or a social context. That person may act very differently in another setting. It bothers me at times to hear people using the term "feeling type" or "thinking type," as if that term describes everything one needs to know about that person. Admittedly, it is a very handy and sometimes useful way to think about differences in people. But it also tends to put people in boxes and limits their complexity and versatility. I much prefer the wordier but more accurate description: "He has a dominate thinking function," or "She tends to be more introverted around strangers." I doubt that my preference will ever become very popular. People tend to prefer simple and consistent explanations of their world. But it is good to be reminded that human nature can be quite flexible and dynamic.

We are not limited to those qualities that are simply automatic according to our type. We can access competencies from both sides of our temperament continuum. We can learn how to open up in some situations and clam up in others. We can learn when to plan things out and when to be flexible, when to analyze and when to trust our gut. Are you stuck with your personality type? That is not actually the right question. The Myers-Briggs type indicator is designed to evaluate your preferences. Your consistent preferences become a good predictor of how you will behave in many contexts of your life. Understanding and accepting your inherited temperament is important for self-awareness and self-acceptance. It is also important to enable you to focus more on what you enjoy and what you are good at. A better question to ask is, "How can I be at home in my familiar preferences and still cultivate other temperament strengths as well?"

Below are some ideas about how to access other dimensions of your personality. The ideal for your growth is to become more flexible with a variety of temperament strengths.

Developing Temperament Strengths

- Understand that personality traits can be fluid, depending on the situation, and that you may behave differently depending on the context.
- Recognize where you already are competent in areas that are different from your accustomed personality traits.
- Find references (e.g., texts, websites, articles, etc.) that provide a thorough list of contrasting characteristics from each of the four MBTI temperament continuums.
- Rank your typical personality traits using the terms "always," "frequently," "occasionally," "seldom," or "never." Notice that you rarely respond with always or never.
- Ranking your personality traits, as above, you may find yourself thinking that it depends. Ask yourself what conditions affect which trait.
- After deciding which traits are automatic for you, determine which are complimentary traits—that is, traits that are not automatic but may be useful to access in certain situations.
- PRACTICE. Here are two examples: David Keirsey has labeled the thinking function utilitarian and the feeling function cooperative. When communicating, if you

have a dominant feeling function, practice getting to the point more quickly. If you have a dominate thinking function, be a little more patient. If you have a dominant judging function, try to enjoy a weekend without any plans. If you are more perceptive, enjoy completing a task that you have been putting off.

- Ask friends and family members about your personality traits. You may be surprised that they see more of your personality style than you see (or want to see).
- Accept that your brain is surprisingly flexible and adaptable and that, with practice, you can acquire additional competencies that are valuable to you.

Spiritual Gifts

If you are a Christian, you have a spiritual gift. A spiritual gift is given by the Holy Spirt for specific tasks in the church. The gifts recorded in Romans 12:3–9 relate to gifts that God gives us to motivate us for a specific type of service. I think of these gifts on a continuum from truth to grace. The apostle John wrote that "the Word became flesh and dwelt among us. ... full of grace and truth" (John 1:14). Jesus embodies all of the spiritual gifts. He can be fiercely truthful and completely gracious—and He is the only one. The rest of us tend to find ourselves on one side of the continuum or the other. Clearly, this is God's plan. We, the body of Christ, need each other to fulfill Christ's mission. In Romans 12:6, Paul writes:

> We have different gifts, according to the grace given to each of us. If your gift is prophesying, then prophesy in accordance with your faith; if it is serving, then serve; if it is teaching, then teach; if it is to encourage, then give encouragement; if it is giving, then give generously; if it is to lead, do it diligently; if it is to show mercy, do it cheerfully.

I think that Paul's spiritual gift was probably encouragement. He was always exhorting the churches to find and use their spiritual gifts. In this letter to the Romans, we find the ways in which God gives gifts to motivate Christians to participate in Christ's body. Paul is saying that if you have a particular motivation, use it in ministry. The ministry gifts are listed in Ephesian 4:11 and I Corinthians 12:23. When a person is motivated to serve Christ in some way and does so regularly, that person has a ministry. Through the ongoing operation of a ministry, people experience the manifestation of the spirit. The gifts of manifestation are listed in 1 Corinthians 7–11. Motivation, ministry, and manifestation are the lists of spiritual gifts that enable Christians to extend God's work in the world.

For example, the prophet is motivated to *declare* truth. They are less interested in accommodating the listener than in being forthright, even when the truth may be painful to hear. The teacher wants to *explain* truth, providing a logical rational for why something is the way it is. The encourager tries to make truth *reasonable*, accommodating the listener when possible. I recall that the apostle Paul often sought face-to-face meetings where he could explain the logic of the Gospel. The administrator is skilled at *connecting* gifted people with needed tasks. The server likes to *accomplish tasks* that promote ministry. The server seems to be content to work in the background. The giver is gifted at *resourcing* ministry. They respond quickly and skillfully to locate and supply needs. The gift of mercy is located on the farthest end of the truth-grace continuum. This person is empathetic compassionate, less interested in admonishing than in *restoration*. Clearly, God intends us to value, respect, and accept our many different interests and directions and learn to work together. The apostle Paul reminds us that we are all different parts of the body of Christ and to be successful in God's work requires all members of Christ's body functioning together.

It would not work if the church were only prophetic (although some might wish it were). The church also needs to be gracious and accepting. The church needs to be well organized, but that is the means, not the ends. The church needs to be instructive, serve the needs of the community, and fund mission outreach. But, again, these are means to an end, the end being the fullest expression of the ministry of Christ in the world. We need to accept each other's gifts and areas of interest and work successfully with each other to fulfill Christ's mission.

Temperament and Gifts

What is the connection between an individual's temperament and their spiritual gift? When people receive Jesus into their heart and become followers, their temperament may or may not change, but their tastes and life trajectory certainly will. It seems that often God uses a person's existing temperament and talents and empowers a new vitality and direction. That new direction is to be in Christ's service.

David Keirsey (1998), a Jungian analyst, has thoroughly written and lectured on the 16 different MBTI type configurations and provides a detailed and comprehensive website on the MBTI (https://www.keirsey.com). A person with a dominant introverted, sensing, thinking, and perceptive temperament (ISTP), according to Keirsey, tends to be very good at making and fixing things. He calls this type a "crafter." Keirsey calls a person with dominant extroversion, sensing, feeling, and judging (ESFJ) a "provider." Does God need people who are good at making, fixing, or providing? He may call them into the ministry of service or helps. The INFP temperament is by nature a caring, healing person. The Holy Spirit will likely give this person the gift of mercy to minister compassion to hurting people.

In my days as a pastor, I learned early to have as many different gifts represented on my committees as possible. I learned that lesson (as I do most lessons) the hard way. I once organized a very successful banquet for the graduating seniors at our church. After the 300 people left, and left quite a mess, it dawned on me that I had not delegated anyone to help me clean up. Fortunately, a few folks saw my plight and pitched in. After that, I made sure that I had a server on my committee to remind me about details, an encourager to reassure me, an administrator to help me organize, and a profit to tell me that it would be too expensive. Thank God for gifted people.

Sometimes gifts are given for specific purposes. In 1979, Peter Wagner from Fuller Seminary wrote *Your Spiritual Gifts Can Help Your Church Grow*. Dr. Wagner cites specific gifts that are often overlooked. These are gifts that God gives as needed and when needed. The gift of missionary, the gift of celibacy, and the gift of intercessory prayer, for example, are not listed in Scripture but may, at times, be exactly what is required for specific purposes.

In this book, Dr. Wagner includes insights into helping people discover their gifts. I used the plural for "gifts" because certainly there are times when God needs us to multitask. In my experience, God gifts his people with an extra measure of motivation and energy for a special work. When that motivation and energy provides a consistent source of joy, that may be your gift and your ministry.

Gifts and Calling

In the first section of the chapter, I stated that because everyone is created in the image of God, everyone has the gift of being able to find a direction for their life. Recall that Carl Rogers called this blueprint for your life "the actualizing tendency." Also, recall that Jim Hillman called that actualizing tendency the acorn theory. Maslow believed that it was possible for human beings to reach a confluence of their doing with their being and become self-actualized. Jung called this "individuation." The last of Erikson's eight stages of the life cycle would be to realize a sense of "integrity"—an appreciation for a life well lived. Evidently, psychologists believe that it is possible for people to know who they are and why they are here. Where do you think God is in this?

Where is God in anything? What do you believe? Has human nature evolved? Is the idea of a "calling" an instinctive process, a biological imperative, as Rogers believes or something else? It comes down to what *you* would like to believe. If I were arguing a theological position, I would quote from *A Matter of Days* by Hugh Ross (2015), who confirms that geology and astrophysics shows us that God did his work slowly. This is what the astronomer and professor Owen Gingerich believes in *God's Universe* (2006) and Francis Collins believes in *The Language of God: A Scientist Presents Evidence for Belief* (2007). What do you believe?

For me, the tragic conclusion of spending decades observing human behavior is that many people do not have the courage, the motivation, or the luxury to think about whether or not they have a calling in their lives. This is a tragedy because they are missing out on the gift of a soul that God has given to each of us, a soul that is capable of knowing Him and knowing the value of our own life. When a person *fully* grasps their value, that person will surely find the means to authenticate that value in some sort of direction and function in life—a calling.

God speaks to everyone when He says that "if you search for me you will find me" (Jeremiah 29:13). I would add that when you understand your temperament, evaluate your talents, and become a follower of Christ, God fills you with His spirit and with gifts for His work. The next step is to search for and find your unique calling.

I would like to mention some additional resources for those interested in the relationship between temperament and style of worship:

- McHugh, A. (2017). *Introverts in the church: Finding our place in an extroverted culture.*
- Harbaugh, G. (1990). *God's gifted people: Discovering your personality as a gift.*
- Oswald, R., & Kroeger, O. (1988). *Personality type and religious leadership.*

Also, for a more in-depth treatment of personality types, read:

- Beebe, J. (2016). *Energies and patterns in psychological type: The reservoir of consciousness.*
- Hunziker, M. (2016). *Depth typology: C. G. Jung, Isabel Myers, John Beebe and the guide map to becoming who we are.*
- Keirsey, D. (2006). *Please understand me II: Temperament, character, intelligence.*
- Nardi, D. (2011). *The neuroscience of personality: Brain savvy insights for all types of people.*

Questions for Review, Reflection, and Discussion

1. What is your MBTI temperament?
2. What is/are your spiritual gift(s)?
3. In what ways might you use the MBTI in counseling?
4. In what ways would knowing someone's spiritual gift benefit them?
5. In what ways would knowing someone's spiritual gift benefit you as a therapist?

CHAPTER 14

On the Psychology of Worship

> "Thou shalt worship the Lord thy God and Him only shalt thou serve."
>
> —Luke 4:8

Chapter Preview and Learning Objectives

Worship is an investment in someone or something to return something of value. Everyone worships something. The first directive our Heavenly Father gave us is not to worship anyone or anything but Him. This is for our own good since nothing else works. Nothing will hold up over time as a sufficient source of well-being. We need to be careful not to get caught up in misplaced worship. Most people who seek therapy suffer from one or another form of misplaced worship. Forms of worship vary with different personalities and the personality of the clergy. The church symbols are explored with a view to a greater appreciation of the wealth of experience available in worship.

Learning Objectives

Students will do the following in this chapter:

- Consider in what way worship is an investment.
- Gain an understanding of the psychology of worship.
- Learn the ways misplaced worship is harmful.
- Understand the difference between a sign and a symbol.

On the Nature of Worship

In Professor Reza Aslan's 2017 book, *God: A Human History*, he convincingly states that from the beginning, "Human beings intuitively knew that they are embodied souls. It is a belief so primal and innate, so deep-rooted and widespread, that it must be considered nothing less than the hallmark of the human experience" (p. 6).

This has been true from earliest human history when our ancestors placed objects in graves and carved or painted sacred images on the walls of caves. Human beings worship. *Worship* (from the old English "to ascribe worth") is an investment in someone or something to return a sense of security and significance. So people worship their ancestors, their spouse, their children, their stock portfolio, their new car, their addictions, and their golf handicap, spending hours and hours on the driving range. Sometimes people worship themselves. That was Lucifer's downfall: misplaced worship.

I could easily say that the majority of clients I have seen over the years suffered the consequences of misplaced worship. Giving too much power to something or someone other than God never works. Religion might be understood as an effort to control your investment. It is not a good idea to worship your spouse or your kids. You end up controlling them or being controlled by them. It is not a good idea to put your faith in the stock market or, worse, your addiction. You will give away time and money to something that does not bring happiness. Being a religious person does not work either. Religion can be an end in itself. The idea is that "if I get it right, I'll be okay." But as humans, we never get it completely right. The reason that God tells us not to worship anything or anyone other than Him is because that is the only form of worship that works. It makes sense that God made that commandment Number 1 on His list of 10. Nothing else will do the job of helping us to become more joyful and loving.

In its broadest sense, worship is an investment—an investment in something or someone that can return a sense of stability and significance. Almost anything will do as an investment. When I think of the term "investment," I usually think of the process of putting money into an account with the hope of an increase. But that is a very limited way of thinking. A farmer planting a seed is making an investment. Crossing a room to greet someone you do not know is an investment. Spending time practicing the piano or taking a college class is an investment. So is maintaining a beautiful garden or home. If you go to a place of worship on a regular basis, you are making an investment.

What do you hope to gain by your investment? You can ask the same question by asking, "What does my brain want?" I stated in a previous chapter that your brain wants three things: sanity, stability, and significance. The brain achieves sanity with the ability to predict a range of outcomes. There is enough predictability in the universe to mediate an adequate amount of sanity. The brain tends to hold on to what has become familiar in order to maintain sanity. So God protects our sanity by limiting the number of miracles we might want.

The brain wants stability and consistency. You do not have to have roast turkey at Thanksgiving, unless that is something you have always had. I have friends from an Italian background who enjoy lasagna for Christmas dinner. I am pretty sure they would not order Chinese takeout. They want the stability of maintaining their traditions. I was once given a bag of tamales as a Christmas present. The family that offered them to me said that the real enjoyment was their annual family get-together to make them. The brain wants stability: what is familiar, what is traditional, and what brings people together.

The brain wants significance. "Life is difficult" is the opening sentence in *The Road Less Traveled* (Peck, 1978), the bestselling textbook on the art of living life. A major life challenge is trying to make sense of life itself. Because human beings are both biological and spiritual, our quest for significance takes on a two-fold challenge. Biologically, we need to feel significant (valued) so that we can survive. Our most primitive need is to belong to the herd so that we do not get eaten. Being rejected by people is not just painful; at a biological level, it is terrifying. On a spiritual level, we need to feel that our life matters. God has created us with an awareness that our life has value. Attending a place of worship on a regular basis meets all three needs. Our brain loves the familiar services of worship. We are greeted by other church members and feel valued, and maybe even significant. Regular worship is a valuable resource for spirit, soul, and body—an essential investment in emotional well-being.

How is worship an investment? The answer is that it meets important needs, which is why God made worshiping Him the very first commandment: "I am the Lord thy God ... Thou shalt have no other gods before me" (Exodus 20:2–3). God is not jealous; he is omniscient. He knows that no other object or person will work as a focus of worship. It is tempting to make someone or something too important. Where I live, people wear LA Dodger hats or shirts. In some cases, they have amassed scores of Dodger memorabilia. So when their team is in a slump, so are they. Speaking of slumps, do not worship the stock market. Make wise investments, but do not make it your god. Otherwise, you will ride the roller coaster right along with the market.

If worship is an investment, then religion could be understood as an effort to control the object of your investment. People spend a great deal of time, thought, and effort focusing on the objects of their worship. Golfers are religious about showing up at the driving range. Gamers are religious about achieving higher levels. Shoppers can be religious about finding bargains. We need to be careful about the focus of our investments. God knows what is in your heart. He can tell the difference between showing up at church to safeguard your investment versus showing up with a heart full of gratitude for His unfailing goodness.

You have to be especially vigilant about making your spouse or your children too important. It is very tempting. I love my wife, but if I make her too responsible for my happiness, I will end up attempting to control her, making sure that I get a return on my investment. I confess that I am a bit codependent, which is to say, I am very alert to her moods and too solicitous about doing things that make her happy. There isn't anything wrong with wanting to make your spouse happy. But there is something wrong with *needing* to make them happy. That is misplaced worship. The same is true with your children. Of course, you want to make them happy. Good luck with that. If you are overly invested in your children's happiness (or safety), you will end up being overcontrolling. You will achieve the opposite of what you hope for. And do not overly invest your personal significance in how your children turn out or even whether or not they stick around. It is wonderful when they do, but it is their choice. If you hold on too tight and invest too much of your well-being in whether their home for every single holiday, that is misplaced worship. I realize this may be difficult to hear, but we need to be careful that our happiness and well-being are firmly established in our relationship with God. If not, we have broken the very first of His commandments.

Misplaced Worship

Nowhere, that I know of, in the literature of psychology is a discussion of the problem of misplaced worship. That surprises me because it appears that the idea of worship has been a part of the human story from the beginning. Before recorded history, archeologists digging around in the strata of prehistory have found evidence of human beings worshiping something or someone. Cave paintings, standing stones, and burial objects attest to a primitive sense that there is a world beyond this one.

Recall that term "worship" is used to ascribe value. As I have said, worship is a psychological investment in something or someone to return a sense of value or significance. People will worship something, anything: their spouse, their children, their marriage, their stock portfolio, their home, their job, their new luxury car, their golf handicap. Whatever someone spends a great deal of time taking care of, attending to, or being fearful about losing is likely an object of worship—an investment in something that returns a sense of sanity, stability, or significance.

Speaking of golf, I had a client whose husband retired early and spent nearly every day playing golf and drinking with his buddies. That is what I would call a religion, but not a very good one. It is not uncommon to find folks spending all of their free time in the garage, the workshop, the garden, or keeping up the house. There is nothing wrong with any of these hobbies when they do not become a religion. I once had a subscription to *Los Angeles Magazine*. Sometimes the articles were interesting, but mostly, I enjoyed the restaurant reviews. I also found many opportunities for misplaced worship: beautiful estates, fashions, cars, ads for money managers, and high-end vacations. There was even a section for parents. How nice. These were ads for boarding schools.

Why is God's first commandment so important? Because nothing else is worth worshiping. Nothing else is worth investing large sums of time, energy, or thought. Obviously, all of God's commandments are for our benefit. You would think that it would be obvious that nothing other than what is ultimately valuable is worth worshiping. Marriages end. Kids leave home. Pets pass away. Stocks go up and down. Nothing in life is a safe investment, only God. Why, I wonder, does that seem like such a hard concept to grasp? Maybe it is not a hard concept; maybe it is only hard to put into practice. It may seem easier to invest in something more tangible, something that we could control. This way we could religiously check to make sure our investment was paying off.

I could easily say that the majority of problems I deal with in therapy have to do with the consequences of misplaced worship. For example, people with addictions have found substitutes for the need to escape, to anesthetize, or for the euphoria of intoxication. I actually believe that people need intoxication—need to find ways to be lifted out of their humdrum routine—to experience transcendence. They need to find sources of intoxication that are healthy and life enhancing. Listening to a beautiful piece of music, enjoying nature, helping others, belonging to a group of loving people, finding a sport or pastime that you really enjoy, savoring a sunset with a loved one, or just sitting quietly by yourself, breathing in God's love—all of these can be genuine and life-enhancing forms of intoxication. Alcohol and drugs are short-lived, inadequate, and poisonous substitutes for the authentic intoxication that can happen when you are worshiping and spending time with God. I do not think that humans have a choice in needing to experience some sort of intoxication. But we have many choices in finding healthy ones.

More frequently than the time I have spent treating people addicted to substances were the many hundreds of hours I have spent treating people for the misplaced worship of their spouse, children, or themselves. The Righteous Brothers (1966) sang, "You're my life and my heart's inspiration, without you, Baby, what good am I." That is misplaced worship. Your value should not be invested in whether or not someone you love is having a good day or is able to be consistent in love. People will let you down. If you need them too much, you are not loving them; you are using them. The same is true for your kids. They will have bad days. Their bad day does not make you a bad parent.

I have treated adults who grew up with an anxious or addicted parent. I cannot imagine what it must be like to be exposed to someone disabled by anxiety or substances. Breathing in that atmosphere day in and day out can be toxic. But just as bad is the tendency for kids to invest their well-being in taking care of their parent(s). The psychologist Alice Miller wrote about this in *The Drama of the Gifted Child* in 1979. Self-abandoning in the service of caretaking a parent is a sure road to depression.

People often ask about why psychotherapists seem so interested in childhood experiences. In her TED Talk, *The Power of Vulnerability*, Brené Brown (2014) got a laugh from the audience when she talked about her first time seeing a therapist and said, "None of this childhood &%$!" It is very uncomfortable for many people to talk about their childhood, but young brains soak up a great deal of what is around them, good and bad. And brains tend to hold on to what has been soaked up. So it is good to understand the origin of some of our not-so-healthy thoughts and emotions. Understanding makes it easier to accept the challenge of change and gives therapists some idea of the direction to take. The best direction for us to take was given to us by the apostle Paul in Romans 12:2: "Do not conform to the pattern of this world but be transformed by the renewing of your mind." How can that happen?

A Life Devoted to Worship

Change usually requires effort. We work at what we value. Loving God and worshiping Him is the best of all possible investments. And the good news is that a life devoted to worshiping God is the best of all possible ways to live life. But do not put the cart before the horse. The best way to read Paul's advice above is as an indicative, not as an imperative. Yes, Paul probably meant his words as imperative (i.e., "This is what you should do"). Paul is asking us to refocus our attention from the world around us to our relationship with God. That is great advice, but it is very hard to do. If you were to ask me how to go about rewiring your brain, how to unlearn the habits of a lifetime (e.g., the need for external validation, the security of having enough money, the tendency to compare and compete, and the lifelong habit of worrying), my response might be, "Good luck with that." Then I might remind you of what Jesus said in a lesson on a mountainside: "Seek ye first the kingdom of God, and his righteousness; and all these things shall be added unto you" (Mathew 6:33). Those words are the "horse" I was referring to. The "cart" is the slow transformation of our mind that is possible in our daily efforts to put God first in our thoughts, our appetites, and our choices.

When we seek first the kingdom of God, the things that will be added to us are the manifold blessings of living with a ready source of good intoxication: the peace, joy, and golden moments of transcendence when we sense God's nearness. With these good things added to us, it is easier (but not easy) to let go of the brain's habits of comparing, competing, storing up, playing safe, and worrying about tomorrow.

"A life devoted to worship" may sound like a sermon title or a tract from an ancient and wise church father. But psychologically, living that life just makes good sense. Jesus told us that His yoke is easy and His burden is light. I would like to think that it is not as hard as it sounds to put God first in everything we do. But as I said, anything of value typically requires effort. Renewing our minds to live in line with Christ's teaching will require daily effort, but it is the best possible way to live.

Worship—Opening to the Heart of God

That daily effort of worshiping rightly requires learning to become vulnerable. The word *vulnerable* means a willingness to suffer. It can also mean unguarded. You could say that a company of soldiers found themselves in a vulnerable, unguarded position. The vulnerability I am describing is a choice, a choice to be open hearted. You can make that choice every day. Once you have set your mind to it, it is surprising how easy it is to become practiced at opening your heart, to living your life devoted to worship.

I love the little book the *Practice of the Presence of God*, a book of teaching and letters from the 17th-century Carmelite friar Brother Laurence, compiled by Father Joseph de Beaufort. The book records conversations in which Brother Laurence shares his simple, steadfast commitment to making the worship of God a daily choice even in the midst of mundane and menial tasks. Worship, in its simplest form, is a choice to be vulnerable, aware, and open-hearted to God's presence, if possible, at every moment. Brother Laurence made it clear: This is something that can be improved with practice.

And when you practice vulnerability, over time, it becomes easier to see God in the face of every person you meet. It is easier to hear God in the song of the birds and the rustling of the leaves. You carry a melody in your heart, and your heart is open to the heart of God. So you are more vulnerable and open to His love. The Irish poet John O'Donohue wrote *Beauty: The Invisible Embrace* in 2003. Where I use the term "vulnerability," O'Donohue uses the term "reverence." He said that "when we walk on the earth with reverence, beauty will decide to trust us. The rushed heart and the arrogant mind lack the gentleness and patience to enter that embrace" (O'Donohue, 2003, p. 24).

The Sweet Spot

The Oxford Dictionary tells us that a *sweet spot* is "the point or area on a bat, club, or racket at which it makes most effective contact with the ball" (Lexico, n.d.-b). In the Christian life, a sweet spot is the perfect balance of loving self and others. You may be able to find the sweet spot on a golf club or tennis racket, but you will rarely, if ever, hit the sweet spot in your Christian walk. Why? Because it is very hard to find that balance. When Jesus told us to love others as we love ourselves, he was giving us very wise, but very difficult, direction.

That wisdom is that it is the best way to find happiness in this life. The difficulty, as in any sport, is that it requires constant practice and attention. I am using a sports analogy here because, even if we do not regularly play a sport, most of us understand the work involved. Playing tennis, for example, requires moving about the court while continually keeping your eye on the ball. Sports typically require split-second decisions. In my introduction, I refer to the myriad of decisions that a ball player must make in order to hit the ball out of the park. It takes lots of practice. So does loving.

How do I practice being a loving person? How do I know what genuine love is? How can I tell if my motive is sufficiently selfless or controlling? Can success at loving be measured, and if so, how is it measured? What about loving myself? That is also a commandment. Like the Sabbath, loving myself is essential self-care. God is as concerned with my well-being as much as He is with anyone's. Moreover, maintaining a balance of loving others and loving oneself is the only way it can work. I cannot just love others and neglect myself. In time there would be nothing left of me to love with. I can't simply love myself without regard to others. In time there would be no others. The hard thing about what Jesus told us to do is finding and maintaining that balance.

Keeping one's eye on the ball isn't especially difficult in a 2-hour game of tennis. Can I keep my eye on the ball for a lifetime? Can I keep making balanced decisions when it comes to love? I think I understand why God recommends marriage. When it works, a committed relationship is the best "love lab," the best way to work on finding that sweet spot of balance in loving self and others.

It may be John Gottman (1986) who is best known for introducing the term "love lab." Gottman is known for his rapid and effective evaluation of the potential success of a relationship in therapy. When a couple's motivation to love has been compromised by hurts, betrayals, or neglect, progress in couples therapy may be impossible. M. Scott Peck (1978) correctly affirmed that love begins with the will: "the will to extend one's self for the purpose of nurturing one's own or another's spiritual growth" (p. 81). It is precisely here that the directive to take up one's cross daily enters the picture. The cross we bear daily is the willingness to extend ourselves, to choose carefully, compassionately, and wisely how to balance nurturing our own and another's spiritual growth. That means the work of being honest with ourselves and being honest with the ones we love.

I can certainly appreciate God's promise of sending me a "helper suitable for me." She really is. We are alike enough to enjoy each other and different enough to have "opportunities to grow." Becoming mature is doing difficult things until they are not—or, at least, less—difficult. Again, vulnerability is what is needed for the work of maturing. Vulnerability—the willingness to suffer—means learning to tolerate unsettling emotions.

The apostle Peter tells us that "love covers over a multitude of sins" (Peter 4:8). It isn't that another's hurtful comments or actions are invisible. Rather, love simply chooses not to see them, which does not mean that love is blind. Rather, love is selective.

Love is very willing to turn the other cheek. When someone is either passive or controlling by nature, however, when they have not learned to check their automatic fight-flight impulses, they are not turning the other cheek. They are simply immature. Turning the other cheek requires a choice: the choice to suffer unfair comments or actions or a choice to lovingly confront the offender. Turning the other cheek requires wisdom to know how love would respond. Love is always in the center of choosing. Taking up your cross daily is keeping your eye on the ball. Jesus promised that would become easy and light. Easy and light, golf pros tell you, is the surest way to find the sweet spot. But oh my, it takes practice.

Personality and Worship

People are different and so are the ways they prefer to worship. I will refer you back to Chapter 13 where I discussed personality differences based on the Myers-Briggs type indicator. Does it make sense that people with a dominant extraverted temperament like an enthusiastic form of worship? Perhaps people who are more introverted prefer a quieter, worshipful atmosphere. My guess is that people with a dominant sensing function like straightforward Bible teaching, and intuitive folks may prefer metaphor and a more symbolic form of worship.

Notice how tentative I was in the paragraph above. That is because I do not think there are any hard and fast rules to apply to how people prefer to worship. There are many variables involved. The quality of preaching, the friendliness of the people, the edifying liturgy or style of worship, the worship music, and even a church's location are all involved in why we like the churches we like. But it is interesting to see why different personality types gravitate toward certain churches. It might be fun for someone to do some research for a graduate project relating personality type to various preferences in worship.

The temperament of the pastor is certainly a large factor in what attracts people to a particular church and form of worship. Some pastors are teachers, some pastors are encouragers, and some pastors are very concerned about social justice. Some pastors are very warm and personable, and others are very dynamic and persuasive. So many of the different styles of worship can be influenced by the different personalities of the pastor. But not always. And maybe it shouldn't be.

I was confirmed in the United Church of Christ (the former term was "Congregational"). My family attended the First Congregational Church of Glendale. Later I was baptized by John MacArthur at Grace Community Church in Sun Valley, CA. I had a reawakening of my Christian walk at a Full Gospel Businessmen's conference in 1972, and for a while, we attended a Four Square church and enjoyed the preaching of Jack Hayford. My in-laws attended Hollywood Presbyterian Church when Lloyd Ogilvie was preaching. I do not know who I enjoyed the most. John, Jack, and Lloyd were all amazing preachers. Each one had a different style of preaching, led a different style of worship, and likely had some different points of theology, but their dynamic love of Jesus was infectious. I attended a Baptist church for 6 months when my ship was in Pearl Harbor, and after seminary, I was ordained in the Presbyterian Church. After leaving pastoral ministry for a counseling ministry, I heard great things about a local Episcopal Church, and my wife and I attended there for a few years. Before finding our present church, we "gypsied" around for a time and visited our local Lutheran and Catholic Churches. Today I am going to an independent church in Thousand Oaks with the trendy name, Atmosphere, and a great worship band. Pastor Jim is among the handful of preachers I can listen to without finding my mind wandering.

I said all that in order to say this: I find church fascinating. I find God's people, in all of their diverse forms of worship, fascinating. I love worshiping God in the wonderful diversity of His people. I will take a risk and muse that, for me, a perfect church might have the polity and theology of the Presbyterian Church, the Liturgy and choral perfection of the Episcopal Church, the zeal of the Baptist Church, and the exuberance and friendliness of Atmosphere. It is rare for anyone to find a perfect church. And that is good because "church" is made up of people. And God needs all kinds of people and many forms of worship in His church.

People attend church for many significant psychological benefits. In no special order, people go to church to be lifted out of the weekly blur of day-to-day business. Some go to pray, some to seek forgiveness. Some people need healing or to hear again that God loves them and that they have value. Some like to learn, some to feel closer to God. Some people enjoy the music, and some enjoy the preaching. Many people go to church to make friends and to experience community. Moreover, there are many more reasons I have not mentioned. Different strokes for different folks.

Undressing the Clergy

In the early 1980s the senior pastor and I were doing lots of weddings. He suggested to me that for weddings we wear something other than the somber black "Geneva gown" that we typically wore for Sunday Services. The Geneva gown got its name from its origin as an academic gown worn by the "teaching elders," John Calvin, and others in Geneva, Switzerland. The idea in the Reformation was to do away with priestly vestments in favor of academic attire. But black is not the best color for weddings, so we invested in off-white linen robes complete with cotton belt and liturgical stole—not very Presbyterian but it worked better for weddings.

If I were asked to preach on a Sunday, I think it would be fun to be in front of the congregation wearing that linen robe. I would take it off to reveal a black academic gown underneath. I would take off the Geneva gown to reveal a classic business suit and tie. Under that would be an aloha shirt and under that a colored t-shirt. I would reassure the congregation that that would be it—nothing else was coming off. This would be a visual lesson in church history. All of these garments have, at one time or another, been worn by clergy preaching on Sunday morning. And throughout the decades, each garment has signified something vital to the worship of God.

Sign and Symbol

A *sign* points to something specific. A stop sign means stop. A triangle on a restroom door means men's room. A *symbol* opens to deeper and varied meanings. The American flag is a symbol. So is the cross. Those symbols evoke both mental and emotional content. The flag, accompanied by the National Anthem, can bring tears. So can the cross when accompanied by the congregation singing "Amazing Grace."

Clergy vestments are highly symbolic. In the Catholic, Episcopal (or Anglican) churches, and in many Lutheran churches, priests and pastors typically where white robes, often accompanied by an overlaid chasuble and liturgical stole. The clergy in Eastern and Oriental Orthodox Churches generally wear very colorful, elaborate robes. Vestments symbolize ordination: persons who have been given special instruction and a commission to administer the sacraments and preach the word of God. Psychologically, a priest acts as a representative of Jesus Christ, given the sacred task of representing Christ's final instructions to His disciples at the last supper. For millions of Christ followers in these denominations, a priest is, themselves, an important symbol in facilitating worship.

After the reformation, many Protestant churches were encouraged to affirm the "priesthood of all believers." The clergy were no longer seen as priests, but as "teaching elders." The academic robe symbolized that role. Today, depending on the denomination, it is more common for clergy to dress more casually in a suit and tie, shirt and tie, or colorful shirt. This symbolizes comfortable approachability. This style of clergy dress may say, "I'm not anyone special. We are all equally commissioned by Christ to spread the gospel." My pastor sometimes wears an untucked dress shirt, a polo shirt, or even a nice t-shirt. What is he telling us symbolically? In my pastoral days, I was very mindful, wearing my Geneva gown and standing at the communion table, that as I repeated our Lord's words at the last supper, I was stepping into a highly symbolic role. I often felt, palpably, the sacred awesomeness of that role. After the service, I was eager to take off the robe and be myself again.

Symbols have been extremely important in the history of the Christian Church. The cross, the fish, the winged lion, the ox, the alpha, and the omega all have symbolic meaning, as do statues of saints and martyrs. Artistically, it is a shame that so much Christian art and statuary was defaced or destroyed in the early years of the Protestant reformation. Sadly, well-meaning Christians have been at war with each other since the beginning. The many different forms of worship and artistic means to express the sacred have suffered as a result.

I had a surprise a few years ago when I sat down to talk with a reenactor of an Anglican priest sitting in a garden in Williamsburg, Virginia. I was interested in his work "here in the colonies." He was astonishingly well versed in the history of the Anglican church in Virginia and about his ministry among the colonists. I told him that I was also a clergyman, a pastor in the Presbyterian Church. Without hesitation, he lightly touched my knee and said in a whisper, "You may rely on my discretion." That was the surprise. I had forgotten the prejudice against Catholics, Presbyterians, Quakers, and others in colonial America. Whereas Bruton Parish, the Episcopal Church in Williamsburg, was beautifully appointed, the Presbyterian meeting house was drab and barren. Apparently, it wasn't the building that had significance but the fellowship of the believers and their freedom to worship.

The building in which the church meets has great symbolic significance. I love visiting cathedrals. The beauty of the sacred space lifts the soul and inspires awe. Worshipers are dwarfed by the grandeur, enthralled by the architecture, and held captive by radiant light streaming through stained glass. But in all of its grandeur, what does the cathedral symbolize? In an earlier chapter, I mentioned the theological concepts of immanence and transcendence. A cathedral lifts worshipers into the experience of transcendence. That is so important. Can it also inspire community?

The church is a community of believers worshiping together. A cathedral is a beautiful place to visit and an inspiring place to worship. But perhaps a rented space in a warehouse, a home, or a community center would do just as a well as a true symbol of where the "church" is. The church is where God's spirit is. God's spirit is in the people who are worshiping him and in the place where they have come together to worship. Homes typically reflect the tastes and traditions of the family within. So the rich diversity of the people of God is also symbolized in the places of their worship.

The University of Redlands presents an annual carol performance at Christmas time called "A Feast of Lights." The performance is a miraculous blend of classical and contemporary music song by over 100 student and alumni choir members. The highlight of the evening is when the lights are turned off in the vast university chapel auditorium and everything is dark save the light from a single candle. From that candle the choir members file past, lighting their own candle, then lighting the many candelabra on the stage and attached to the walls of the chapel. Soon the entire auditorium is ablaze with light. The symbolism is evident in the light overcoming the darkness and the inextinguishable expansion of the flame, the symbol of the Spirit of God moving from one to another: each flame identical, with equal amounts of warmth and illumination. So it is with God's gifted people. The indwelling Holy Spirit is available to all, bringing God's comfort, warmth, and light to each.

Freedom to Worship

Freedom to worship how, where, what, or with whom one pleases is among the most significant freedoms granted to Americans by our constitution. The framers of the constitution undoubtedly realized that the diversity of people in the colonies and the diversity of their religious expressions needed protection. The psychological benefits of worship are immense. Faith provides support and succor in challenging times. Faith meets existential needs. Faith, when benevolent, encourages kindness and compassion, Faith encourages care for the environment and the community. Faith, when practiced by well-meaning, caring Christian people, is an example and model for how people should be treated.

Christians understand the power of worship. They understand the value of belonging to a worshiping community. There is also a great deal of value in grasping the psychological benefits that regular worship provides. Looking deeply into the human psyche, understanding the pull of God's Spirit toward the goal of becoming more like Christ, the potency of communion and the transformative, therapeutic power of prayer are all made wonderfully evident when one looks at the work of psyche in worship.

Questions for Review, Reflection, and Discussion

1. In what way might worship be thought of as an investment?
2. How would you characterize the psychology of religion?
3. What areas of your life might represent misplaced worship?
4. How is psychotherapy mostly about treating the consequences of misplaced worship?
5. How would you describe the difference between a sign and a symbol?
6. What Christian symbols have particular meaning for you?

CHAPTER 15

Counseling and the Laity

> Carry each other's burdens, and in this way you will fulfill the law of Christ."
>
> —Galatians 6:2

Chapter Preview and Learning Objectives

Pastoral care ought to be a normal part of the ministry of every church. Many pastors are gifted at counseling and, if not, are able to direct parishioners to elders or members of the congregation who are. The apostle Paul said the gifts of the Holy Spirit enable members of Christ's body to function in many different ways within the church family. Stephen Ministry is an excellent example of how laypersons can be trained and equipped to do some of the counseling and pastoral ministry in the church. There are some basic skills in people helping that anyone can learn.

Learning Objectives

Students will do the following in this chapter:

- Come to an appreciation of the heart of therapy.
- Appreciate how laypersons can be trained to do pastoral ministry.
- Be introduced to the work of Stephen Ministry.
- Be exposed to fundamental helping skills, such as active listening and attunement.
- Learn the value of "joining" and processing emotions.

Counseling by Laypersons

At this moment someone is pouring out their heart to a fellow believer. Later today three guys will be praying for each other. Two friends are walking together, and one is sharing her struggles in her marriage. Her friend is doing a great job of helping. She is listening, letting herself feel her own emotions, and not offering any advice. It is quiet for a few moments before her friend says, "I'm so sorry you're going through all of this." Those words might seem like an insufficient response to a person in pain, but the few moments of silence gave this "counselor" friend time to connect with her own feelings of sadness for her friend. When she did respond, it was from her heart. Her words were genuine, and her simple response perfectly met the needs of her friend and she felt loved.

The heart of therapy is careful listening and a compassionate response. Many people are able to do that for their friends, family members, or other believers. It seems that some people are gifted in this area. Whether by temperament or a spiritual gift, some believers are simply good at listening and being compassionate. Others in the congregation may be eager to learn some of the skills of effective counseling.

I have frequently taught lay-counseling training courses at various churches. I have often used Gary Collins's *How to be a People Helper*. It was first available in 1976 and has been updated since then. Collins also wrote an excellent book entitled *Christian Counseling*. The third edition was published in 2007. *How to be a People Helper* is especially designed for training laypeople to be effective counselors in a variety of contexts. In addition, I have also served as an advisor for Stephen Ministry training at a local church. Stephen Ministry is an excellent program for equipping lay persons to do some of the pastoral care in the church. Their website explains that "Stephen Ministry offers a proven and effective way to organize, equip, and supervise a team of congregation members—called *Stephen Ministers*—to provide high-quality, one-to-one, Christ-centered care to people in the congregation and the community experiencing life difficulties" (Stephen Ministries, n.d., What Is Stephen Ministry? section).

Limitations to Lay Counseling

Stephen ministers are also instructed about the types of persons and problems that they are not equipped to handle. Brief crisis counseling, support for grieving persons, help with moderate depression and anxiety, brief relationship therapy, support through divorce or other life changes can, in most cases, be competently handled by a Stephen minster. However, severe mental illness, severe depression and anxiety, suicidality, entrenched and hostile relationships, addictions, personality disorders, child custody issues, domestic violence, and abuse are among the problem areas that should be treated by a professional.

Pastoral Counseling

As I mentioned in Chapter 11, pastors or elders ought to be the first ones to be contacted for support. Many pastors have been trained to provide pastoral counseling and are an excellent resource for many types of problems. Even if your pastor is not a gifted counselor, they may be able to refer you to a member of the congregation who is skilled, compassionate, and perhaps even trained in counseling. In addition, many churches keep a list of licensed professionals in the area who provide Christian counseling.

Spiritual Gifts

At Fuller Seminary in 1976, I took a class from James Dunn, a visiting professor from Nottingham, UK. Dr. Dunn's Scottish accent was engaging but more so was the text for his class, *Jesus and the Spirit* (Dunn, 1975). Dunn had so immersed himself in the life and work of the apostle Paul that it seemed as if he knew him personally. In his detailed study of the early church, Dunn (1975) writes, "The common experience of the Spirit could stand as the one necessary and sufficient term in Paul's definition of belonging to Christ" (p. 260). He then goes to say:

> If it is the experienced Spirit who creates community in the first place, so it is the Spirit experienced in charismata who sustains community. At no time does Paul conceive of two kinds of Christians—those who minister to others and those who are ministered to, those who manifest charismata and those who do not. To be a Christian is to be charismatic; one cannot be a member of the body without sharing the charismatic Spirit. ... To belong to the body is to have a function within the body, a contribution which the member must make; otherwise, the health of the whole suffers. ... the Spirit's gifts are the living movement of Christ's body. (Dunn, 1975, pp. 262–264)

Finally, Dunn (1975) discusses the lack of formal leadership in the early church. Dunn stresses Paul's belief in the value of Christian community working together, not from assigned leadership, but from gifted individuals within the community:

> Paul never addresses himself to a leadership group within a community. His instructions and exhortations are generally addressed to the community as a whole. This could only mean that responsibility for responding to such exhortations lay with the congregation as such and not merely with one or two individuals within it. Hence the lack of mention of any leadership group, overseer or whatever, Paul does not even seem to envisage the prophets giving a lead ... each member having a function and responsibility for its common life and worship. (pp. 291–292)

It seems from Dunn's study of the early church and especially the specific instructions given to the churches by the apostle Paul that the Body of Christ was, at first, not a hierarchal organization but rather a charismatic community. Unfortunately, it seems inevitable that the church evolved into what we see today.

I am not suggesting that God has sat shaking His head on the sidelines. But I am suggesting that we human beings have a tendency to mess things up. Paul probably was shaking his head, as the early church struggled with different ideas about who it was and how it ought to function. In the book of Acts, Scripture records the necessity of appointing elders and deacons and giving them various responsibilities to care for the flock. Paul's ideal of a purely charismatic community began to evolve, perhaps out of necessity, to accommodate the consequences of people's egos into an institution. The original idea of creating a hierarchy to protect and to serve ultimately divided Christs body in two: a clergy of pastors, priests, and bishops and everyone else. It seems that many Christians do not realize that they are not the audience but the actors, actors who are gifted to be response-able and, thus, are responsible for each other.

Equipping the Laity

If you are a Christian, you are a member of Christ's body and gifted to perform a function within the body. In Romans 12:3–9, Paul describes these functions. If you have a *prophetic* gift, you tend to have a strong sense of right, wrong, and fairness and an urge to speak up. If your gift is *teaching*, you value both learning and educating. If you are an *encourager*, you find joy in helping others reach their potential. Some people prefer to work behind the scenes with acts of *service*. Others have a gift for *leadership* and organization. Some people have a keen insight into money and are wise about the benefits of *giving*, while the gift that others give is the gift of *mercy* and compassion. All of Christ's followers are gifted. God uses these gifts to equip us for the work He wants us to do—whether to give, or serve, or teach, and so forth.

So not just for those God has gifted to be encouragers, prophets, or teachers, but to everyone who is in a relationship with Jesus and His people, there are some basic skills that are good to learn and practice. I emphasize practice because these skills, while easy to grasp, are very difficult to put into practice. I will list these skills below and emphasize, again, that all of us need to know how to care about one another.

Counseling Skills—The Basics

When someone asks to talk with you, here are some things to keep in mind.

Preparation

- Make sure to find a quiet, comfortable, private place to talk.
- It is good to set a time limit. An hour is typical, but it can be more or less time if agreed upon.
- Plan to follow up by text, email, phone, or in person.
- Prepare your hearts. Ask God's blessing on your time together.

Listening

Suppose you are listening to a story. The person telling their story is inviting you to walk alongside.

- Listen for the emotions inside of the story.
- Ask yourself, "What must this feel like?"
- Try to get inside the story. Imagine what it may be like to be the other person facing their struggles and challenges. Have you had a similar experience that might help you relate to the other's story?

- Feel your feelings in response to the story; this is the root of compassion. It is okay to tear up, but remember this is their story, not yours.
- Suspend any judgement or suggestions. It is okay to ask for clarification, but stay focused on the emotions. You are a companion on another's journey. Your goal is for the other to know that you are with them on this leg of their journey. In psychological language, this is referred to as the quality of "attunement."

Attunement

The goal of good listening and of a good counseling experience is for the person you are helping to "feel felt." This is the term that Dan Siegel (2007) uses in his book *The Mindful Brain*:

> The process of attunement creates a neural state of integration that forms the foundation of the receptive dimension of reflective awareness. Within interpersonal integration, we come to "feel felt" by another person, we feel not only aligned with the other but our brain likely establishes a state of ... "neuroception" of safety. (p. 120)

The qualitative feel of such an open state is the foundation of love. You are listening to the other's story and listening to how the story impacts you. Your job is not to help, heal, convert, or fix, but to *be with* the other. It is this "withness" that is healing. It is bad enough to have to go through challenges; it is worse when you feel that you are all alone. If you are doing your job and genuinely connecting with the other, when their story winds down, you may not know what to say. That is good. You have sufficiently emptied yourself so that the Holy Spirit can work more effectively through you.

Joining

Joining is continuing to come alongside but now with some suggestions and direction. There is an art to this. Many counselors make the mistake of rushing into fixing mode. It is tempting to want to encourage the person you are helping, but be patient. Probably three quarters of your time together is simply listening. What genuinely helps someone is processing feelings. Remember my explanation of neural integration. Telling one's story, feeling the feelings, maybe allowing some tears or anger to well up, and experiencing a release of emotion is the heart of healing. The art of counseling is knowing when it is your turn to say something and knowing what to say.

Counselors can make the mistake of saying things like "I know how you feel," "This happened to me," "What I do when this happens," and so forth. Do not call attention to yourself. Stay focused on the person you are helping. Here are some things you can do: Think of an ARC, a connection between the two of you: **A** stands for affirm, **R** is for repeat/reflect, and **C** is clarify. That will help you to remember how to listen well.

Affirming is acknowledging what someone is saying. You are letting the other know that you get it. You understand. Here are some examples:

- I hear you.
- I understand.

- That must feel awful.
- I can see why, could feel/think/imagine that.
- How awful!

Unless you have done the work of creating attunement, of letting yourself genuinely connect emotionally, these responses may seem and feel ingenuine and trite. When you are inside of the other's story, it is more likely that your emotional response will sound and feel real.

Repeating/reflecting is probably the most effective form of active listening. This is what professional psychotherapists do most often. "What I hear you say" sounds dumb, but it is exactly what you are doing. There are more interesting, less cliched ways of saying the same thing. You can say, "So you're telling me that ..." or "Okay, what you're saying is ..." Then you fill in what you have heard. It is good to try to repeat verbatim. That way, your speaker will know that you truly are listening. However, sometimes it is even better to repeat what you have heard at a deeper level. Your speaker may become aware of deeper feelings that were previously hidden. For example, as you listen to your client tell their story, you hear anger, but it seems like underneath the anger is a layer of bitterness. You might say, "I hear some bitterness in what you're saying." In a way, your comments can also be a way of clarifying.

Clarifying is checking with your listener to find out if you are hearing them correctly and/or if you would like some additional information. You can say, "Am I hearing you correctly?" "What else were you feeling?" "What happened next?" and so forth. Be careful with this, but it is okay to interrupt your speaker for the purpose of active listening. An example would be when you say, "May I stop you for a moment? What were you aware of at the time?" Be careful not to make your speaker feel interrogated. And never, ever pull a Doctor Phil: "What were you thinking!?"

Practice

Professional therapists practice these steps until they become (or should become) second nature. So, if you truly want to be available to help people, if you would like to be known in your church as the person to contact when they need help, practice. Practice with a friend, your spouse, or your adult child. Ask your pastor for 20 minutes. Ask them to share a challenge. Alert your pastor that you do not plan to help; you simply need to practice being a good listener. Get feedback.

In your practice sessions, listen to your inner family. What is your inner *child* feeling? What is the *parent* in you thinking or wanting to say? Listen to them, but do not let them say anything. Your adult is your wise executive and the one, ultimately, who will speak up when appropriate. Bear in mind that you are mainly practicing *not speaking up*. You are practicing allowing yourself to become empty—joining, attuning, listening within to the voice and wisdom of the Holy Spirit. I will include a one-page handout for basic listening skills in the Appendix.

Questions for Review, Reflection, and Discussion

1. What are some of the benefits of having lay counseling in the church?
2. What are some limitations to lay counseling?
3. Would your congregation be open to lay-counseling training?
4. Explain the steps of active listening.

CHAPTER 16

Church Hurts

> "The Spirit of the Lord is on me, because he has anointed me to preach the gospel to the poor. He has sent me to heal the brokenhearted, to preach freedom for the prisoners, and recovering of sight for the blind, to set the oppressed free."
>
> —Luke 4:18

Chapter Preview and Learning Objectives

The Body of Christ, the church, is a place of healing and restoration. Or, at least, it ought to be. There are times when the church itself inflicts the wounds. This is true when immature Christians use Scripture to criticize, judge, and shun people. And it is especially true when people in positions of trust abuse that trust by betraying, abandoning, and abusing others. Our earthly father may be a model of protection, provision, and love, reflecting the attributes of our Heavenly Father. However, our earthly father often falls far short of this model. As a result, many of God's children have a difficult time trusting God or believing that He is actually loving.

Learning Objectives

Students will do the following in this chapter:

- Explore what it means to be a mature Christian.
- Understand the relationship between vulnerability and maturity.
- Grasp the value of perspective.

- Explore the relationship between earthly fathers and our Heavenly Father.
- Discover the harm inflicted when a church member betrays trust.
- Review how the church can be a healing "corrective emotional experience."

In the passage above, Jesus described His mission: to proclaim the good news that God's kingdom has come, present in Himself. Proof of His calling was the work He has been sent to do: healing, delivering new sight, and freedom from wounds. The church continues His work. But what happens when the church itself becomes a source of wounding?

Maturity

At times, it hurts to be a Christian. It hurts to be reminded of how often we fall short of God's best. We make bad decisions, act unkindly, and are reminded again and again of how very human we are. At times it is good to hurt. Pain is instructive. I often think that reaching maturity is doing hard things until they are not (or are at least less) hard. I suppose that the difference between a mature and immature person is a mature person's willingness to suffer pain in the service of growth.

Willingness is everything. The choice to be open to learning life lessons, according to Peck (1978), is the road *less* traveled. Walking down that road with a heart open to looking honestly at oneself is painful. But it is redemptive pain, pain that is chosen in the service of growth. Walking down that road with an open heart, one sees and feels the pain that is all around. Jesus was described as a man of sorrows and acquainted with grief. Of course He was. His heart was open to the people around Him.

Perspective

You cannot be on that road and stay open to the pain you see, feel, and cause without God's help. The Holy Spirit, the teacher and comforter, is always with you with compassion, wisdom, and the perspective you need for the journey. Willingness is everything, but so is perspective. It must be that every brother or sister in Christ who has suffered on the road and had something of value to share with us must have acquired God's perspective. However large the challenge, knowing that the shepherd is leading with his rod and staff surely helps us to fear no evil.

The heart of cognitive behavioral therapy is finding perspective. Cognitive distortions walk about as roaring lions waiting to devour. They come to steal, to kill, and to destroy. We are reminded that Jesus is with us that we may have life and have it abundantly. The battle in our minds is the battle for perspective. We cannot face pain without perspective. In the letter to the Romans, Paul tells us that "our sufferings of this present time are not worth comparing with the glory that is to be revealed to us" (Romans 8:18).

It may be that the most valuable psychological intervention available to the human race, after the resurrection of Jesus Christ, is God's amazing reassurance: the perspective of Scripture. Scripture is God's affirmation of our value and acceptance. We are reminded that we are never alone, never without hope, and never without love.

But we have heard all this before. Do we believe it? More importantly, do we deeply believe it? Has God's word penetrated our heart? Can we feel the truth of it: the joy and peace of God's promises, protection, and provision? Can we say with Carl Jung, "I don't have to believe; I know"? I wonder how many Christians deeply believe what God has said about who He is, who we are, and what He is doing in our life.

As I have said above, brains are hard to convince. Brains like facts that they can see, predict, and use. The apostle Thomas was voicing our doubts when he said, "Show me." Even then, even when we have been given the evidence of answered prayer, we still wonder, "Even if it's true, is it true for me?" The answer to our doubting, our questioning, is God's promise that if we search for Him with our whole heart, we will find Him. I believe that. I believe that God would not lie. I believe that as psychologists and counselors, we understand the value of cognitive reframing and reconstruction. In time, if we search for God with our whole heart, in our daily life, and in His word, we will experience that renewal of our mind and of our faith.

Fathers

Describe your father. Can you describe him in a couple of sentences? Probably not. Fathers tend to be difficult to capsulize. I think that is because fathers are typically not all good or all bad. I would describe my father as kindly and loving. I could also describe him as passive and preoccupied. It wasn't until much later in my life that I heard "I love you" from my dad. That is not uncommon. Men of my father's generation were not socialized to be very emotionally expressive. Many of my clients never heard "I love you" from their fathers. They would tell me that, somehow, they knew they were loved even though they never heard the words. That may be one of the reasons that it is hard to hear "I love you" from our Heavenly Father.

It is sad that so many of my clients suffer father wounds. I have listened to story after story of rejection, abandonment, and abuse by earthly fathers. Because the brain soaks up and holds onto early childhood impressions, the word "father" can certainly evoke mixed emotions. Even those of us who have been fortunate enough to have experienced loving fathers can be held back by our own human tendency to locate our value and acceptance in relation to a history of a felt need to perform for Dad's approval—so that Dad will be proud of us.

In 1985 Linda Schierse Leonard wrote *The Wounded Woman: Healing the Father-Daughter Relationship*. Dr. Leonard writes about her experience with her father. In this she talks about the experience of way too many wounded women. Growing up in chaos, abuse, addictions, seduction, abandonment, and so many less horrific, subtle forms of mistreatment, many women have a difficult time relating to God the Father.

The tagline for the trailer of the 1999 film *The General's Daughter* was "What's worse than rape?" Of course, nothing is. So moviegoers wondered. At the end of the film, we discover betrayal of the worst kind. "For the good of the army," the general covers up the rape of his daughter by the soldiers in her platoon. The chief responsibility of fathers and mothers is to love and protect their children. The general's behavior betrayed his daughter, his responsibility to her, and his responsibility to God. When a father wounds his daughter by betraying love, how is she ever going to trust love? The same is true when a person in a position of trust in the church and abuses that trust by physically, sexually, mentally, or spiritually injuring another member of the church. Jesus, normally meek and mild, said that such a person "ought to have a millstone hung around their neck and be drowned in the sea" (Matthew 18:6).

At Church

Among other things, Jesus commissioned the church to heal hurts. It is possible that a wounded person could experience a quality of love and steadfastness from brothers and sisters in Christ that, over time, would be the corrective emotional experience that could heal betrayal and restore the ability to trust. It is also possible that the church could inflict even more betrayal. If the representative of Christ on earth, the church, betrays its commission to love and heal hurts, where does one turn?

I once had a client who suffered a loveless, abusive marriage for many years. She was dying, which we are supposed to do (but in a way that creates growth and ultimately joy). For her there was no growth and no joy, only death. My ethical standards as a marriage and family therapist prohibited me from encouraging her toward divorce. As a Christian I worked hard to try to find a way to repair this marriage. Her husband was unwilling to come in for therapy. She tried many ways to reach him and finally decided to give up. I had mixed feelings when she told me that she was planning to see an attorney. Mostly, I felt sad. I knew what this family was about to go through with a divorce. The other feeling I had was a sense of relief that this woman would no longer have to tolerate abuse from her husband. Scripture declares that God hates divorce. Who wouldn't? Divorce is hard on everyone: spouses, children, extended family, and friends. But God certainly understands that when trust has been repeatedly betrayed and His child is suffering ongoing abuse and injury, it may be time to leave a marriage.

Fortunately, the couple attended a church. Of course, no one knew what was going on at home. I thought that, certainly, her church family would understand and be a resource of love and acceptance. They were not. In fact many of the congregation turned against her. They viewed her as the one betraying her marriage by pursuing a divorce. I do not think that her husband was a sociopath, but he was very clever at protecting his "nice guy" image at church. He was the one people sympathized with. She suffered in silence. She had a close friend who knew the truth and stood by her, but because of her children, she was reluctant to say anything against her husband. Christians are warned not to gossip, but for some, gossip is hard to resist, and children can be the worst offenders. Before long, her children refused to go back to church because of the hurt they suffered from other children, and she eventually quit going herself.

Where do you turn when your church family abandons you? How do you deal with the pain of betrayal when the wrong person is vilified? Do you still trust God? Where is He? Why hasn't He protected you? Then, perhaps, you recall the words Jesus uttered when He cried out from the cross, *Eli Eli lama sabachthani*, "My God, why have you forsaken me?" And you realize that Jesus also suffered betrayal. In fact, He suffered every form of sin, and

He did that for you. As Paul reminds us in his second letter to the church at Corinth, "For He made Him who knew no sin *to be sin* for us, that we might become the righteousness of God in Him" (2 Corinthians 5:21). Reminded that Jesus was betrayed by ones who love him and strengthened and humbled by Christ's sacrifice on the cross, you begin to wonder about the ways that you, too, have fallen short. The cross changes everything, especially our perspectives.

It hurts when people in the world are unkind, selfish, and even cruel. It hurts, but you are not surprised. That is how people are when they are not following Christ. When people say they are following Christ and are unkind, selfish, and cruel, what then? That is when church hurts. That is when the body of Christ has failed to live up to its commission to love. When people are supposed to act one way and act in the opposite way, they are called hypocrites. That has been the accusation most commonly heard from people in the world. My former client would agree. She was abused by her husband and then from her church family. I do not know if she has every returned to church.

Church hurts when it ought to be a resource, a place of acceptance and healing, and it does just the opposite. By betraying its commission, the body of Christ wounds itself. Our Heavenly Father's representatives on Earth must not betray what has been entrusted to them, the responsibilities of love. Our Lord's commandment to love one another means that no one should ever feel judged, shunned, rejected, abandoned, or betrayed. No one should ever be abused sexually, slandered, held up to ridicule, or gossiped against. No one should feel prejudice or made to feel less than, unwanted or disqualified for Christ's love. If the church hurts someone, the church has a responsibility to help to heal.

The shepherd David once sang, "If I ascend up into heaven, thou art there: if I make my bed in hell, behold, thou art there" (Psalm 139:8). David reminds us that God is always present, even when the church betrays His trust. People hurt each other: We always have and we always will. Sometimes the hurts are intentional, sometimes not. But because it is people who hurt each other, it is people who can help to heal each other.

The Healing Work of the Church

In the previous chapter, I discussed the role that lay counselors can play in extending the pastoral ministry of the church. This can happen in a formal context when the church equips its laity with the training necessary to come alongside people in pain. It is just as important that the church equip the congregation to appreciate that all Christians, not just those identified as pastors or lay counselors, have a role to play in creating the safety and trust required for healing. Scripture tells us that all of us have responsibilities to extend Christ's work. In one place and another, Scripture directs us to *speak the truth* in love. Through love *serve* one another, *teach* and *help* one another, *encourage* one another daily, freely you have received, freely *give, manage* your household and put on a heart of *compassion.*

I have frequently discussed the concept of a "corrective emotional experience." Imagine if all Christians took Christ's commission to heart and offered the kindness, compassion, and consistency that an injured person had never before experienced. What a difference that would make in a person's life. I stated above that we are all psychologists. We are all interested in people: how we think, how we act, why we make the decisions we make. If we are following Christ and belong to his body, we may not be trained to function in the role of psychologist, but we are all called into the ministry of caring for one another.

Questions for Review, Reflection, and Discussion

1. What characterizes a mature person?
2. What are the benefits of being vulnerable?
3. How does the church facilitate reframing and alternative perspectives?
4. How does our earthly father help or hinder our relationship with our Heavenly Father?
5. In what ways can the church do more harm than good?
6. In what ways can the church be a healing, corrective emotional experience?

CHAPTER 17

The Psychology of Survival

> "At that time many will turn away from the faith and will betray and hate each other, and many false prophets will appear and deceive many people. Because of the increase of wickedness, the love of most will grow cold, but the one who stands firm to the end will be saved."
>
> —Matthew 24:11–13

Chapter Preview and Learning Objectives

What are the core strengths of being human? How do we stand firm and survive life's challenges? We need strength training in each area of our existence: body, soul, and spirit. How is this strength training accomplished? How do you know what work you are called to do, and how do you survive the work?

Learning Objectives

Students will do the following in this chapter:

- Explore the metaphor of "core strength."
- Grasp that to be human is to be aware of choices.
- Question whether the soul is the core of our core strength.
- Discover how to build spiritual muscle.
- Consider God's calling on your life.
- Explore ways to survive the work He has given you to do.

Standing Firm

The year before COVID-19 hit, I was working with a trainer at a local gym. I came in early one morning and started my routine. My trainer walked over stifling a laugh and asked me what I was doing. "Pull downs," I said. "I'm working my shoulders." "Pull downs are for your back," he said, instructively. "Oh," I responded, and he showed me the correct way to do pull downs by tightening my back muscles as, with both hands, I pulled down on the bar above my head. Pull downs, I discovered, did help to strengthen my back muscles. And not just pull downs: My trainer had me do a host of other exercises to strengthen my core. At 72, I still have pretty good back muscles. As I get older, I still want to be able to stand upright and firm.

Strengthening one's core is a key to being able to do many things that elderly people sometimes find difficult. But strengthening one's core is also a metaphor. Survival requires core strength. If we look at survival from a holistic perspective, we can appreciate that a strong body, a strong faith, and a strong connection to others are what is required for mental, physical, and spiritual core strength: longevity and well-being.

Recall from Chapter 7 that what defines human beings, existentially, is freedom to choose. In a 2018 article for *Areo* entitled "What Is Existential Freedom?" Dolan Cummings described freedom to choose as "not an object to be manipulated, but a subject capable of agency. That goes to the heart of what I'll call *existential freedom*: i.e. the inner freedom to choose, even when your choices are externally constrained" (para. 3). That quote reminded me of a passage from Victor Frankl's (1959) *Man's Search for Meaning*:

> When man cannot express himself in positive action, when his only achievement may consist in enduring his sufferings in the right way—in and honorable way—in such a position man can, through loving contemplation of the image he carries of his beloved, achieve fulfillment. For the first time in my life, I was able to understand the meaning of the words, "the Angels are lost in perpetual contemplation of an infinite glory." (p. 37)

Victor Frankl had core strength. He survived. He was able to stand firm in three years of horrific loss in concentration camps where his father, mother, and wife of nine months all perished. According to Frankl, we always have choices. Love gave him the strength to survive because the ability to love is our primary core strength.

Our core strength, theologically, relates to our ability to choose to love. Recall that this ability is what makes us human. We are able to respond to Him, to the needs of the planet, and to each other. We are able to choose love. We are less human when we fail to respond according to God's commission to love ourselves and to love others. We live with our choices. And in view of what our planet is facing, like Captain Ahab and the white whale, we may end up being tied to our choices.

Choices

Recall the words of Joshua: "Choose this day whom you will serve" (Joshua 24:15). This day is the day God has given us. What choices will we make? It may be that the choices we make are the core strengths of our life on Earth. And like all types of strength training, we need to build that strength. We build core strength in three arenas: body, soul, and spirit.

I do not need to dwell on physical strength training. It seems that western culture is obsessed with physical strength and beauty. Stack up the magazines, podcasts, and internet articles related to physical fitness and activities against any other subject matter. I haven't done that yet—and probably won't—but I can imagine that there is no contest. Wait, I forgot video games. I will not say much about video games. I will lose most of my younger readers.

However, in the physical arena, we do face challenging choices daily. In her TED Talk *The Power of Vulnerability*, Brené Brown (2014) said that Americans are the most addicted people on Earth. She may be right. She points to the epidemic of obesity, painkillers, and other distractions. She calls it our efforts to numb ourselves. I think she was connecting our need to numb with, among other things, what Vivek Murthy (2020) called America's epidemic of loneliness. We are a competitive society. Early in life we develop the habit of comparing ourselves to others. A competitive society does not encourage vulnerability, and without vulnerability, there is no genuine connecting. In Chapter 12 I discussed the "miracle of Roseta." The miracle was the power of connection. Without the stresses endemic to other American communities, the close-knit community created a culture of connection that helped them to survive. Can the Christian church follow God's commandment to love and care about each other? Can we overcome our cultural conditioning that shuns vulnerability and remains competitive? I will ask again, what choices are we making?

When it comes to survival, after attending to our physical health, the next arena on the list is the health of our soul. Jesus warned us that if we make too many wrong choices, we may be in peril of losing our soul. In Chapter 7 I described the soul. Recall that the soul is what connects the animating spirit of God's breath to our muddy biology. Soul is connective tissue. Our soul is the core of our core strength. It is the place of relating to God and to others. It is the place of wrestling and of choosing. If we become too preoccupied with distractions, we lose our soul, our connection to everything in life that has value.

In his letter to the church in Rome, the apostle Paul courageously wrote about his own struggles and the all-too-human struggle with choices:

> For I have the desire to do what is good, but I cannot carry it out. For I do not do the good I want to do, but the evil I do not want to do—this I keep on doing. Now if I do what I do not want to do, it is no longer I who do it, but it is sin living in me that does it. (Romans 7:19–20)

Sin, for Paul, is about choices: the choices that move us toward or away from God and from life. Every day we make both large and small choices to move toward life or toward death. Paul continues this theme in his letter to the Galatians: "For the flesh desires what is contrary to the Spirit, and the Spirit what is contrary to the flesh. They are in conflict with each other, so that you are not able to do whatever you want" (Galatians 5:17).

I would like to think that people in the field of psychology grasp that the heart of their work is the tending of the soul. For many years it has seemed to me that my work as a therapist was to help people to appreciate that everything in life has to do with the choices we make. I tried to help people to become more aware of the options they had in thinking, feeling, behaving, and even in their choice of perceptions—how to view their experiences. The heart of psychology is helping people to develop this core strength. And in any form of strength training, core strength is not acquired by information alone, but from practice.

Certainly, people with organic mental disorders—people struggling with addictions, people who have been abused and brutalized as children, people suffering from malnutrition and poverty, and others facing impossible life challenges—have a very limited capacity to choose how they perceive or respond to these horrible conditions. Still, choices can be made to accept help. People have been trained and equipped to help people in intolerable conditions. God bless and strengthen these people.

I heard a fascinating teaching many years ago comparing the ancient temple of Solomon to the nature of the soul. The outer court of Solomon's temple contained the brazen alter and brazen laver, representing the physical sacrifices and self-cleansing efforts we make to approach God. The holy of holies contained the arc of the covenant where God appeared to the high priest. The holy of holy represented our spiritual connection to God. The middle court, according to this teaching, represented the soul, the midplace, and connection between our outer life and our inner, spiritual life. This space is called the holy place. In the holy place there were three things: the alter of incense, representing our emotions and praises rising up to God; the seven-branch lamp, representing the illumination of our intellect; and the table of 12 loaves of showbread, or *the bread presence*, symbolic of God's provision for the 12 tribes of Israel and representative of our will. The lesson was called "the way into the holiest." The instructor pointed out that one could think of the holy place as the soul, consisting of intellect, emotions, and will. What was memorable about this lesson and is relevant to our discussion about learning and practicing making better choices was the reference to the table of bread. Bread, in order to be palatable, needs to be ground, kneaded, molded, and baked. So it is with the human will. If we submit ourselves to the master baker, He will collect the ingredients of our will, lovingly knead us into compliance with His design, and mold us into shape. We are then baked through life's challenges until we are savory to God and able to love others.

The first phase of bread making may be the most relevant to this discussion of response-ability, the human capacity for choice. Wheat must first be ground. When Jesus said in Mathew 10:39, "Whoever finds their life will lose it, and whoever loses their life for my sake will find it," He was referring to the essential grinding down of our ego: anything that we position in our life that stands in the way of following Christ. Interestingly, Carl Jung also discussed the letting go of the ego in his 1933 book *Modern Man in Search of a Soul.* Jung spoke of the arc of life—coming into life and going out. The first half of life must be about acquiring ego strength, the ability to live, successfully, in the outer world. In the second half of life, one's ego must turn inward, away from achieving, accomplishing, and acquiring, and direct one's attention to pursing the development of one's inner world. Gradually, we let go of our ego agendas in favor of seeking spiritual maturity. We lose our life in order to find it. Jung (1933) goes on to say:

> We moderns are faced with the necessity of rediscovering the life of the spirit; we must experience it anew for ourselves. It is the only way in which we can break the spell that binds us to the cycle of biological events. (p. 122)

What is the cross that Jesus told us we must pick up daily? The cross symbolizes the often-painful choices we must make daily if we are to follow Him. These choices, Paul said, are hard to make. I think Paul's confessing to the impossibility of doing what he so wished he could do caused him genuine pain. Grinding down the ego is painful. Paul had been a Pharisee, "a Hebrew of Hebrews," and was likely proud of his achievements in being able to keep the law perfectly. How painful it must have been for Paul to realize he had nothing to boast about: "May I never boast except in the cross of our Lord Jesus Christ, through which the world has been crucified to me and I to the world" (Galatians 6:14). There is nothing that we have achieved or acquired in the outer world that will advance the life of our soul. If we are to stand firm, our core strength must be achieved from the strength of our connection to God and the work He has given us to do in the world.

Spiritual Strength Training

The third arena of vital strength training is our spirit. Soul is our connection to Spirit, and spirit is the connection to God. Notice the I used both lower and upper cases for the word "spirit." Our spirit is connected to the Spirit of God. In fact, our spirit is a particularization of that part of God's Spirit that has been assigned to us. It would be true to say that who we truly are as a human being is spirit. We have a soul and we live in a body. Our body will die, but we never will. How do you strengthen your spirit?

You already know the answer to that question. How do you strengthen anything? By committing to it. There is no other choice if you genuinely want to grow spiritually. There are no half measures. If you believe that God has called you to a particular work, you commit to it. You do what is required. You do it with your whole heart.

Here is another thing you already know: Everything you need to know for your spiritual life and walk (the wisdom and direction you need for encouragement on your journey) is within in the pages of Scripture. The people of God have had a long history. Learn from them. They made the same mistakes that you probably will. They learned valuable lessons. And the best lessons will come from your Rabbi, Jesus. Spend time with him. He invited you to learn from him. Here are some things you need to do to develop spiritual core strength:

- **Know who you are:** What is your personality type? What is your spiritual gift? What motivates you? What are your spiritual goals?
- **Embrace your value:** God has chosen you for a specific work. No one can touch the lives that you have been assigned to touch. You are one of a kind. No one is *more* important or valuable.

- **Find your courage:** "He gives strength to the weary and increases the power of the weak" (Isaiah 40:29). "I am with you; do not be dismayed, for I am your God. I will strengthen you and help you; I will uphold you with my righteous right hand" (Isaiah 41:10).
- **Ask for direction:** "If any of you lacks wisdom, let him ask of God, who gives to all liberally and without reproach, and it will be given to him" (James 1:5). "However, when He, the Spirit of Truth, is come, He will guide you into all truth" (John 16:13).
- **Know that God is with you:** "He leads me beside still waters. He restores my soul. He leads me in paths of righteousness" (Psalm 23:2–3). "I will never leave thee, nor forsake thee" (Hebrews 13:5).

Surviving Your Calling

If you are a Christian, you have been called to God's work. There is the larger work to which every Christian is directed: to be lovers and gardeners. We have been called to love one another and to tend to that patch of God's creation that has been given to us. Then there is that specific work that has been assigned to you. A way to know what that work is (I will quote Marie Kondo) is to discover that which "sparks joy." Ideally, the work God has given us to do creates a confluence of our doing with our being. There ought to be the feeling of a right fit when the work we do is a direct extension of who we are. Some people might say that they feel as if they were born to do this work.

Admittedly, not everyone will have that strong sense of right fit. And it might take some time, possibly years, to find the right work, the work that one feels called to. In many parts of the world, where people are struggling to survive, the idea of a right fit may be eclipsed by what "just has to be done." However, there can still be joy in doing what needs to be done. When love is your core strength, there is joy in offering love to someone in need. Victor Frankl was able to survive by finding meaning in his suffering. There was very little he could do in a concentration camp. But as a former physician, he was able to offer some medical attention to fellow prisoners and feed small bits of bread to others who were starving. It is surprising how being able to choose to be a loving person, caring for others, can help you find the strength to go on.

Every day serving God is a good day. Note that I did not say "easy day." In fact, serving God, at times, may be the hardest work there is. Joining someone on a road to healing after they have experienced dehumanizing abuse and betrayal is heart-wrenching. It is a long road. And you are right there with them as they talk about and relive what they went through.

I think that the hardest part of that journey for me is learning, again, how cruel people can be. I wish I could pretend that people were good. Many are. And many are not. I should not be surprised. Paul spoke of how some people can be in the first section of his letter to the church in Rome. He explained that some people prefer to worship themselves. Their cruelty and inhumanity to others stems from a need to feel superior, from a need to inflict their own pain onto others or to act out their selfish warped desires. I should not be surprised, yet time after time, I am shocked at what people can do to each other. When God has called you to do the work of helping hurting people, how do you survive the pain of the collateral damage you signed up to suffer?

The Work of the Cross

The last words Jesus spoke on the cross, "It is finished," recorded in the Greek language, is rendered in the perfect tense. It is finished. It is complete. It is perfectly perfect. The work of redemption is perfect: perfect in every respect and perfect in every aspect. Nothing more needs to be done to open heaven. And heaven can be present for those who ask for it. How does one survive the work of ministering healing and restoring hope to people who have lost hope and, in some cases, lost the will to live? The answer is by looking toward the cross.

I had a 40-minute drive home from the counseling center where I worked for a number of years. Some days were easy to transition from work to home. I could listen to the radio, sing along with some "oldies," and repair myself from the day. On other days I felt like the most tired person alive, emotionally wrung out and drained. In the *Divine Comedy*, Dante Alighieri reminded us that sometimes you have to go in deeper in order to get out. On those days, trying to distract myself by listening to oldies was not going to work. I needed to go deeper into the pain. I needed to feel the feelings and allow the cleansing work of catharsis to help metabolize the suffering I had absorbed and shared.

The work of the cross is more than Christ's demonstration of loving sacrifice. Rightly understood, the work of the cross makes it possible for us to do our work. Knowing that He did the work he did for us makes it much more possible for us to do our work for Him. We can count on the extra strength and wisdom He offers and can know that He is with us in the work. Looking toward the cross is knowing that we can do the work He has asked us to do even when it is difficult. Below are some practical suggestions for surviving the work.

Survival Skills

1. Pray before you start your day and pray before each client or person you are asked to help.
2. Reassure yourself that the Holy Spirit is with you and will offer guidance and wisdom.
3. Listen with one ear to the story being told and one ear to what you are hearing inside.
4. If you are seeing several people in one day:
   - Be sure to set boundaries around your time so that you can repair yourself in between.
   - Give yourself some quiet time to breathe.
   - Go for a short walk.
   - Listen to some relaxing music.
5. Remember that you only have so many *productive* hours in you per week. If you try to do more, you may end up accomplishing less. Trying to do more than is

reasonable for you, you will likely make mistakes, like forgetting appointments, not answering phone calls, double booking, and not doing good work. Worst of all, you may not be giving your best to your clients or the people you are helping. If you see too many people, you may unconsciously push people away.

6. Do not make the common mistake of neglecting your family and friends. They may be the best way to repair yourself for the journey. This means setting boundaries around your family time, staying in touch with friends, and connecting with others doing similar work.
7. Go on vacations, take time off, get out in nature, and find sources of entertainment that make you laugh.
8. Give yourself time with God. You need some time during the day or a weekend retreat to get insight and encouragement from the "Comforter."
9. Try to have some fun—whatever works for you. Think of fun as "energy in" to balance the "energy out" from one day to the next.
10. Make a list of things you enjoy doing, both large and small. It helps to know that you will be periodically rewarding yourself for the hard work you have chosen to do.

I said earlier that I get tired at the end of a long day seeing clients. I get tired, but not depressed, and I typically look forward to the next day. Recall that when you are doing the right work, the energy for the work is in the work. I include a light-hearted check list of survival skills in the Appendix. I call it the Buckley Burnout Prevention Inventory (BBPI). It may give you more ideas for surviving the work.

Questions for Review, Reflection, and Discussion

1. What do you do to build your spiritual "core strength"?
2. In what ways do you feel God's calling on your life?
3. How will you repair yourself from an emotionally draining day?
4. How will you know how many productive hours you can do in a week?
5. How will you stay healthy and vital for the journey?

CHAPTER 18

On the Sacredness of Therapy

> "In whom (Jesus) the whole structure is joined together, and it continues [to increase] growing into a holy temple in the Lord [a sanctuary dedicated, set apart, and sacred to the presence of the Lord]."
>
> —Ephesians 2:21

Chapter Preview and Learning Objectives

This chapter is an encouragement to students to appreciate the sacredness of their work as therapists. Erich Fromm (1941) emphasized five existential needs for human happiness. He stressed the value of a frame of orientation for finding order and meaning in life. For Christian therapists, that order and meaning is found in the specific work God has gifted them to do. The word *sacred* means to be "set apart." Therapists set apart each hour for the work of being with a person in pain.

Learning Objectives

Students will do the following in this chapter:

- Come to appreciate their special calling.
- Acquire a deep understanding of the concept of "sacred."
- Learn the value of drawing on God's strength for the work of healing.

A Frame of Orientation

I wrote about the sacredness of therapy for my graduate students many years ago. I am sure they knew that I was a Christian. In course introductions, I mentioned having gone to seminary and spending time as a pastor before becoming a therapist. I was never preachy or proselytizing in class; however, I hope that the person I was as an instructor was a good witness to the Christian faith. I also hope that it was clear to students that it is so very important for them to have a supportive and sustaining belief system as a foundation for their work as therapists.

The psychologist Erich Fromm (1941) believed that it was important for everyone to have relationships as well as an individuality identity. He also believed that we need roots as well as some sort of experience of transcendence. It seems that, in the ideal, these existential needs ought to be in balance. Figure 18.1 is a diagram of what Fromm was saying.

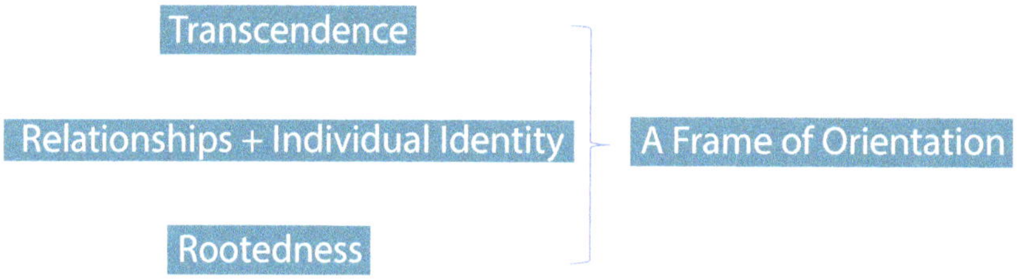

FIGURE 18.1 *Frame of Orientation*

One does not want relationships at the expense of individual identity or an identity at the expense of relationships. It seems good to have familiar surroundings (roots) but not to become entombed in the familiar. We also need to get above and beyond what we are used to and experience novelty and change. Connecting all of these existential needs, Fromm (1973) said that we need a "frame of orientation." By that he meant a belief system that connects and makes sense of the various elements of our life. For me, that frame of orientation is faith in Jesus Christ and His plan for my life.

For my students who do not share my faith, I still encourage them to have a frame of orientation that supports and sustains their work as therapists. I hope to have imparted to them that the profession of therapy is a sacred endeavor. I created the piece below ("On the Sacredness of Therapy") for that reason. I am reprinting it here from the last chapter of my book *Growing Groups: A Journey of Healing, Growth, and Transformation* (2021).

On The Sacredness of Therapy

Doctors ask, "Where does it hurt?" Historians and biographers ask, "What was it like?" Friends may ask you, "How did you manage?" But no one will ask you, "What is it like to be you?" People do not ask that question because there is too much at stake: too much responsibility for exploring the answer. What do you do with the information? People must be paid to ask that question and trained to manage the consequences of listening, deeply listening to what it is like to be another human being. It is not a bad thing that some people are paid to listen. Thank God for it. Asking the question, "What is it like to be you?" carries a great deal of responsibility. The compensation one receives from listening to a friend is in the reciprocal nature of the friendship; they will listen to you as well. The problem is that people will often protect their friends from how they truly feel. The best of friends cannot be completely unguarded. We fear that our friend may catch our anxieties and depressions and may not have the stamina to fight them off or may judge us for feeling the way we do.

Family members may fare better, at times, at getting unguarded information. But sharing comes with a price. Family members, like friends, have a great deal at stake in the relationship. The closeness and interdependence of family members calls for caution. What price may one have to pay for getting a completely honest answer to the question, "What is it like to be you?" And what if someone were genuinely willing to ask me that question? Would I even want to know the answer? Do I truly want to know who I am or how I feel? There are days when the last thing I want to do is to check in with myself. It is safer just to watch television. I suppose that what defines a professional listener or psychotherapist is the fact of being paid, as well as the required training and experience. But I do not think that most therapists are primarily interested in money. That is not why they became therapists: There are easier and more reliable ways to earn a living. I think that most therapists would also say that it is not a simple matter of wanting to help people. Therapists in training come to terms with the reality that not everyone in therapy is helped or even genuinely wants to be helped. There is something more than money or helping people that draws certain people to the work of psychotherapy. I think it is the work itself.

What is the work of psychotherapy? In his book *Re-Visioning Psychology*, James Hillman (1976/1992) points to the root meaning of words *psyche* as "soul" and *therapy* as "attendant" or "servant." People are drawn to the work of psychotherapy because of the significance of the work itself. In that work, one is invited to tend soul—one's own and another's. In that work, one is permitted to ask the question, "What is it like to be you?" Much of the education and training a therapist receives is to know how to deal with the awesome responsibility of listening to and attending to the soul of another. The existential psychologist Abraham Maslow (1971) warns us not to run away from the significance of our work by turning people into patients, focusing solely on symptoms, and hiding behind diagnoses and treatment plans. Maslow calls this "desacralizing." *Desacralizing* is robbing the soul of its depth, complexity, awe-fullness, and wonder. There are moments in therapy where it is possible to feel overwhelmed by the enormity of courage and the depths of suffering and love that exist in that place. In the presence of that sacred space, I sometimes feel the urge to take off my shoes.

What is a "sacred" space? One of the meanings of the word *sacred* is to "set apart." The work of therapy requires a setting apart, not just of a particular place and time but of a quality of openness, trust, and caring that transforms those who participate in that space. Peck (1978) saw into the work of creating a sacred space when he defined *love* as "a willingness to extend oneself for the purpose of nurturing one's own or another's spiritual growth" (p. 81). So also, the authors of *A General Theory of Love* spoke to the work of creating that space when they said, "Love is not only an end for therapy; it is also the means whereby every end is reached" (Lewis et al., 2000, p. 169). It is love, then, the attitude of self-extension, the "I-Thou" connection that Martin Buber described, that sets apart a particular time and place for the work of being open to truly knowing another and to the willingness to ask and deeply listen to the question, "What is it like to be you?"

In the section above, I was hoping to impress my students with the awesomeness and privilege of being invited to make a difference in someone's life. The question, "What is it like to be you?" ought to be the central question in the mind of the helping person. We are treating people, not just symptoms. Above everything else, the person we are helping needs to feel uniquely valued. This is why I entitled this piece "On the Sacredness of Therapy."

A few years ago, my wife and I had the opportunity to travel to Ireland. Going through security and passport control, we had our first taste of Irish friendliness. It seems that most customs officials are not especially friendly, but this red-haired Irishman was an exception. He must have looked at our landing cards and saw our professions as marriage and family therapists when he asked, "Well then, tell me, how is marriage like a bath?" We stood with our mouths open, shocked that a customs official was not only friendly but also about to tell a joke. "I don't know," I said. "How is marriage like a bath?" "Well," he replied in his wonderful Irish accent, "It's lovely at first but after a while it's not so hot." All over Ireland, we found people reaching out with warmth and friendliness. One fellow in particular talked about having a few pints of Guinness and looking for the crack. "The crack," I later discovered, was his humorous reference to one of the most intriguing pieces of Irish folklore, the "Thin Place."

The Thin Place

The idea of a "thin place" originated in ancient times when people believed that special places on Earth with exceptional or unusual natural beauty could act as portals into sacred spaces. In a March 9, 2012, article for *The New York Times*, Eric Weiner wrote:

> It's not clear who first uttered the term "thin places," but they almost certainly spoke with an Irish brogue. The ancient pagan Celts, and later, Christians, used the term to describe mesmerizing places like the wind-swept isle of Iona (now part of Scotland) or the rocky peaks of Croagh Patrick. Heaven and earth, the Celtic saying goes, are only three feet apart, but in thin places that distance is even shorter. (para. 4)

The author was referring to the ancient idea that a thin place was a transitional space where spirits could transit from this side to the other. They were places of special spiritual significance.

Reading about the Irish thin place, I am reminded of the sacred circles of the Native Americans, sometimes referred to as "medicine circles," a place of symbolic power and healing. The medicine wheel in the Bighorn National Forest in Wyoming was, historically, been a space of sacred prayer and healing.

Tom Yellowtail of the Crow Nation related a wonderful legend of the healing of "Burnt Face." The legend tells of a young boy racing through his village and carelessly falling into a fire pit. After the accident, the villagers called him "Burnt Face." The humiliated boy leaves the village and wanders in the wilderness until he finds a level place on which to build a circle of rocks. Day after day, the boy adds another rock to the circle as a prayer, but each day the boy grows weaker. One day a whirlwind appears and threatens to unearth the boy, but he holds his footing, and a great eagle appears from within the whirlwind. The eagle asks a favor of the boy. He is asked to kill a giant river otter that threatens the eagle's children. The boy summons his courage, faces, and defeats the otter. He is rewarded with an eagle feather and the promise of the eagle's protection. The boy, now a young man, returns to the village. He is no longer ashamed but proud and confident, and the villagers welcome him. That prayer wheel remains to this day; it is now called the "Fort Smith Wheel."

The significance to our study is the power of connection. Thin places, medicine circles, and vortex sites are the human soul craving locations for accessing the sacred. But the sacred, healing place is within people, not in places. There may be places on Earth where, according to some, energy fields can be sensed or places on Earth of exceptional beauty or mystery that inspire awe or even reverence. The apostle Paul reminds us in his letter to the church in Rome that "since the creation of the world God's invisible qualities—his eternal power and divine nature—have been clearly seen, being understood from what has been made" (Romans 1:20). So it is not surprising that people can sense the presence of the nearness of the sacred. But that nearness is not found in places on Earth but by the quiet calling within one's own heart.

When a group of people are truly open to each other, working together, caring for each other, the warmth, acceptance, and sense of connection is miraculous. In my mind, the openness and connection they experience in that place of caring is a "thin place" or a "healing circle." "For where two or three gather in my name, there am I with them" (Matthew 18:20). This is where deep healing can take place.

The Irish think of a thin place as permeable space. I think of it the church's vulnerable space: the stage M. Scott Peck (1998) described in his book *A Different Drum* as "emptiness." The emptiness that Peck referred to is the product of the courage and faith of a group to open their hearts without judgement or agenda and deeply care about one another. A heart that is empty is able to be filled. It is not, of course, necessary to empty yourself of your thoughts, feelings, values, and beliefs, only of your ego's agenda. You empty yourself so that you are able to hear from the Holy Spirit. He knows best what you need, what the church needs, and how to bring about healing and growth.

Learning to Die

The central task of the Christian life is to learn how to die. Early in life we come to terms with the limitations of our divinity. What do I mean by that? Scripture tells us that we were created to be children of God. We can imagine all kinds of reasons why God might want children, but Scripture does not have a great deal to tell us about that. What we do know is that we were created in God's image for fellowship with Him. To be created in God's image is, at once, the most amazing fact of creation and the most problematic.

In Genesis 1:28 we read that "God blessed them, and God *said* (emphasis added) to them." God spoke creation into existence but He spoke directly *to* us. The image of God is the promise of relationship. It is the ability to respond. That ability is good news, and other news. The good news is that we can relate to God. We are response-able. The other news is that we are responsible for our response-ability.

The relationship God is offering is built on His love. Our responsibility is to love Him in return. And because God loves the world, so must we. This means that we must learn how to die to whatever is in the way of our ability to love. Learning to love well means learning to die. Jesus told us to carry our cross daily. He also said that His yoke is easy and His burden is light. I do not completely agree. No doubt, the yoke Jesus was referring to is not the yoke of the Jewish law. That yoke is impossible to bear. Jesus is contrasting His yoke with that. His yoke is easy in the sense that loving one another ought to be easy. And maybe it should be, but it is hard for me and probably for others. The problem is the ego.

One's ego does not die easily, and it shouldn't. Psychologists use the term "ego" to describe our ability to relate competently to the outer world. We develop "ego strengths" as we mature. We learn how to behave socially, we acquire abilities and experiences, and we achieve a sense of identity and, hopefully, a sense of purpose and direction in life. In his book *Modern Man in Search of a Soul*, Carl Jung (1933) describes the "arc of life." Theoretically, the top of that arc, according to Jung, ought to be the zenith of the ego's adaption to the outer world. After midlife, having acquired sufficient ego strengths, the ego can then look inward toward developing one's Self. What Jung referred to as the "Self," Christians could call "spirit." Jung's term *individuation* is the process of becoming a fully functioning Self. Similarly, *sanctification* is the process of becoming a mature spirit, set apart for God's use. Whether one refers to individuation or sanctification, the journey of spiritual growth requires learning to let go of the demands and habits of one's ego.

When people are fortunate enough to have the time and resources to look inward, they find that particularization of God's Spirit that has been assigned to them: their own spirit. Our spirit is intimately connected to God's Sprit. "For in Him we live and move and have our being" (Acts 17:28). His Spirit is the Holy Spirit from whom we receive courage, comfort, wisdom, and direction. There is no separation between our spirit and the Spirit of God.

The Heart of Christian Psychology

The heart of Christian psychology is knowing the heart of Christ. Many religions share disciplines and concepts that are similar to the disciplines and concepts of Christianity. In fact, learning about other spiritual walks can sometimes amplify and confirm Christian truths. But it is knowing Jesus Christ, in a personal and intimate relationship, that is the center of Christian psychology.

No other approach to psychology is as powerfully transformative as walking daily with Jesus. And all other approaches to psychology are found, in one form or another, in the pages of Scripture. The New Testament confirms your existential value. It directs you to explore and confess your failures, receive forgiveness, and learn the language of faith. The apostles remind us of the importance of our words, of our fellowship together, and how to be in community with others and with our spouses and children. We are invited to appreciate the role of the Holy Spirit to bring us guidance and peace and that God is at work daily, helping us to grow, to get over bad habits, and to experience a deep sense of being loved. In other words, all of the languages of psychotherapy—existential, psychodynamic, cognitive behavioral, and systemic—are mirrored in the pages of Scripture. The fifth psychological language, that of physical and biological healing, are accessed through prayer. Physicians are servants of the Great Physician. Prayer is able to connect the two so that, guided by God, physicians are able to prescribe the best path toward healing.

There *is* such a thing as a Christian psychology. It is existential, person-centered, systemic, cognitive and behavioral, and powerfully psychodynamic in providing the incentive and courage to look honestly at who we are and how we are. These fundamental approaches to psychological healing are all reflected and activated in the Gospel. Jesus, the teacher, and the Holy Spirit, the counselor and guide, can be relied upon for every form of healing work. What makes psychology Christian is Christ's presence in the heart of the therapist and the willingness of a wounded person to be open to Christ's touch.

Questions for Review, Reflection, and Discussion

1. How do you experience the idea of the "sacred" in your life?
2. Have you had a transcendent "peak" experience?
3. What do you believe absolutely?
4. Why do you want to live?
5. Do you feel "called"?
6. How would you describe a "calling"?
7. What values guide your life?
8. Recall a moment when you felt a deep sense of joy. Can you describe it? What made that moment memorable?
9. How would you like to be remembered?

Appendix

Speaking of Psychology: You Know More Than You Think

Mark the terms with

1. If you can define it
2. If you think you know what it means
3. Have no idea

_____ Ego
_____ Super Ego
_____ Id
_____ Denial
_____ Repression
_____ Suppression
_____ Projection
_____ Object Permanence
_____ Transitional Object
_____ Regression
_____ Schema
_____ Displacement
_____ Inferiority Complex
_____ Manic
_____ Depressive

_____ Anxiety
_____ Transference
_____ Attachment
_____ Neurotic
_____ Psychotic
_____ Personality Disorder
_____ Adjustment Disorder
_____ Borderline
_____ Narcissism
_____ Internal Boundaries
_____ External Boundaries
_____ Existentialism
_____ Positive Reinforcement
_____ Negative Reinforcement

How did you do?

Family Rules Exercise

A *family rule* is an explicit (overt, verbalized) or implicit (covert, nonverbalized) directive regarding expectations of behaviors, emotions, attitudes, and even thoughts and opinions. Family rules along with family rituals (e.g., celebrating special events and occasions) and family myths (e.g., our family is ...) combine to inform our inner scripts or narratives: the stories we tell ourselves about who we are and what is correct and expected. The family rules we learn growing up can continue to influence every aspect of our life: morality, relationships, self-care, health, spirituality, sexuality, and so forth. A good way to get in touch with some of these family rules is to write out all of the rules that you are aware of (many of them were unspoken). Write out Dad's rules and Mom's rules. Notice if the rules are similar or competitive. What rules have you kept over the years? What rules have you reacted against or modified? What rules have you made for yourself? Here are some typical categories to explore: spending money, school grades, expressing feelings, health issues, religious involvement, acceptable dinner conversation, neatness, politics, responsibilities, and so on. You or your clients may have grown up not knowing their father or mother. In some cases, a rule may be "Don't expect me to be in your life." In cases where the absence was unavoidable, a rule might be "Don't expect life to be fair." You get the idea. Write out as many of these spoken and unspoken rules as you can think of. This will take a while. Keep a notebook handy as you recall more examples. You should end up with three or four pages, at least.

Family Roles Exercise

Family members typically take on specific roles within a family. Functional roles create order, consistency, and distribute responsibilities among family members. In a healthy marriage, partners love, support, and share the workload equally. The chief roles of parents are to nurture, train, and safeguard children. The role of a child is to grow and learn to be a mature adult. A healthy family system supports the needs of the family as well as the individual members. An unhealthy family system is characterized by the misuse or abuse of power where individual roles function to avoid or manage threats and to maintain stability at the expense of individual growth and well-being. Here are some good questions to ask yourself or your clients about the role(s) they may have played in their family of origin:

- How was power distributed in your family? Who had what kind of power, and how was it used?
- What were some of the roles people played in your family?
- Were the family roles rigid or flexible?
- What role might you have played in your family as a child?
- Do you still function in a familiar role in your family of origin or in your present relationships?

Typical Roles for Kids: Hero, little parent, victim, Dad's buddy, family counselor, genius, scapegoat, underachiever, addict, surrogate spouse, lost child, little princess, rebel, perfect one, mommy's helper, religious one, clown, heroine, sickly one, family referee, star, athlete, peacemaker, troublemaker, martyr, little sunshine, perfectionist, caretaker, criminal, loser, beauty queen, drama queen, actor, entitled one.

Understanding and Helping Families

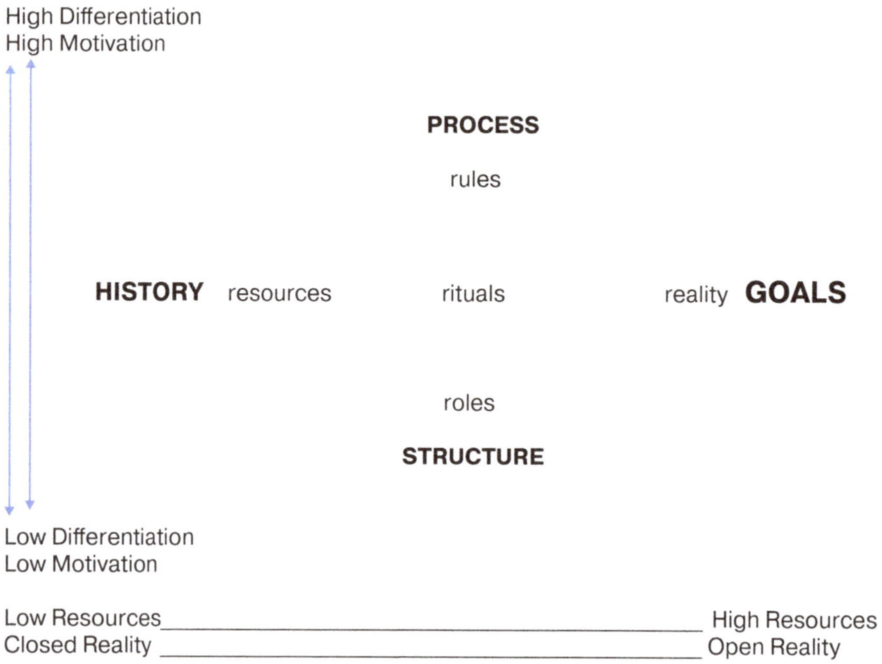

Families are like noses. They are all alike and they are all different. A typical family system is comprised of family rules: rules governing conduct, language, what should be believed, what should or should not be thought, and what should be felt or not felt. Family members have roles: roles governing who is supposed to function in a particular way. Families have rituals: enacted traditions that facilitate connection and consistency. *Process*, consisting mainly of rules, governs how families convey information. *Structure*, consisting mainly of roles, governs behavior: who does what or acts a certain way in the family. *History* identifies the *resources* of traditions, beliefs, and myths as well as the resources of caring people and financial adequacy. *Goals* describe what is important to a family and where the family is headed. The family may have an "open reality," describing a willingness to change, grow, and adapt, or a "closed reality," describing a family that is resistant to change and prefers homeostasis.

Therapeutic Approaches

A family systems therapist selects from a variety of treatment approaches and chooses the one that best fits the family system. If the family has a high level of differentiation (mature functioning), the therapist may use a process-oriented "experiential" or "narrative" approach to improve family communication. A low level of differentiation indicates that a family is stuck with rigid roles and rules. The therapist may use a "structural" or "strategic" approach to unbalance the homeostasis to create change. If a family has few financial resources, the therapist will use a brief solution-focused approach. All therapeutic approaches will also use some elements of cognitive and behavioral therapy to provide insight and behavioral change.

Guidelines for Good Communication

I have condensed the most important steps to good communication to these seven guidelines. The goal is to reduce defensiveness by taking turns and practicing openness in both speaking and listening.

Speaker	Listener
1. **Use good timing and discretion.** 2. **Talk about yourself (your own feelings).** 3. **Stay current, and be brief.**	4. **Give feedback.** 5. **Wait your turn to be the speaker.**
Goal: to be vulnerable, to be open, and to trust that your feelings and concerns are being heard and accepted	**Goal:** to open your heart, to truly hear what your speaker is saying, and to enable your speaker to feel heard
Briefly state the context. For example: When you ... When this happens ... Sometimes I feel ...	**Listen with your heart.** Try to validate, comfort, and reassure. Be open-hearted, or at least try to be curious and not competitive.
Identify your feelings. For example: I feel angry. I feel hurt. I feel scared.	**Give Feedback** Feedback is about what you hear, not what you think. Think about creating an **ARC** between you and your speaker. **A:** Affirm or acknowledge. **R:** Repeat back or reflect. **C:** Clarify/be curious.

6. **Take a time out.**
When things get too frustrating and you need time to cool down, take a time-out no less than 20 minutes or more than 48 hours or some other agreed-upon time.

7. **Have a postmortem.**
Take time to have a discussion after your time-out to explore themes and issues that got triggered.

Taking Turns

Making the transition from one speaker to another can be tricky. It feels unfamiliar and a little too formal to take turns, but it is very important to know who is doing what. You are trying to help each other to remember the rules, not to get competitive, and to remember that *when you're the listener, you're not the speaker.* The best way to do this, if you are the speaker, is to say, "Thanks for listening," "I'm done," or something similar that lets the listener know that they can now take a turn. If you are the listener, politely ask if your speaker feels heard and if you can take your turn being the speaker.

Don'ts for the Speaker	Don'ts for the Listener
Tax the listener with too much info.	Square the record, justify, or defend.
Overuse examples and illustrations.	Grab the speaker role.

Don'ts for the Speaker	Don'ts for the Listener
Hog the speaker role.	Resist letting information in.
Use the speaker role as an opportunity to berate the listener.	Be technically correct with no heart.
Go on and on without pausing.	Require agreement.
	Have agendas in listening responses.

The Heart of the Work: The Goals and Breadth of Psychotherapy

The Goals of Therapy

For the mind: Process = *Integration* (the brain's ability to create new internal narratives that more successfully integrate difficult emotions with conscious and adaptive cognitions)

Goal = *Differentiation* (from Murray Bowen, the ability to differentiate thoughts and feelings, enabling greater freedom to make independent choices)

Fruit = **Maturity and freedom to choose**

For the heart: Process = *Involvement* (taking risks, reaching out, practicing vulnerability)

From M. Scott Peck's (1978) *The Road Less Traveled*, this is "the willingness to extend oneself."

Goal = *Individuation* (from Carl Jung, the ability to integrate one's shadow, masculine and feminine energy, psychological complexes, and discover one's true path and Self)

Fruit = **Self-acceptance and freedom to love**

For the soul: Process = *Reflection* (from Siegel, cultivating mindfulness, practicing growth and conscious awareness, and reaching toward the capacity for "vision logic")

Goal = *Self-actualization* (from Maslow, resolving biological and relational needs, integrating "being" and "doing," cultivating spiritual qualities, beauty and truth)

Fruit = **The joy of Being**

The Breadth of Therapy

Human nature exists in the tension of biology (necessity) and spirit (possibility). Psyche (soul) encompasses and relates biology to spirit and manages the tension and tasks of being alive. Psychology assists people physically, emotionally, relationally, and spiritually to be fully alive. Psyche and psychology span a continuum between measurement and metaphor. From Ken Wilbur's (2000) *Integral Psychology*:

The Self as **Biological**	The Self as **Relational**	The Self as **Spiritual**
Concern for the organism	Concern for connection to self/others	Concern for meaning/value
An interest in truth	An interest in goodness	An interest in beauty
The domain of "its"	The domain of "we"	The domain of "I"
Science	*Morals*	*Creativity*

The Heart of Therapy

From Lewis et al. (2000), Cozolino (2010), Kottler (2010), and Siegel (2007), the heart of therapy is the therapist ... your traits, talents, training, your calling, your sense of purpose and Self.

From Covey's (2004) *The 8th Habit*, your experience, discipline, conscience, vision, and passion.

From Buckley (2021), when you arere doing the right work, the energy for the work is in the work.

BBPI: The Buckley Burnout Prevention Inventory

Please check only the items that are true for you.

1. _____ I don't mind being bored or wasting time once in a while.
2. _____ I read for fun, not just for work.
3. _____ I exercise regularly.
4. _____ I frequently watch the golf channel (or other mindless TV).
5. _____ I don't feel guilty when I take a nap.
6. _____ I sometimes catch myself daydreaming.
7. _____ I let my inner child out to play.
8. _____ I like to hang out with friends.
9. _____ I have chosen the right career.
10. _____ I take risks and try new things.
11. _____ I enjoy taking time during the day to breathe and relax.
12. _____ I can laugh at myself.
13. _____ I can help people but I can't do their work for them.
14. _____ I usually know when to let go.
15. _____ I seldom repress the urge to yodel (or act silly).
16. _____ I am able to access spiritual resources.
17. _____ I try to be open and accepting of life.
18. _____ I am able to accept and forgive myself.
19. _____ I am able to accept and forgive others.
20. _____ I often daydream about snorkeling in Tahiti (or other fun things).
21. _____ I like seeing animal shapes in the clouds.
22. _____ I try hard to get enough rest and to eat properly.
23. _____ I have someone with whom I can be real.
24. _____ I can usually see things positively.
25. _____ I try to bring beauty into my life.
26. _____ I like to get out into nature.

If you checked ...

under 6 items ... you should seek therapy.

7–12 items ... you are about average.

13–20 items ... you are doing great.

Over 20 items ... you should teach stress-management workshops.

References

Adler, A. (1979). *Superiority and social interest*. Norton.

Ansbacher, H. L. (1956). *The individual psychology of Alfred Adler, a systematic presentation in selections of his writings*. Harper & Row.

American Psychiatric Association. (2013). *Diagnostic and statistical manual of mental disorders* (5th ed.).

Anderson, R. S. (1975). *Historical transcendence and the reality of God: A Christological critique*. Eerdmans.

Anderson, R. S. (1976). *Theology of personhood* [Lecture]. Fuller Theological Seminary, Pasadena, CA.

Anderson, R. S. (1976). *On being human: A theological paradigm of personhood* [Lecture]. Fuller Seminary.

Arraj, T. (2015). *A Jungian analyst talks about psychological types: A visit with John Beebe* [Video]. YouTube. https://www.youtube.com/watch?v=770FrOmZbuU

Aslan, R. (2017). *God: A human history*. Random House.

Barnhouse, D. G. (1965). *The invisible war*. Zondervan.

Barth, K. (1948). *Church dogmatics* (Vol. 3). Bloomsbury.

Becker, E. (1973). *The denial of death*. Free Press.

Beebe, J. (2002). *Terror, violence and the impulse to destroy*. Daimon Verlag.

Beebe, J. (2016). *Energies and patterns in psychological type: The reservoir of consciousness*. Routledge.

Berne, E. (1961). *Transactional analysis in psychotherapy: A systematic individual and social psychiatry*. Grove Press.

Berne, E. (1967). *Games people play*. Ballantine Books.

Bowen, M. (1985). *Family therapy in clinical practice*. Jason Aronson.

Bowlby, J. (1969). *Attachment and loss. Vol. 1: Attachment*. New York: Basic Books.

Bowlby, J. (1973). *Attachment and loss. Vol. 2: Separation: Anxiety and anger*. New York: Basic Books.

Bowlby, J. (I980). *Attachment and loss. Vol. 3: Loss: Sadness and depression*. New York: Basic Books.

Bradshaw, J. (1988). *Healing the shame that binds you*. Health Communications.

Brown, B. (2014, June). *The power of vulnerability* [Video]. TED Conferences. https://www.ted.com/talks/brene_brown_the_power_of_vulnerability?language=en

Brown, C. G. (2012, February 16). Should scientists test prayer? Why prayer should be studied empirically. *Psychology Today*. https://www.psychologytoday.com/us/blog/testing-prayer/201202/should-scientists-test-prayer

Buckley, G. (2021). *Growing groups: A journey of healing, growth, and renewal*. Cognella Academic Publishing.

Burns, D. D. (1980). *Feeling good: The new mood therapy*. William Morrow & Co.

Burns, D. D. (1989). *The feeling good handbook*. William Morrow & Co.

BuzzFeedVideo. (2015, December 9). *I jumped off the Golden Gate Bridge* [Video]. YouTube. https://www.youtube.com/watch?v=WcSUs9iZv-g

Calvin, J. (1975). *Calvin: Institutes of the Christian religion* (J. T. McNeill, Ed.). The Westminster Press. (Original work published 1536)

Centers for Disease Control and Prevention. (2020). *Symptoms of depression among adults: United States, 2019* (Report No. 379). https://www.cdc.gov/nchs/products/databriefs/db379.htm

Christensen, A. (2010). A unified protocol for couple therapy. In K. Hahlweg, M. Grawe-Gerber, & D. H. Baucom (Eds.), *Enhancing couples: The shape of couple therapy to come* (pp. 33–46). Hogrefe Publishing.

Collins, F. S. (2007). *Language of God: A scientist presents evidence for belief.* Free Press.

Collins, G. R. (1976). *How to be a people helper.* Vision House.

Covey, S. (2005). *The 8th habit.* Free Press.

Cozolino, L. (2004). *The making of a therapist.* W. W. Norton & Co.

Cozolino, L. (2010). *The neuroscience of psychotherapy.* W. W. Norton & Co.

Cummings, D. (2018, July 31). What is existential freedom? *Areo Magazine.* https://areomagazine.com/2018/07/31/what-is-existential-freedom

Dessen, S. (2008). *Just listen.* Puffin Books.

Dunn, J. D. G. (1975). *Jesus and the spirit: A study of the religious and charismatic experience of Jesus and the first Christians as reflected in the New Testament.* Westminster Press.

Estés, C. P. (2003). Explaining evil. In J. Beebe (Ed.), *Terror, violence and the impulse to destroy: Perspectives from analytical psychology* (pp. x–x). Daimon Verlag.

Ellis, A., Harper R. (1997). *A guide to rational living.* Wilshire Book Co. (Original work published 1961)

Emmons, R. A. (2000). Is spirituality an intelligence? Motivation, cognition, and the psychology of ultimate concern. *The International Journal for the Psychology of Religion, 10*(1), 3–26. https://doi.org/10.1207/S15327582IJPR1001_2

Feist, J., Feist, G., & Roberts, T-A. (2017). *Theories of personality* (9th ed.). McGraw-Hill Education.

Frankl, V. E. (1959). *Man's search for meaning.* Beacon Press.

Freed, A. M., & Faul-Jansen, R. (1976). *T.A. for teens and other important people.* Jalmar Pr.

Fromm, E. (1941). *Escape from freedom.* Farrar & Rinehart.

Fromm, E. (1964). *The heart of man: Its genius for good and evil.* Harper & Row.

Fromm, E. (1973). *The anatomy of human destructiveness.* Open Road Media.

Fromm, E. (2013). *The art of loving.* Open Road Media. (Original work published 1956)

Gingerich, O. (2006). *God's universe.* Harvard University Press.

Harbaugh, G. L. (1990). *God's gifted people: Discovering your personality as a gift.* Augsburg Books.

Harlow, H. F., Dodsworth, R. O., & Harlow, M. K. (1965, July). Total social isolation in monkeys. *Proceedings of the National Academy of Sciences of the U.S.A., 54*(1), 90–97. doi: 10.1073/pnas.54.1.90

Herbert, G. (1983). Love. In A. Allison (Ed.), *The Norton anthology of poetry* (3rd ed.; p. 141). W. W. Norton & Co.

Hendrix, H. (1988). *Getting the love you want: A guide for couples.* Henry Holt & Co.

Hillman, J. (1992). *Re-visioning psychology.* New York: Harper Perennial. (Original work published 1976)

Hillman, J. (1996). *The soul's code: In search of character and calling.* Grand Central Publishing.

Hillsong United. (2017). *So will I.* Hillsong Music, Sparrow Records.

Holt-Lunstad, J., Smith, T. B., & Layton, J. B. (2010, July 27). Social relationships and mortality risk: A meta-analytic review. *PLOS Medicine, 7*(7): e1000316. https://doi.org/10.1371/journal.pmed.1000316

Horney, K. (1972). *Our inner conflicts.* Norton.

Hunziker, M. (2016). *Depth typology: C. G. Jung, Isabel Myers, John Beebe and the guide map to becoming who we are.* Write Way Publishing Co.

Ingram, B. L. (2006). *Clinical case formulations: Matching the integrative treatment plan to the client.* Wiley.

James, M. (1973). *Born to love: Transactional analysis in the church.* Addison-Wesley.

James, M. (1974). *Transactional analysis for moms and dads.* Addison-Wesley.

James, M., & Jongeward, D. (1972). *Born to win: Transactional analysis with gestalt experiments.* Da Capo Press.

Jung, C. G. (1921). *Psychological types.* Rascher Verlag.

Jung, C. G. (1933). *Modern man in search of a soul.* Harcourt, Brace.

Jung, C. G. (1971). *Collected works of C. G. Jung. Volume 6: Psychological types.* Princeton University Press.

Jung, C. G. (1977). *The collected works of C. G. Jung. Volume 18: The symbolic life: Miscellaneous writings.* Princeton University Press.

Keirsey, D. (1998). *Please understand me II: Temperament, character, intelligence.* Prometheus Nemesis.

Kernberg, O. F. (1975). *Borderline conditions and pathological narcissism.* Jason Aronson.

Kierkegaard, S. (1844). *The concept of dread.* Bianco Luno.

Kierkegaard, S. (1941). *The sickness unto death* (Walter Lowrie, Trans.). Princeton University Press. (Original work published 1849)

Klein, M. (2002). Love, guilt and reparation: And other works 1921–1945. In *The writings of Melanie Klein, Volume 1.* Free Press.

Kohut, H. (1977). *The restoration of the self.* University of Chicago Press.

Kottler, J. (2010). *On being a therapist* (4th ed.). Jossey-Bass.

Leonard, L. S. (1985). *The wounded woman: Healing the father-daughter relationship.* Shambhala.

Lewis, C. S. (1940). Christianity and culture. *Theology, 40*(237), 166–179. https://doi.org/10.1177/0040571X4004023702

Lewis, C. S. (2014). *The screwtape letters.* Project Gutenberg. https://gutenberg.ca/ebooks/lewiscs-screwtape-letters/lewiscs-screwtapeletters-00-h.html (Original work published 1942)

Lewis, T., Amini, F., & Lannon, R. (2000). *A general theory of love.* Random House.

Lexico. (n.d.-a). Personality. In *Lexico.com dictionary.* Retrieved November 5, 2021, from https://www.lexico.com/definition/personality

Lexico. (n.d.-b). Sweet spot. In *Lexico.com dictionary.* Retrieved November 5, 2021, from https://www.lexico.com/definition/sweet_spot

Luther, M. (1529). *A mighty fortress is our God* [song].

Malony, H. N. (1983). *Wholeness and holiness: Readings in the psychology/theology of mental health.* Baker Publishing Group.

Maslow, A. (1954). *Motivation and personality.* Harper and Row.

Maslow, A. (1971). *The farther reaches of human nature.* Viking.

May, R. (1975). *The courage to create.* Norton.

McAdams, D. P. (1993). *The stories we live by: Personal myths and the making of the self.* William Morrow & Co.

Mchugh, A. S. (2017). *Introverts in the church: Finding our place in an extroverted culture.* IVP Books.

Melville, H. (2001). *Moby-Dick; or the whale.* Project Gutenberg. https://marist.libanswers.com/faq/336133 (Original work published 1851)

Mikulincer, M., & Goodman, G. S. (Eds.). (2006). *Dynamics of romantic love: Attachment, caregiving, and sex.* The Guilford Press.

Miller, A. (1979). *The drama of the gifted child.* Basic Books.

Miller, W. R. (Ed.). (1999). *Integrating spirituality into treatment: Resources for practitioners.* American Psychological Association.

Murthy, V. (2020). *Together: The healing power of human connection in a sometimes lonely world.* Harper Wave.

Nardi, D. (2011). Neuroscience of personality: *Brain savvy insights for all types of people.* Radiance House.

Nee, W. (1957). *Sit, walk, stand.* Gospel Literature Service.

O'Donohue, J. (2003). *Beauty: The invisible embrace.* Harper Perennial.

Office for National Statistics. (2017, September 27). *People who were abused as children are more likely to be abused as an adult.* https://www.ons.gov.uk/peoplepopulationandcommunity/crimeandjustice/articles/peoplewhowereabusedaschildrenaremorelikelytobeabusedasanadult/2017-09-27

Oswald, R. M., & Kroeger, O. (1988). *Personality type and religious leadership.* Rowman & Littlefield.

Peale, N. V. (1952). *The power of positive thinking.* Prentice Hall.

Peck, M. S. (1978). *The road less traveled: A new psychology of love, traditional values and spiritual growth.* Simon and Schuster.

Peck, M. S. (1983). *People of the lie: The hope for healing human evil.* Simon and Schuster.

Peck, M. S. (1998). *A different drum: Community making and peace.* Simon and Schuster.

Peterson, J. (2019, June 8). *Who dares say he believes in God?* [Video]. YouTube. https://www.youtube.com/watch?v=MnUfXYGtT5Q

Protestant Episcopal Church. (1842). *The book of common prayer.* H & S Raynor.

The Righteous Brothers. (1966). (You're my) soul and inspiration [Song]. *Soul and inspiration.* Sony/ATV Music Publishing.

Rogers, C. (1951). *Client-centered therapy.* Houghton Mifflin.

Ross, H. (2015). *A matter of days: Resolving a creation controversy.* RTB Press.

Rothschild, B. (2000). *The body remembers: The psychophysiology of trauma and trauma treatment.* W. W. Norton & Co.

Siegel, D. (1999). *The developing mind: How relationships and the brain interact to shape who we are.* The Guilford Press.

Siegel, D. (2007). *The mindful brain: Reflection and attunement in the cultivation of well-being.* W. W. Norton & Co.

Schuller, R. H. (1988). *Living positively one day at a time.* Berkley.

Sockol, L. (2006). *The man who mistook a whale for pure evil: A diagnostic assessment of Captain Ahab* [Student paper]. Serendip. https://serendipstudio.org/sci_cult/courses/emotion/web2/lsockol.html

Vance, E. (2016, November 23). Unlocking the healing power of you. *National Geographic.* https://www.nationalgeographic.com/magazine/article/healing-science-belief-placebo

Venkatakrishnan, H. (2018). *Mental health—Neurosis vs psychosis.* Medindia. https://www.medindia.net/patients/patientinfo/mental-health-neurosis-vs-psychosis.htm

Vogler, C. (2007). *The writer's journey: Mythic structure for writers* (3rd ed.). Michael Wiese Productions.

Wagner, P. (1979). *Your spiritual gifts can help your church grow.* Gospel Light Publications.

Warren, R. (2012). *The purpose driven life: What on Earth am I here for?* Zondervan.

Weiner, E. (2012, March 9). Where heaven and Earth come closer. *The New York Times.* https://www.nytimes.com/2012/03/11/travel/thin-places-where-we-are-jolted-out-of-old-ways-of-seeing-the-world.html

Wilber, K. (2000). *Integral psychology: Consciousness, spirit, psychology, therapy.* Shambhala.

Williamson, M. (1992). *A return to love: Reflections on the principles of a course on miracles.* HarperCollins.

Woolley, S. R., & Johnson, S. M. (2005). Creating secure connections: Emotionally focused couples therapy. In J. L. Lebow (Ed.), *Handbook of clinical family therapy* (pp. 384–405). John Wiley & Sons.

Index

A

Actualizing tendency, 14
Adler, A., 13, 90
Affirming, 145–146
Ainsworth, M., 18, 69–70
American Nurses Credentialing Center, 82
Anderson, R., 12, 43, 66
Anxiety, 74–75
  existential, 76–77
Art of Loving (Fromm), 67
Aslan, R., 130
Attachment (Bowlby), 18, 69
Autonomy *vs.* shame and doubt, 15

B

Barnhouse, D., 96
Barth, K., 66
Beck, A., 72
Becker, E., 47, 49, 91
Beebe, J., 128
Being human, 63–70
  fully human, 66–68
  living spirit, 66
  psyche, 68–69
  relatedness, 69–70
Berne, E., 114–115
The Body Remembers (Rothschild), 27
Borderline Conditions and Pathological Narcissism (Kernberg), 87
Born To Win (James and Jongeward), 115
Bowen, M., 75
Bowlby, J., 18, 69–70
Bradshaw, J., 77, 90
Brown, B., 93
Brown, G., 59
Buckley Burnout Prevention Inventory (BBPI), 179

C

Calling, gifts and, 40–41, 127–128
Calvin, J., 64, 97
Centers for Disease Control and Prevention (CDC), 72
Christenson, A., 59
Christian counseling, 39, 61
Christian psychology, 168–169
Church Dogmatics (Barth), 66
Church hurts, 149–154
  at church, 152–153
  fathers, 151–152
  healing work of, 153–154
  maturity, 150
  perspective, 150–151
Clarifying, 146
Classical behavioral conditioning, 17
Classical conditioning, 17
Client-centered therapy, 6
Clinical Case Formulations (Ingram), 36, 59
Cognitive and behavioral languages, 6–7
Cognitive behavioral therapy (CBT), 7, 17
Cognitive therapy for depression, 72–73
Collins, F., 2
Community and connection
  corrective emotional experience, 113–114
  costs of isolation, 111–112
  life groups, 112–113
  mean people, 116
  parent, adult, child (PAC) model, 114–116
  psychology of, 109–117
  value of, 110–111
Concept of Dread (Kierkegaard), 48, 76
Corrective emotional experience, 113–114
Counseling
  attunement, 145
  by laypersons, 142
  joining, 145–146
  limitations to lay, 142
  listening, 144–145
  pastoral, 142–143
  practice, 146
  preparation, 144
  skills, 144–146
  spiritual gifts, 143–144

Couple relationships
kinds of pain, 103–104
limbic regulation, 101–102
limbic resonance, 100–101
limbic revision, 102
psychology of, 99–106
reenactment, 104–106
stretching, 102–103
two ways to die, 104
Courage to Create (May), 49, 92
Covey, S., 17
Cozolino, L., 28–29
Crockett, D., 46

D

Damascus, 2
Defense mechanisms, 49–53
Denial, 45–53
bad kind, 47
defense mechanisms, 49–53
existential, 47–48
good kind, 46
three paths, 48–49
Denial of Death (Becker), 47, 49
Depression, 72
cognitive therapy for, 72–73
existential therapy for, 73–74
Desacralization, 39
The Developing Mind (Siegel), 18, 69
Diagnostic and Statistical Manuel of Mental Illness (DSM), 57–58
Dissociation, 29
Dissociative identity disorder (DID), 30

E

Egypt, 7
The 8h Habit (Covey), 17
Ellis, A., 17, 43
Emmons, R. A., 59
Emotion, 25–28
Empirical languages, 57
Enhancing Couples (Christenson), 59
Erikson, E., 14–15, 90, 127
Escape from Freedom (Fromm), 87
Escape, mechanics of, 45–53
Evil, 86
Existential anxiety, 48–49, 76–77
Existential denial, 47–48
Existential therapy, 48
for depression, 73–74
Extroversion, sensing, feeling, and judging (ESFJ), 126

F

Fallen world, 90–92
Families
roles exercise, 173
rules exercise, 172
systems, 13
understanding and helping, 174
Family Therapy in Clinical Practice (Bowen), 75
Fear, 86–87
Feeling Good (Beck), 72
Feelings, 24–25
Fight defenses, 52
Flashback, described, 27
Flight defenses, 52
Forgiveness, 32
Freud, S., 12–14, 49, 57
From Effectiveness to Greatness (Covey), 17
Fromm, E., 67, 86, 94, 163–164
Functional magnetic resonance imaging (fMRI), 13

G

Games People Play (Berne), 115
General Theory of Love (Lewis), 67, 100
Generativity *vs.* stagnation, 15
Gifts, 120
calling and, 40–41, 127–128
spiritual, 125–126
temperament and, 126–127
Gingerich, O., 2
Gladwell, M., 110
God: A Human History (Aslan), 130
God's Universe (Gingerich), 2
Good communication, guidelines, 175–176
Greece, 7

H

Harbaugh, G., 127
Healing, 77–78
Healing, holding, and helping, 32–34
Healing Power of Human Connection in a Sometimes Lonely World (Murthy), 67
Healing the Shame that Binds You (Bradshaw), 77
Helping professions, 79–84
licensed clinical psychologists, 81–82
licensed clinical social worker (LCSW), 81
marriage and family therapist (MFT), 81
needs, 80
physicians, 84
psychiatric nurse, 82
psychiatrists, 82–84
Herbert, G., 42
Hillman, J., 41

Historical Transcendence and the Reality of God (Anderson), 12
Horney, K., 90
Human development, stages, 15–17
Humanism, 6
Humanistic and existential languages, 6
Humanistic-existential therapy, 6
Humanistic/human potential movement, 6
Hunziker, M., 128
Hypothalamic-pituitary-adrenal (HPA), 112

I

Identity *vs.* role confusion, 15
Individuation, 14
Industry *vs.* inferiority, 15
Ingram, B., 36, 59
Initiative *vs.* guilt, 15
Institutes of the Christian Religion (Calvin), 64
Integrity *vs.* despair, 15
Interpretation of Dreams (Freud), 12
Intimacy *vs.* isolation, 15
Invisible War (Barnhouse), 96
ISTP (introverted, sensing, thinking, and perceptive temperament), 126

J

James, M., 115
Jongeward, D., 115
Jung, C., 14–15, 65–67, 123

K

Keirsey, D., 126, 128
Kenyon, E. W., 43
Kernberg, O. F., 87
Kierkegaard, S., 19, 48, 75, 92
Kinds of pain, 103–104
Klein, M., 70
Kottler, J., 28
Kroeger, O., 127

L

Laity, 144
The Language of God (Collins), 2
Languages
  cognitive and behavioral, 6–7
  empirical, 57
  humanistic and existential, 6
  medical and biological, 7
  metaphorical, 57
  psychodynamic, 6
  psychological, 57–58
  systemic, 7
Lay counseling, 142
Lewis, C. S., 3, 67, 86, 96
Licensed clinical psychologists, 81–82
Licensed clinical social worker (LCSW), 81
Life groups, 112–113
Limbic regulation, 101–102
Limbic resonance, 100–101
Limbic revision, 102
Living Positively One Day at a Time (Schuller), 22
Living spirit, 66
Loss (Bowlby), 69
Luther, M., 97

M

The Making of a Therapist (Cozolino), 29
Malony, H. N., 84
Marriage and family therapist (MFT), 81
Maslow, A., 6, 16, 37, 40, 65, 165
Maturity, 150
May, R., 49, 76, 92
MBTI. *See* Myers-Briggs type indicator (MBTI)
MBTI explained, 123–124
McAdams, D., 69
McHugh, A., 127
Mean people, 116
Mechanics of escape, 45–53
Medical and biological languages, 7
Melville, H., 87
Memory, 25–28
Metaphorical languages, 57
Mighty Fortress Is Our God (Luther), 97
Mindful Brain (Siegel), 73, 145
Misplaced worship, 132–133
Modern Man in Search of a Soul (Jung), 65–66, 168
Murthy, V., 16, 67–68, 109
Myers-Briggs type indicator (MBTI), 120
Myers, J., 22

N

Nardi, D., 128
Needs, 80
Nee, W., 42
Neural integration, 26, 29
The Neuroscience of Psychotherapy (Cozolino), 28
Neurosis, 88–89
New Creation Realities (Kenyon), 43
New York Times, 166
Niebuhr, R., 23

O

On Being a Therapist (Kottler), 28
Operant conditioning, 17
Oswald, R., 127

P

Parent, adult, child (PAC) model, 114–116
Pastoral counseling, 142–143
Peale, N. V., 22
Peck, M. S., 47, 85–86, 165, 167
People of the Lie (Peck), 86
Personality, 136–137
Peterson, J., 76
Philippi, 3
Physicians, 84
Posttraumatic stress disorder (PTSD), 25
The Power of Positive Thinking (Peale), 22
Pride, 87–88
Promise, 58–60
Psyche, 68–69
Psychiatric mental health nurses (PMHN), 82
Psychiatric nurse, 82
Psychiatrists, 82–84
Psychic distance, 25
Psychodynamic languages, 6
Psychological languages, 57–58
Psychology, 1–9
  Christian counseling, 61
  current time, 19
  defined, 4–5
  denial, 45–53
  developments, 18–19
  forward movement in, 12–15
  history of, 11–19
  human development, stages, 15–17
  integrating psychological languages, 57–58
  languages. *See* Languages
  of community and connection, 109–117
  of couple relationships, 99–106
  of survival, 155–162
  of worship, 129–139
  problems with, 55–58
  promise, 58–60
Psychosis versus neurosis, 88–89
Psychotherapy, goals and breadth of, 177–178
The Purpose Driven Life (Warren), 16

R

Reenactment, 104–106
Relatedness, 69–70
Repeating/reflecting, 146
Return to Love (Williamson), 92
Re-Visioning Psychology (Hillman), 165
Road Less Traveled (Peck), 47, 131
Rogers, C., 6, 37–38, 40, 60
Ross, E. K., 33
Rothschild, B., 27

S

Sacredness of therapy, 163–169
  Christian psychology, 168–169
  frame of orientation, 164
  learning to die, 167–168
  thin place, 166–167
Sanctification, 16
Schuller, M. R., 22
Seasonal bonding, 33
Self-actualization, 16, 37, 40, 65
Seminary, F., 43
Separation (Bowlby), 69
Shame, 77
Siegel, D., 8, 18, 69, 73, 77, 145
Sign and symbol in worship, 138–139
Sit, Walk, Stand (Nee), 42
Skinner, B. F., 17
Social interest, 13
The Soul's Code (Hillman), 41
Spiritual gifts, 125–126, 143–144
Stories We Live By (McAdams), 69
Stretching, 102–103
Suppression, 27
Survival
  calling, 160–161
  choices, 156–159
  psychology of, 155–162
  skills, 161–162
  spiritual strength training, 159–160
  standing firm, 156
  work of the cross, 161
Systemic languages, 7

T

Talk therapy, 28–32
Tarsus, 2–4
Temperament, 120–122
  gifts and, 126–127
  strengths, 124–125
Theology of Personhood (Anderson), 66
Therapeutic person, 39–40
Therapist
  approaches, 36–39
  Christian counseling, 39
  gifts and calling, 40–41
  journey, 41–43
  therapeutic person, 39–40
  therapy and, 35–43
Therapy, 21–34
  emotion, 25–28
  existential. *See* Existential therapy
  feelings, 24–25

healing, holding, and helping, 32–34
memory, 25–28
sacredness of, 163–169
talk, 28–32
therapist and, 35–43
Together: The Healing Power of Human Connection in a Sometimes Lonely World (Murthy), 16, 109, 111
Tranquilized in trivia, 48
Transactional Analysis in Psychotherapy (Berne), 115
Trust *vs.* mistrust, 15
Two ways to die, 104

U

Understanding and helping families, 174

V

Vance, E., 59
Venkatakrishnan, H., 88
Vogler, C., 41
Vulnerability, 28

W

Wagner, P., 126–127
Warren, R., 16
Weiner, E., 166
Williamson, M., 92
Worship
clergy, 137
freedom to, 139
life devoted to, 133–134
misplaced, 132–133
nature of, 130–132
opening to the heart of god, 134
personality and, 136–137
psychology of, 129–139
sign and symbol, 138–139
sweet spot, 135–136
Writer's Journey (Vogler), 41
Wundt, W., 7

Y

Young, S., 22